The Theatre of Protest and Paradox:
Developments in the Avant-Garde Drama

George Wellwarth

The Theatre
of Protest and Paradox
Developments in the Avant-
Garde Drama

MACGIBBON & KEE : LONDON

First published by MacGibbon & Kee Ltd 1965
Copyright © New York University 1964
Printed in Great Britain by
Cox & Wyman Limited
London, Fakenham and Reading

In Memoriam Erwin Wellwarth

1890-1948

ACKNOWLEDGMENTS

I should like to acknowledge the assistance and advice of Professor Leo Hamalian of City College of New York, Professor Myron Taube of Long Island University, Professors Robert Clements, Henry Popkin, and Oscar Cargill of New York University, Miss Louise Gruner, Mr. Kurt Hellmer, and my wife Marcia. Without their help and encouragement this book might not have been completed.

Several of the chapters in this book first appeared in somewhat different form as articles in the following journals: *Tulane Drama Review*, Fall, 1963 (Dürrenmatt and Frisch); *Tulane Drama Review*, Fall, 1963 (Ghelderode); *Drama Survey*, Winter, 1963 (Artaud); *Drama Survey*, Spring, 1962 (Genet); *Ararat*, Spring, 1961 (Adamov); *University of Kansas City Review*, Autumn, 1961 (Beckett); *Southern Speech Journal*, Fall, 1961 (Dennis); *Southern Speech Journal*, Fall, 1962 (Ionesco); *Texas Studies in Literature and Language*, Autumn, 1962 (Audiberti); *Quarterly Journal of Speech*, Autumn, 1963 (Hochwälder); *Literary Review* (published by Fairleigh Dickinson University, Teaneck, N.J.), Autumn, 1963 (New American Drama); the chapter on Alfred Jarry is reprinted from *Criticism, a Quarterly for Literature and the Arts*, Vol. IV, No. 2 (Spring, 1962) by permission of the Wayne State University Press. Permission of the editors of these periodicals, who hold copyright on these respective items, is gratefully acknowledged.

PREFACE

THIS BOOK is a critical study of the extraordinary outburst of drama in the French, German, English, and American theaters since the end of the second World War. Ever since 1950, when Eugene Ionesco's first play *The Bald Soprano* was produced, the theater has been vibrant with the excitement of a new movement of artistic creation. In France this movement has taken the form of "avant-garde" theater or "theatre of the absurd," as Martin Esslin has more satisfactorily called it. In the German-speaking theater it has taken the form of the brilliantly constructed dramatic conundrums of the Swiss writers Friedrich Dürrenmatt and Max Frisch and the Swiss-based Austrian Fritz Hochwälder. England has seen the rise of the "angry young man," writers whose plays have a potentially high intellectual significance that is unfortunately smothered by the ineptness of their practical execution. In addition, England has produced the "neo-absurdist" theater of Harold Pinter and N. F. Simpson, that, although rather enigmatic and esoteric for the literalness of the Anglo-Saxon taste, will yet prove to be more lasting and significant than the angry-young-man drama. America alone has been unable to produce enough dramatists working at the same time in a sufficiently similar vein to be called a "movement." It has, however, produced a small number of remarkable, if uneven, individual playwrights, such as Edward Albee, Jack Gelber, Arthur Kopit, and, above all, Jack Richardson.

At first glance the plays written in French, English, and German since the end of the second World War are entirely dissimilar. It is the purpose of this book to explain the meanings of these plays, set them in their proper place in the history of dramatic literature, and point out their basic similarities. These similarities consist of a common theme (protest) and a common technique (paradox). Since intellectual drama (as distinct from box-office drama, which reflects popular social mores) always reflects current philosophical trends, it is only natural to find an outburst of profound dissatisfaction after a great war. Just as the first World War produced the immature frenzy of expressionism and the contemptuous rejection of surrealism and Dada, so the second World War has stimulated a philosophy of protest against the social order (in the English- and German-speaking drama) and against the human condition (in the French-speaking drama and in a few English-speaking ones). The protest no longer takes the form of hair-clutching hysteria, as it did in so many of the World War I dramas, but rather of a quiescent cynicism born of bitter experience. The cumulative knowledge of two World Wars in less than half a century, not to mention sundry atrocities and diverse obscenities thrown in every now and then as a bonus from the gods, so to speak, has made of today's intellectuals men without faith. They can no longer scream because they can no longer hope. They can no longer speak directly to their hearers because they can no longer believe that they are heard. They can only express themselves indirectly in sardonic paradoxes.

In the French section I have endeavored to show that there is a direct relationship between the avant-garde writers of today and the dramatic principles of Antonin Artaud and Alfred Jarry. The theatre of the absurd began, I believe, abruptly and suddenly on the evening of December 10, 1896 with the first performance of Alfred Jarry's *Ubu roi*. This play was the perfect example of artistic primitivism, a play literally without forebears, totally uninfluenced by any previous work. The attempt by some critics to relate *Ubu roi* to previous works by pointing out that Jarry had obviously read these works because he mentions them in the play is futile and illogical. Literary influence cannot be demonstrated by citing a reading list. Nor does a thumbnail history of nonsense literature prove that the nonsense literature which Jarry composed and which is being written today belongs in a literary continuum. Jarry's nonsense is, as a matter of fact,

entirely different, both in style and purpose, from previous nonsense literature. The German, English, and American writers
have more recognizable antecedents in the conventional drama
of ideas.

George Wellwarth

November, 1963

CONTENTS

xiii

Hope Deferred:
The New American Drama

The Theatre of Protest and Paradox:
Developments in the Avant-Garde Drama

The French-Speaking Drama

ALFRED JARRY
The Sower of the Avant-Garde Drama

ON THE EVENING of December 10, 1896, the Paris theater world was shocked by an extraordinary and unprecedented event. All the leading critics and members of the literary demimonde had assembled to see Lugné-Poë's Théâtre de l'Oeuvre company perform Alfred Jarry's new play, *Ubu roi* (King Ubu), at the Théâtre Nouveau. The curtain opened and Fermin Gémier stepped forward to say a word that had never before been pronounced on stage. The theater was never the same again.

Thus began the avant-garde drama.

Alfred Jarry died in 1907 at the age of thirty-four. Thanks in large measure to his own considerable ability for self-advertisement, he was by no means entirely neglected during his lifetime. Jarry's critical reputation, however, presents a rather peculiar picture. While he was still alive, those who wrote about him were, understandably enough, more concerned with his personal peculiarities than with his works. After his death, little of any significance was written about him for a long time. There was a brief revival of interest in him during the short-lived Dada movement of the early twenties; and Charles Chassé unwittingly contributed to the Jarry legend by publishing a book in which he accused him of plagiarizing the character of

1

Ubu from two old schoolfellows. In 1927 Antonin Artaud and
Roger Vitrac founded the Théâtre Alfred Jarry for the production of avant-garde drama. In 1938 Artaud, the direct ancestor
of the current avant-garde drama, laid down the rules for the
new drama in Le Théâtre et son Double (The Theatre and Its
Double). But it was not until the College of 'Pataphysics was
founded by a group of Jarry disciples in 1948 that Jarry came
back into his own. With the increased popularity of the current avant-garde drama—the drama of Ionesco, Beckett, Genet,
Adamov, Audiberti, etc.—interest in Jarry has revived steadily
as it has become evident that there is some similarity between
the style of the new plays and that of the Ubu plays.

It will be necessary first to clear up what is meant by the
term "avant-garde." Roughly speaking, the term means "out in
front of everybody else." Now, a person who is out in front of
everybody else is fully exposed to the fire of the enemy. Such
intrepidity, whether fearless or merely foolhardy, is shocking to
the timid, the cautious, and the prudent who comprise the
majority; all the more so because the majority—instinctively
and in all innocence—always considers its position sacred and
inviolate. The power to shock is, then, the chief characteristic
of the avant-garde drama and at the same time its chief source
of strength.

Avant-garde drama has always been with us, and the modern
avant-garde drama is merely the successor to, although not the
lineal descendant of, the Robertsonian cup-and-saucer drama,
the society drama of the Pinero-Jones axis (difficult though it may
be now to realize that these were considered shocking in their
day), and the Ibsen-Shaw social drama. The twentieth-century
avant-garde drama is unlike any previous avant-garde drama.
Previously the forefront was always created by means of a logical, if unexpected, development of some aspect of the currently popular drama. Thus the Robertsonian drama rose out
of an increased emphasis on physical realism in stage production; the "Pinerotico-Jonesian" drama shocked because it
introduced moral problems that had previously been thought
unfit for public discussion; the Ibsen-Shaw drama shocked
even more by actually discussing these moral problems seriously

instead of just titillatingly skittering around them in the fey manner of Pinero and Jones. The current avant-garde drama, however, has no such respectable antecedents. It sprang into existence with explosive suddenness on the evening of December 10, 1896.

Jarry was one of the very few true primitives in the history of literature. Some critics have seen the influence of Rabelais in the tone of raucous vulgarity that pervades the Ubu plays,[1] but a common interest in scatology hardly proves influence. Others have professed to see Hamlet in Bougrelas, the vengeful son of the Polish king whom Ubu kills,[2] but—again—parody does not imply literary influence. No, Jarry was simply an anomaly. In the continuum of literary history he suddenly appears, mysteriously crystallized, as it were, out of the elements of his own uniquely slanted mind.

The superficial childishness of the Ubu plays should not prevent the reader from taking them seriously. That Jarry's mind remained in many essentials a child's in no way diminishes his importance as the originator of the scream of protest later to be decreed by Artaud the official theme of the avant-garde drama. Jarry never formulated a coherent philosophy: he presented everything with the simplicity and immediacy of a child slinging mud pies. With the intuition of genius he was able to perceive an elaborate philosophy that he did not have the intellectual staying power to work out and understand, and to which, consequently, he succumbed.

When Jarry wrote *Ubu roi*, he was rebelling not only against the outmoded conventions of the current drama, as the previous "avant-gardists" had done, but against absolutely everything. Jarry rebelled against all things, both physical and metaphysical, to the point where he had to invent a new "reality" beyond the physical and metaphysical worlds—and thus the calculated insanity of 'Pataphysics came into being. The inverted world of 'Pataphysics is important in the history of

1. For example, Roger Shattuck, *The Banquet Years* (New York: Harcourt, Brace & World, Inc., 1958), p. 204.
2. Martin Esslin, "The Theatre of the Absurd," *Tulane Drama Review*, IV (Summer, 1960), p. 7.

drama only in so far as it symbolizes Jarry's total rejection of the world and the cosmos. Jarry, fortunately, was not a practical and active person, for he was the ultimate rebel who insisted on building up his own dream world after completely rejecting all existing reality.

Jarry's revolt was both seminal and instinctive. The blasé audiences of today are accustomed to hearing the most extreme forms of verbal obscenity casually mentioned in everyday conversations. Consequently, obscenity as a symbol of protest against the rigidities of convention has lost all effect. To us the famous opening line of *Ubu roi* seems mildly amusing, perhaps even a little trite, and certainly innocuous. But in 1896 the public utterance of that one word *"merdre"* (slightly altered to make it Jarryesque) had an absolutely cataclysmic effect. It was a slap in the face of society. When Fermin Gémier uttered the famous *mot d'Ubu* on that riotous night in 1896 the shock was electric. It did not matter that the performance was marred by continual catcalls and outbreaks of rioting, or that all the respectable critics excoriated the play on the following morning, or that Jarry was taken seriously only by a small coterie he had gathered round him, or that "Ubuism" had no direct, immediate influence on the drama. The point was that the word had been spoken, that the event had occurred. In the theater, as in life, events are irreversible. Once something has happened, it has happened; and once it has happened, it can happen again. In art, setting the precedent is the important thing. After the production of *Ubu roi* the theater could not be the same again: *Ubu roi* had happened, and the totality of theatrical experience had instantly and irretrievably been translated into a new perspective.

Ubu roi begins with the tremendous thunderclap of *le mot d'Ubu*, which set the expectant first-night audience off into a maniacal frenzy, if contemporary accounts do not exaggerate. The word shocked propriety. But the rebellion implicit in the utterance of the word on a public stage was a rebellion against all society and, indeed, all life. It was an evocation of disgust so deep that conventional language was powerless to express it, and at the same time the very unconventionality of the word was a gesture of defiance itself. The various scatological references sprinkled through the play represent rebellion on its most instinctive and elementary level—that of a child's refusal to bow to bathroom training. The purpose is deeper, however. Jarry's protest against the human condition was primitive and untutored; it was protest based on blind nihilism. Jarry's urges are those of a blinkered colt champing at the bit: *"Cornegidouille!"* says Père Ubu at one point, *"Nous n'aurons point tout démoli si nous ne démolissons même les ruines!"* Even the ruins must be pulled down.

The cosmic malignity that hovers invisibly over the characters in present-day avant-garde dramas is tangible and personified in Jarry's plays. Instead of being a helpless pawn (like Vladimir and Estragon in *Waiting for Godot*, or the employee in Adamov's *La Parodie*, or Maurice in Genet's *Deathwatch*), Jarry's protagonist, Père Ubu, is dirty, treacherous, greedy, ungrateful, cowardly, and cruel. In other words, the grotesquely bloated but still human figure of Father Ubu has all the attributes of the cosmic malignant force that pervades the avantgarde drama. Present in Ubu's elaborate "disembraining" machine, in his impaling people he doesn't like, and in the offhand mass slaughters he constantly orders, is the cruelty that Artaud later wanted to put into drama to show man's subjection to the hostile powers of the universe.

The story of *Ubu roi* is basically a naïve childish fantasy. The play is Jarry's warped version of the typical fairy tale—a king killed by a wicked usurper, the young and virtuous rightful heir to the throne as avenger, battles fought between troops who resemble the little tin soldiers of a toy box, eerie (but not too eerie) "supernatural" events, a fight with a make-believe bear, and so on.

At the beginning of the play, Ubu, an ugly, dirty, smelly, and grotesquely fat person, is being urged by his wife to kill Wenceslas, king of Poland, and usurp the throne himself. Ubu was formerly king of Aragon but is now captain of Wenceslas's dragoons. On the following day King Wenceslas is butchered by Ubu and his supporters as he reviews a parade of his troops. Ubu immediately slaughters the remaining members of the royal family (except Bougrelas, the heroic heir, who escapes with his mother) and takes over the kingdom. Basically, Ubu's idea of ruling is to kill all the people who have any money so that he can have it all for himself. Thus we see a long procession of noblemen, judges, and financiers fall into the trap door of the "disembraining" machine. Once Ubu has gathered unto himself all the money (or, as he prefers to call it, the "phynances") in Poland, he sets out to fight the czar of Russia, who is determined to avenge his cousin Wenceslas. Ubu is routed in the battle and flees with two of his followers to a cave, where they kill a bear while Father Ubu perches on a high rock reciting a paternoster. After this, Ubu is joined by his wife, and off they sail for France.

Ubu cocu (Cuckold Ubu, written 1897 or 1898) shows us Ubu as a private man once again. Except that he is no longer king, nothing is changed. He is still the same totally self-centered juggernaut of evil, crushing everyone in his path—a naïvely personified symbol of cosmic maliciousness and cruelty. Jarry has Ubu describe himself exactly when he first appears as an interpolation in the early work *César-Antechrist:* "*Semblable à un oeuf, une citrouille ou un fulgurant météore, je roule sur cette terre où je ferai ce qu'il me plaira.*" This is Ubu's constant watchword: he will do just as he pleases. Like the cosmic evil he represents, Ubu rolls over everyone in his path with the obliviousness of a robot-controlled tank. And so, when Ubu takes over the house of M. Achras, the harmless, bumbling student of polyhedrals, he cheerfully takes over everything and, after consulting his conscience, impales M. Achras. The scene with Ubu's Conscience is illuminating as an example of Jarry's satiric qualities. Ubu asks his Conscience whether he should kill M. Achras for insulting him. "Monsieur," his Conscience answers, "it is not proper for a civilized man to answer good with evil. M. Achras has sheltered you, M. Achras has opened his arms and his collection of polyhedrals to you, M. Achras, and so forth, is a very fine gentleman, completely inoffensive, and it would be a terrible thing and so forth to kill a poor old

man who is incapable of defending himself." [3] That is enough
for Ubu: he instantly decides to kill M. Achras since there is
no danger in doing so. Jarry's humorous effects are usually
achieved by this forced marriage of cynical satire and broad
farce. He is not even averse to mixing a little playful criticism
of the contemporary theater into his most farcical scenes. When
Ubu is jammed half in and half out of the trapdoor through
which M. Achras has planned to drop him, Jarry, with a little
oblique mocking bow in the direction of Alfred de Musset, has
him say, "*De par ma chandelle verte, il faut qu'une trappe soit
ouverte ou fermée. La beauté du théâtre à phynances gît dans le
bon fonctionnement des trappes.*" [4] The play as a whole is a
hodgepodge of this kind of flippant ridicule. Jarry does not
bother to get together a coherent plan of attack: he prefers to
dance about and flick out an occasional jab. In the later avant-
garde drama this technique becomes less haphazard, more purposeful; but the formlessness and illogicality of plot line remains
and has become one of the avant-garde's identifying character-
istics.

The one other complete Ubu play (Jarry had a tendency
to insert elements of the Ubu plays into other works) is *Ubu
enchaîné* (Ubu Enchained, published 1900). This play is unlike
Jarry's other Ubuesque works in that it is earthbound. He
switches here from the naïve cosmic defiance he originated to
a form of social satire. *Ubu enchaîné* is as formless and haphazard as ever, but it is essentially a sarcastic spoofing of human
nature. Jarry's point—and this too was taken up by the later
avant-garde dramatists—is that human beings are unable to
think straight (i.e., objectively) and consequently act in accordance with the perverted paradoxes to which their ways of thinking lead them. Thus the climax of the play comes when Pisse-
doux shouts, to the acclamation of the mob, "*La liberté, c'est
l'esclavage!*" But we are getting ahead of ourselves. Jarry begins
this spoof of human behavior by spoofing himself. Ubu steps
forward, poises himself, opens his mouth, and says—nothing!
Mère Ubu is aghast. "What!" she says, "You don't say anything

3. Alfred Jarry, *Tout Ubu* (Paris: Le Livre de Poche, 1962), p. 206.
4. *Ibid.*, p. 215.

Père Ubu? Have you forgotten the word?" ". . . I don't want
to say the word," answers Ubu, "It's made too much trouble for
me already." Mère Ubu is deeply grieved by her husband's stubborn refusal to utter the magic word. She reminds him that they
are in France now and that this is no time to forget how to
speak French. But Ubu will have none of it. He is determined
to change his way of life. He has had enough of being a king
and ruling over people: now he wants to work with his hands
and become a slave. It does not prove so easy to change human
nature, however. Even as a slave, Ubu is the same powerful mass
as before. Even as "free men" under an anarchistic social system, the ordinary beings are helpless driven slaves.

Ubu starts out on his quest for slavery by joining the army
(*l'armerdre*), which consists of three "free men" and a corporal.
The free men demonstrate their "freedom" by always doing precisely the opposite of what they are told to do. The corporal
can thus control them with complete effectiveness by simply
telling them to halt when he wants them to move, to stand at
ease when he wants them to snap to attention, and so forth.
The free men are constantly proclaiming their freedom ("*Nous
sommes les hommes libres. . . . Vive la liberté, la liberté, la
liberté! Nous sommes libres*") but are actually as enslaved as
the automatons of a regular army. At the end of the play they
quite naturally choose slavery because Ubu's adoption of it has
made it appear "freer" than anarchy. Ubu himself succeeds in
achieving the lowest rank of slavery—that of a galley slave. As
the coast of France recedes, he assures Mère Ubu that they will
surely be taken to some country extraordinary enough to be
worthy of them, where they will be put on a trireme with at
least four banks of oars.

The bare plot outlines of the Ubu plays give us no inkling
of their real significance. Like the modern avant-garde dramas
to which they gave birth, the Ubu plays mystify by their apparent simplicity. Audiences laugh and scratch their heads in
bewilderment as they watch the Ubu plays or the avant-garde
dramas because they feel that they are being hoaxed—that a
lot of simple-minded nonsense is being jabbered at them by a
tongue-in-cheek author who wants them to rack their brains

in a futile attempt to uncover a nonexistent profound meaning. And having, as they think, found this out, they laugh derisively and congratulate themselves on their perspicacity.

As usual, the audience, whom Jarry called an obstacle to the advance of the theatrical art in his essay *"De l'inutilité du théâtre au théâtre"* has got hold of the wrong end of the paradox. The Ubu plays and the avant-garde drama *appear* to be simplicity disguised as profundity and are actually profundity disguised as simplicity. The simplicity is deceptive, just as the simplicity of *Alice in Wonderland* or the simplicity of the painter Henri Rousseau, with whom Jarry has often been linked, is deceptive.[5] Perhaps we can get some idea of the way in which Jarry conceals profundity under a facade of naïveté and childlike vulgarity by analyzing one of Rousseau's most famous paintings. *Le Rêve* (The Dream) shows a sleeping woman's dream of a primeval wilderness transformed into a child's picture-book jungle. A naked woman on a red couch is set in the midst of a jungle landscape in which we can see two lions, a snake charmer, and a mysterious disembodied eye. The lions stare with vaguely worried expressions out of brilliantly colored hothouse foliage, their round eyes giving them the fixed, staring look of stuffed toy animals. Behind them the fantastic dream figure of the snake charmer rises out of the thick shrubbery like a forgotten caryatid from some overgrown and crumbled temple. And brooding over all is the sinister slanted eye that peeps out of a gap in the foliage just above the edge of the dreamer's couch. The piled-up, random mélange of exotic plants simultaneously gives the impression of being a stifling mephitic nightmare vision and an innocent playroom wallpaper design. Like William Blake, Rousseau interpenetrated works with sinister meaning and naïve, instinctive playfulness. Jarry shared this faculty. Ubu has the large, carefree jollity and buoyancy always associated with excessive corpulence, and the sinister, cruel menace of total evil. He is at the same time a symbol of the oblivious malignity of the cosmos and an evocation of the pathetically ridiculous

5. I am indebted to Roger Shattuck's *The Banquet Years* for the suggestion of the Jarry-Rousseau connection. Professor Shattuck's book is far and away the best treatment of Jarry in English.

high-school physics teacher who served as his original model.[6]
This quality of innocence is lost in the works of the later
avant-garde dramatists, who derived their theories from Antonin
Artaud rather than directly from Jarry. Artaud took the essence
of Jarry's philosophy and applied it to strictly theatrical matters.
He attempted to transmit Jarry's intellectual system (the system of rebellion through paradox) in terms of the theater. Jarry
himself had been primarily interested in the theater, but he had
by no means concentrated his energies on it as single-mindedly
as Artaud was to do. Jarry's sole purpose in life was to rebel,
and this he did not only in his dramas but in his deliberately
bizarre personal behavior and in his straight-faced advocacy of
the "supreme science" of 'Pataphysics as well. 'Pataphysics
("the science of imaginary solutions, which symbolically attributes the properties of objects, described by their virtuality,
to their lineaments") is Jarry's protest against the futility of
thought. Reason and logic and scientific discovery can only
bring us up to a certain point of knowledge; beyond that point
the human mind is powerless. Since that point is the only point
that really matters—the understanding of death—Jarry felt that
all thought was self-defeating and ultimately ridiculous. The
invention of 'Pataphysics, which is dedicated to the use of strict
logic in order to arrive at senseless conclusions, was Jarry's way
of satirizing faith in human endeavor. Jarry's personal habits
were also dictated by his desire to rebel. He seemed to operate
on the theory that the cultivation of deliberately bizarre behavior constituted a rebellion against existing modes of behavior.
He was implying that socially acceptable behavior is as arbitrary
as the behavior he improvised, and that his own eccentric de-
portment destroyed the validity of the conventional behavior.
Thus he became a well-known figure in the Paris of the eighteen-

6. Ubu originated as a caricature of Monsieur Hébert, Jarry's physics
teacher at the *lycée* in Rennes. Hébert seems to have been a classic example
of a man choosing the wrong profession. As a teacher he appears to have
been totally incompetent and utterly incapable of controlling his pupils.
The fact that he was also extremely fat made him the perfect target for
Jarry and his classmates, and they soon began writing puppet plays in which
he appeared as Père Héb. These plays later formed the basis for the Ubu
plays.

nineties because of his peculiar mannerisms. Jarry used to affect an "Ubuesque" way of talking in which each syllable was given an exactly equal stress so that he sounded like a slowed-down recording. He lived in incredibly cluttered apartments where he kept owls, and went about the streets of Paris with firearms ostentatiously displayed. His defeat of the French army compares with Felix Krull's defeat of his German draft board. He was finally discharged on grounds of ill-health after swallowing some acid, but the real reason was probably that the army simply felt that it could not cope with him any longer.

Jarry's greatest gesture of rebellion, however, was his alcoholism. There can be little doubt that he deliberately drank himself to death. Not long after his arrival in Paris, he must have made up his mind to make the supreme rebellious gesture of suicide. He chose alcohol as his medium because it was slow and because the immediate effects of the alcohol enabled him to carry on his eccentricities undisturbed by the restraints of his own personality. Alcohol freed him from himself temporarily; eventually it freed him permanently from the whole burden of his life. In a way it was a heroic death, for it was a death for a cause, and probably it was not as pleasant a one as the casual drinker might suppose. It was certainly not an insane or unreasonable death. Rebellion as Jarry saw it was a quest for total freedom and a protest against the ultimate enslavement, which is death. Jarry chose to rebel against the ultimate by systematically destroying himself. In this way he conquered—paradoxically; for, having consciously sentenced himself to death, having decided to control his own death, as it were, by deliberately bringing it on, he was able to be completely at liberty, completely contemptuous of all manifestations of social order during the period of life that was left to him.

Jarry was as much a rebel and innovator in the field of theatrical technique as he was in the field of personal behavior. He extended his philosophical rebellion against the status quo by suggesting that realism should be eliminated from the theater. He had no use for the theater of the eighteen-nineties, still based for the most part on the even-tempered technique of Scribe and Sardou, whose dramas aimed at an exact-as-possible imitation of contemporary reality in dialogue and in scenic effect. Just about the only contemporary play Jarry admired was Ibsen's *Peer Gynt*, which, in the France of 1896, was still considered wildly heretical because of its poetic expansiveness and its bland disregard of all the current canons of playwriting theory. Jarry himself wished to go back to a theater that frankly admitted it was theater, back to the self-confessedly unrealistic theater that had last been seen in Elizabethan and *commedia dell'arte* times. The oft-quoted letter Jarry wrote to Lugné-Poë about the staging of *Ubu roi* in 1896 is very illuminating in this respect:

> It would be interesting . . . to be able to stage the play . . . on the following lines:
> Mask for the chief character, Ubu . . .
> A cardboard horse's head which he would hang from his neck, as they did in the old English theater, for the only two equestrian scenes, all of whose details are in the spirit of the play, as I intended to make it a "guignol."
> Adoption of a single set, or rather of a plain backcloth, doing away with the raising and lowering of the curtain during the single act. A conventionally dressed character would appear, as in the Guignols, and hang up a placard informing the audience of the location of the scene. (Note that I am certain that the written placard is much more "suggestive" than scenery. Neither scenery nor supers could represent "The Polish Army marching in the Ukraine.")
> No crowds; these are a mistake on the stage and hamper the intelligence. Thus a single soldier in the Review scene, a single one in the scrimmage where Ubu says: "What a gang, what a retreat," etc.
> The adoption of an "accent," or rather, a special "voice" for the chief character.
> The costumes should give as little as possible the impression of local color or chronology (this renders better the idea of something eternal). They should preferably be modern, as the satire is modern; and sordid, to make the play appear more wretched and horrific.[7]

7. Wallace Fowlie, ed., *Four Modern French Comedies* (New York: G. P. Putnam's Sons, 1960), pp. 23–24.

Jarry is here advocating stylization and suggestion as the best means of dramatic communication. For years past, theater people had been committed to the theory that drama was enhanced by imitating real life as precisely as possible. Inevitably this had strangled the drama because plays that imitated reality as precisely as possible were necessarily confined for the most part to a tedious, standardized, repetitive routine of respectable drawing rooms, opulent and plush (though still respectable) bedrooms, and an occasional ballroom or fashionable restaurant. Only in such dramas as Ibsen's *Brand* and *Peer Gynt* was the full potential of the drama realized. Jarry's letter to Lugné-Poë is a sketch of the practical technique that would make the staging of such plays possible.

Artaud formulated a coherent theatrical philosophy on the basis of Jarry's practices and random theoretical remarks. Briefly, Artaud saw drama as a means of expressing rebellion against the human condition. For him all drama was an action that emanated from a perception of man's helplessness in a universe of which he could comprehend only that it was implacably hostile. On a cosmic level man's cry of defiance is only that of a mote whirled around in a trackless void; but on the microcosmic level of the drama, man's protest attains the significance granted to it by its more restricted context. Later this view was to be formulated in nondramatic terms by Albert Camus in his concept of the absurd—the contrast between man's baffled impotence and the apparent malignity of an inscrutable eternity. Camus, also, advocated protest and defiance as a means—the only means possible—of nullifying the cruelty of the cosmic power on a temporal level. In Jarry's dramatic microcosmos this protest takes a far more primitive and instinctive form.

The last of Jarry's Ubu plays closes as Père Ubu fades away into the middle distance. Seated on the galley bench in pot-bellied, mock-heroic defiance, shackles on his legs and sweep oar in his hands, Ubu looks like some grotesque parody of Napoleon on his way to Elba. Like Napoleon, too, Ubu was destined to return. The exile was temporary only. Ubu continued to lie in wait, ready to leap out from his distant Avalon and save the drama from the curse of a too precise mimesis. Every so often he would make forays back to his former haunts. Careful ob-

servers could have dimly perceived him skittering about rather
uncertainly behind the scenes of the post-World War I German
expressionistic drama, giving an occasional uncharacteristically
timid tug on the strings of one of the "*über*marionettes." He
came forward somewhat more boldly in the surrealistic drama
of Apollinaire and the early Cocteau. With the excesses of
Dadaism, which were, however, largely of a nondramatic nature,
Père Ubu was once more thunderously in evidence. And, finally,
when Antonin Artaud created the Théâtre Alfred Jarry in 1927,
and when he published his collection of manifestoes, *Le Théâtre et son Double* in 1938, Père Ubu came into his own again.
Fully rehabilitated, even respectable now, he has waddled back
onto the stage and now pervades the avant-garde drama like
some enormous intangible and interpenetrating influence. Ubu
is back with us—to stay. The seed that Gémier sowed on that
momentous evening in 1896 has finally taken root and sprouted.
With that incredibly simple yet explosively destructive word,
Jarry changed the whole course of the future dramatic continuum. Indeed, the theater would never be the same again.

ANTONIN ARTAUD
The Prophet of the Avant-Garde Theater

ONE OF THE more curious and paradoxical aspects of
modern theatrical history is that trends in the drama have been
started not by the playwrights but by the critics. The dramatist
presents the thesis, but it is the critical commentator who presents the counterthesis that is necessary before the final synthesis of a new theatrical movement can be produced. The
drama of the past (the ancient Greek plays, the Roman comedy,
the medieval mysteries and moralities, the Elizabethan heroic
play, the eighteenth century sentimental drama, the nineteenth
century melodrama and well-made jigsaw puzzle play) was
"written down" to its particular audience: it was designed to
be immediately comprehensible to its spectators. If it was not,

it suffered the relegation to the closet shelf. In modern times,
however, the drama has become more intellectual and sophisticated; and although the goal still is, as it always has been, to
communicate directly to the audience, it has become something
mysterious and puzzling. The simplicity of the drama of the
past was such that dramatic movements were not discovered
until they were dead; today the complexity of the drama is such
that dramatic movements must be discovered by the critic before they can come to life.

The contemporary avant-garde theater—the theater of
Ionesco, Beckett, Adamov, and Genet—is for most people a theater of mystification. Many go to see the plays of these authors
because it is currently the fashionable thing to do. Crowds of
people sit in darkened theaters and stare incredulously at
lighted stages where plays are performed. Much of the confusion caused by these apparently willfully obscure playwrights
might be cleared up by a study of the source of the ideas that
animate them. All of the plays of the current avant-garde experimental drama have a common source in the theories of Antonin
Artaud (1896–1948).

The dramatic theories of Artaud, as outlined in his chief
critical work, *Le Théâtre et son Double*, represent the counterthesis to the thesis of Alfred Jarry's seminal work, *Ubu roi*.
Together they lead to the synthesis of the twentieth century
avant-garde drama. Before Artaud had formulated his theories,
the very real significance of Jarry's drama had passed unnoticed;
and indeed it is only very recently that Jarry has come to be recognized as something more than an infantile prankster. The
situation is in many ways analogous to the start given the modern problem-play movement by Shaw's criticism of Ibsen, who
had previously been shunted aside—by the British public at any
rate—as a tasteless trouble-maker. The spectacular riot that took
place at the opening of *Ubu roi* in 1896 instantly established
Jarry as France's leading enfant terrible. The play itself, however, was brushed aside as a piece of wantonly mischievous nonsense. Only a very few critics had the perceptiveness to observe
the significance behind Jarry's nebulous overlay of apparent
nonsense. One of them was William Butler Yeats, who attended

B

the first performance. Rather wistfully, Yeats recognized that
what he had seen was an important and irrevocable step forward in the development of comedy. Speaking of himself and
the writers of his school, he said, "After us, the Savage God."
Yeats' characterization of Jarry's comedy, and the movement it
would breed, as the comedy of "the Savage God" was one of
those instinctive insights that mark the great critic. "The
Comedy of the Savage God" might almost be a catch phrase
to describe the whole avant-garde movement. It is doubtful
whether Jarry himself realized the full extent of what he was
starting. His play, like the plays of the avant-gardists who came
after him, is a play of pure rebellion, a comedy of the Savage
God remorselessly trampling over everything that exists. The
avant-grade drama is the comedy of nihilism and despair.

It took a critic of Antonin Artaud's temperament to perceive the far-reaching implications of Jarry's play. He saw Ubu
as a powerful destructive force that had eliminated forever the
convention-bound "drama as entertainment" or "drama with a
purpose," which had dominated the stage for so long. After Ubu,
drama had to return to its primal origins as an atavistic folk rite.

As Artaud saw it, what was wrong with drama, as well as
with all the other arts, was culture. By "culture" Artaud meant
the overlay of artificialities that civilization had imposed upon
human nature. The *essence* of human nature, its basic and in-
trinsic quality, had become obscured by the unreal formal masks
—the socially acceptable behavior patterns arbitrarily imposed
on us by custom and tradition. Since art is reality, the artist's
task was to strip away the layers of artificiality and expose the
core of reality that had been hidden for so long. To Artaud this
core was pure emotion; and the emotion was latent, instinctual
savagery. He perceived that men are, as they always have been,
basically barbaric, that the thick protective wall of urbane, civilized behavior they have acquired through centuries of hiding
from psychological self-realization is easily crumbled by a force-
ful appeal to irrational emotion.

Culture, then, must be swept away. Only the instinctive
human desires (anger, hate, longing, the physical desires, etc.)
are worthy of consideration by the artist. Everything must be

elemental—culture and all it implies, including form in art, is out of harmony with instinctive human emotion. We can see from this the real significance of Jarry's Ubu figure. No longer a mere tasteless prank, he becomes, through Artaud's scheme, the prototype of the elemental figure unencumbered by inhibition or respect for the veneer of law and order. The mere existence of a figure like Ubu, whose heedless freedom makes "civilized behavior" look ridiculous, is a protest in itself. And once something has been made to look ridiculous, it can never carry the same authority again.

The apparent perverseness and obscurity of the avant-garde drama is a direct outcome of the Ubu figure and the subsequent Artaud theories. It is an inevitable result of the confusion created in the human mind by its acquired fear of instinct and its ingrained habit of analyzing action. The spectator is confused because he shies away from overt displays of his own instinctual self and because he tries to analyze, i.e., understand, instead of responding and participating emotionally. The vitality of this new drama, despite the puzzlement of the audiences, indicates that the old intensity of instinct is still there, though it has hitherto been stifled.

The function of the drama, according to Artaud, is twofold: it must, by being consistently uninhibited, protest against the artificial hierarchy of values imposed by culture, and it must, by a "drama of cruelty," demonstrate the true reality of the human soul and the relentless conditions under which it lives. The manner in which this violent attack on the everyday is to be accomplished involves a fantastic, larger-than-life callousness that enables the characters to disregard the amenities of social behavior, and a rejection of speech as a means of communication. Speech, according to Artaud, is nontheatrical; therefore, strictly speaking, it has no place in the theater. The paradox forming the basis of Artaud's system of theatrical practice is that instead of clarifying the meaning of drama, instead of using the various elements of the theater (scenery, lighting, costumes, stage movement, etc.) to make the plays easier to understand, it is necessary to make the plays less easy to understand in order to make them the more accessible to instinctive human emotion. What Artaud meant by this was that ever since the theater had descended (as he saw it) from ritual to art form, all the essentially theatrical elements—those elements that distinguish the theater from other forms of expression—had been subordinated to speech. Everything that has ever been done in the theater since ancient Greece has been predicated on the assumption that the function of the theater is communication through speech. But speech—communication of rational thoughts—is the very thing that does not and cannot distinguish the theater from anything else—which makes it, in short, merely a branch of literature. If rational communication through speech is really the ultimate goal of the theater, then, according to Artaud, there is no point at all in going to the enormous trouble and expense of producing a play: it is obviously enough simply to read it. One can obtain information from the written word just as easily as from the spoken. Theater, Artaud decreed, must be theatrical, and speech is not theatrical, but literary. Therefore we must concentrate exclusively on those elements of the theater peculiar to it alone.

Through the ages the true nature of the theater had become obscured. The demands of society shaped theater into something national, even local, reflecting the current mores and points of view of particular segments of humanity rather than universal human feeling. In this way the rational, imitative theater came into being; and problem plays (dealing with some specific aspect of some specific society) or irresponsible comedies designed for superficial entertainment became the vehicles of theatrical expression. Artaud's theater was therefore a return to the original purity of drama.

Artaud did consciously what Jarry had done instinctively when he wrote *Ubu roi*: he went back to the most primitive forms of the theater. To Artaud, theater was something that had been perfect in its beginnings and had been degenerating ever since as a result of contamination by civilized convention. Artaud felt that the theater had originally been the medium through which men expressed their unconscious feelings—the mysterious, nonrational essence of their beings. Inevitably, the first step in Artaud's program was the destruction of the present-day theater. He rebelled against everything that the contemporary theater represented: against society, against convention, against modern dramaturgy, even against the physical structure of the theater itself. Artaud had no wish to compromise or modify: he did not have the temperament to slither deviously to his objective. Revolt, overthrow, and complete, merciless destruction were the steps he recommended. The new theater had to be created as it had been created in the first place—from its original motivating forces.

Artaud rebelled not only against current methods of production, but against the current matter of production as well. He wanted drama to return to its elemental beginnings—yes; but Artaud was not merely an intellectual purist or a passionate dramatic archaeologist with a fetish for restoring originals. His reason for going back to the original form of drama was his conviction that the drama was an expression of the human condition. Unlike the ceremonies of religious worship, in which man abased himself before a superior power with the object of propitiating it, the ritual of the drama was man's assertion of his dignity and independence and was therefore a defiance and *protest* against the superior power. In religious observances man is nothing; in the self-expression of drama he is everything. Both are forms of worship, for both recognize the existence of a superior power. To love and to bow down to that superior power is no more an acknowledgement of its power and superiority than to hate and defy it. And the latter course is the nobler course because it is the truer: man has a right to his own feelings and his own dignity as a being. Reasoning thus, Artaud arrived at his concept of a theater pervaded by a sense of cosmic powers and by an attitude on the part of actors and audiences that simultaneously implied awe and defiance. Like Jarry and like all the other avant-garde writers who came after him, Artaud looked at mankind in much the same way that Pascal did, although the latter drew radically different conclusions from his view: "*Condition de l'homme: inconstance, ennui, inquiétude.*" The condition of man was such because of the unrelenting malignancy of the incomprehensible cosmic powers that govern him. Hence the theater, which reflects the condition of man, must be a "theater of cruelty."

Cruelty in the theater does not mean, as Artaud was careful to emphasize, mere sadism: it is the impersonal, mindless—and therefore implacable—cruelty to which all men are subject. The universe with its violent natural forces was cruel in Artaud's eyes, and this cruelty, he felt, was the one single most important fact of which man must be aware. This cruelty is seen to some extent as viciousness between human beings. But such scenes must be presented in a manner calculated to purge the spectator of the corresponding emotions in him rather than to arouse in him the desire to imitate. At the same time, the spectator must be made aware of the violence dormant within himself and the omnipotence of the forces outside himself: each theatrical performance must shatter the foundations of the spectator's existence. It must show the spectator his own helplessness in the presence of the awesome and ineluctable forces that control the world. The theater must entangle the emotions, for the majority of the people use their senses rather than their intellect. It must be ecstatic. It must crush and hypnotize the onlooker's sense. It must have the same effect on the audience as the dances of the whirling dervishes and the ritual incantations and ceremonies of black magic. Like these ceremonies, the theater must combine submission and mystic union with protest and defiance.

The natural consequence of all this is that theater must be spontaneous. Since theater for Artaud is essentially a primitive ritual, it draws the spectators into the vortex of emotion generated by the actors. Unlike the separated and dispassionate onlookers in the modern theater, the audience should always be like extras who are part of the performance.

If, then, theater is to be spontaneous, it must use only works inspired by the emotion of the moment. In his essay "No More Masterpieces," Artaud explains that all the so-called masterpieces of dramatic literature must either be eliminated or brought up to date. The scholar's slavish cringing before and the layman's passive acceptance of the classics have no place in the

new theater. Artaud maintains that there is no reason whatever
to suppose that a work can be equally valid at all times. Even
if its theme is still as valid as it was in the time the work was
written, its structure must be altered to bring it into close
harmony with the feelings of a contemporary audience. Artaud
attacked the faithful rendition of masterpieces as "bourgeois
conformism"—that clapboard superstructure of civilized behavior so antipathetic to his atavistic spirit. "Bourgeois conformism" makes us confuse sublime ideas with the forms they
have taken in time. What must be said must be said in a way
that is immediately accessible to the masses: "It is idiotic to
reproach the masses for having no sense of the sublime when
the sublime is confused with one or another of its formal
manifestations, which are, moreover, always defunct manifestations." [1] Thus, for example, the themes of Sophocles's *Oedipus
Rex* are as sublime as ever, but the form in which Sophocles
embodied them, i.e., the dramatic form peculiar to the needs
of the ancient Greek theater, is not. Sophocles's stately language,
for one thing, is inappropriate for the "rude and epileptic
rhythm" of our time. *Oedipus Rex* does have all the elements
that Artaud requires in a play. The relentless cruelty of the implacable forces that control man, the violence of human nature,
the defiance of common mores in the incest theme—all are
there. But they mean nothing if presented in the archaic form
and language of the ancient Greek drama:

> . . . a public that shudders at train wrecks, that is familiar
> with earthquakes, plagues, revolutions, wars; that is sensitive
> to the disordered anguish of love, can be affected by all these
> grand notions and asks only to become aware of them, but
> on condition that it is addressed in its own language, and
> that its knowledge of these things does not come to it
> through adulterated trappings and speech that belong to ex-
> tinct eras which will never live again.[2]

1. Antonin Artaud, *The Theatre and Its Double*, translated by Mary
C. Richards. Copyright © 1958 by the Grove Press, Inc. (New York:
Grove Press, Inc., 1958), p. 74.
2. *Ibid.*, p. 75.

cf.
Transl. of content
into form contents
into form
meaning.

This statement crystallizes Artaud's aesthetic theory. Form, as such, has no meaning for him. All that matters is the theme of the play and the technique by which it can be presented most effectively. Plays must be changed in form and language in order to make them clear to the public. The only objection that might be made against this is that form is self-evidently an integral part of a work of art. Change the form of *Oedipus Rex* and you no longer have *Oedipus Rex*. What you have is a different play on the same theme, like the modern reinterpretations of the classical drama by Sartre, Giraudoux, and Anouilh. Artaud's answer to this would be that if modernizing a play means destroying it, then it must be destroyed. In short, Artaud sees drama as a set of important themes floating around amorphously, ready to be shaped into whatever form the all-powerful *metteur en scène* (a combination of producer, director, and author in Artaud's system) wishes to give them.

Artaud was above all a practical—and practicing—theater man. His theories may sound vague, but he described very specifically how he wanted them carried out in actual practice. Artaud maintained that a production should concentrate only on those aspects of the drama that are purely *theatrical,* i.e., that require the medium of the stage to be intelligible. Music, dance, plastic art, pantomime, vocal mimicry, lighting, and scenery fall into this category. When properly combined, they form what Artaud called the "poetry of space." Thus the "poetry of speech," which has always been the theater's chief medium of expression, is eliminated. This is not to say that Artaud intended to transform the theater into a vehicle for pure mime. Speech might still be used in the theater, but not for the communication of ideas and not in such a way as to make it an end in itself. Words can be used on the stage as sound per se —as intonations. As such, their purpose would no longer be to communicate thought, but to bring about an emotional effect. For example, a hoarse, rasping, aspirated roar might indicate a feeling of terror. Artaud's idea of the function of words is rather similar to that of Ionesco's Professor in *The Lesson:* "words charged with significance will fall, weighted down by their meaning, and in the end they always collapse, fall . . . on deaf ears." Like the Professor, Artaud would like to have only "purely irrational assemblages of sounds, denuded of all sense" floating allusively around at high altitudes, where they can charge the atmosphere with a pervading emotion, far above the "deaf ears" of the mind. Insofar as there is to be anything at all even remotely approaching the communication we are accustomed to in the ordinary theater, Artaud would like to convey to the onlookers a generalized impression of a state of mind rather than the communication of facts. Clearly this can only be managed by means of symbols—which on the stage would have to take the form of a formalized sign language. In this "unperverted pantomime" (a term Artaud uses to distinguish it from the type of pantomime ordinarily seen in the theater, which merely substitutes gestures for words as a means of communicating specific ideas) the gestures represent "ideas, attitudes of mind, aspects of nature" instead of words and sentences. As an example Artaud cites the oriental device of representing Night by a tree on which a bird that has already closed one eye is beginning to close the other. This evocation of images or states of mind rather than specific thoughts may be termed a macrocosmic approach to theatrical art rather than the microcosmic one now in use. Like all visionaries, Artaud always saw the large view, the ecstatic, all-embracing concept; thinkers and analyzers, on the other hand, always work through specific instances. In a sense, Artaud was going back to the intellectual method of the Scholastics, rejecting the reform of the inductively minded Renaissance thinkers.

In the drama of Artaud, the *metteur en scène* is responsible both for the text and for the manner of its presentation. The text as written has no authority whatsoever, and the *metteur en scène* is perfectly free to alter it at will. It is his business to transform the text into a set of "animated hieroglyphs" that will involve everyone's emotions. Artaud suggested that this can best be done by a technique of interpenetration of action and audience. That is to say, the old partition between action and audience, which was achieved by the artificial dividing line of the proscenium arch or the barrier of the front-row seats, must be eliminated. The stage will continue to exist, but a great part of the action will be carried on *in* the audience and all around it. Instead of the auditorium being lined-up in front of the stage, as in the theater of conventional design, or around the stage, as in the arena theater, *the stage will surround the audience*. In this way, the audience, seated on swivel chairs, will be encompassed by the action and will feel itself to be part of it instead of hovering over it like students at a surgical demonstration. The theatrical devices that will involve the audience will consist of music, lights, color, masks, and rhythmic physical movement. In addition, Artaud planned to insert novel devices that would serve as hieroglyphs indicating the supernatural forces surrounding man. These would include apparitions, effigies yards high dressed in costumes based on old ritual models, stereophonic sound, and "new and surprising objects." [3] Thus every play would be rewritten by the Supreme Godhead of the New Theater, the Director-Author or *metteur en scène*, in order to fit into the new hieroglyphic language of the stage. The stage will surround the audience, and the auditorium will resound to the eerie wails, the unearthly moans, and the nerve-rending screams of Artaud's apparitions. Often, instead of rearranging already existing plays, the *metteur en scène* will piece together a "drama" on some appropriately awe-inspiring theme as he goes along. A quote from Artaud's tentative repertoire for his new theater makes this clearer:

We shall stage, without regard for text:
1] An adaptation of a work from the time of Shakespeare, a work entirely consistent with our present troubled state of mind, whether one of the apocryphal plays of Shakespeare, such as *Arden of Feversham,* or an entirely different play from the same period.
2] A play of extreme poetic freedom by Léon-Paul Fargue.
3] An extract from the *Zohar*: "The Story of Rabbi

3. For example, the Ubu figure, the "terrible cry" and "menace" in *Waiting for Godot,* the "awful presence" outside the room in *Endgame,* the growing body in Ionesco's *Amédée,* the loud speaker in Adamov's *La grande et la petite Manoeuvre,* Jarry's disembraining machine, the mausoleum in Genet's *The Balcony.*

Simeon," which has the ever-present violence and force of a conflagration.

4] The story of Bluebeard reconstructed according to the historical records and with a new idea of eroticism and cruelty.

5] The Fall of Jerusalem, according to the Bible and history; with the blood-red color that trickles from it and the people's feeling of abandon and panic visible even in the light; and on the other hand the metaphysical disputes of the prophets, the frightful intellectual agitation they create and the repercussions of which physically affect the King, the Temple, the People, and Events themselves.

6] A Tale by the Marquis de Sade, in which the eroticism will be transposed, allegorically mounted and figured, to create a violent exteriorization of cruelty, and a dissimulation of the remainder.

7] One or more romantic melodramas in which the improbability will become an active and concrete element of poetry.

8] Büchner's Wozzeck, in a spirit of reaction against our principles and as an example of what can be drawn from a formal text in terms of the stage.

9] Works from the Elizabethan theater stripped of their text and retaining only the accoutrements of period, situations, characters, and action.[4]

This list of tentative productions was never realized in fact. Artaud's only opportunity to put his theories into practice with absolute freedom came between 1927 and 1929, when he and Roger Vitrac ran their own theater, significantly named the Théâtre Alfred Jarry. Here he produced Les Cenci, which he adapted from the Shelley and Stendhal versions, several of Vitrac's plays, Strindberg's Dream Play, the third act of Claudel's Partage du Midi (acted as a farce), and several other things. But Artaud is not important as a mere transformer of other men's work. He was the catalytic agent for an entirely new drama that used the complex resources of the modern theater to express the age-old cry of fear and protest, the most

4. Artaud, op. cit., pp. 99–100.

elemental human impulse from the most primitive man to the present. Taking the sudden outburst of primitive elemental force that Jarry's *Ubu roi* projected into the theater as his starting point, Artaud continued to define a drama denuded of all the excess and essentially nondramatic elements which had accumulated around the art of the theater through the ages. Artaud's drama may be compared to the bare trunk of a tree stripped of all the shrubbery that usually obscures its reality; but the only tree that would have satisfied Artaud would have been Yggdrasil, the sacred, magical, awe-inspiring ash which penetrates to the center of the earth and to the core of life itself. From this tree sprang the modern avant-garde drama—the plays of Beckett, Ionesco, and Adamov (who in 1947 called Artaud the greatest living poet), of Genet, Audiberti, and Jean Tardieu, and of the other avant-garde playwrights. All their plays are concerned with man's subjection to a malignant fate, all of them discard sociology and psychology as media for building characters, and all of them move in a purely theatric, dreamlike atmosphere. This dreamlike atmosphere (which becomes overt in plays like Adamov's *Professor Taranne*, Ionesco's *Victims of Duty*, and Beckett's *Embers*) is not accidental, but is rather the key to the whole technique. Artaud felt that men see themselves clearly only in dreams; and that it was through dreams that men could reach back to the primeval past when drama was born as the ritual observance of the myths whose creation is coeval with the beginning of human thought itself. Artaud's theory of the dream is allied to the Jungian theory, in which dreams bind men together through their demonstration of an inherited collective unconscious. Artaud opposed Freud's theory of dreams because it showed the effects of individually different psychoneurotic repressions—and so is closely allied to the modern drama of individual character analysis.

The use of the dream technique is basic to Artaud's drama. It enabled him to use speech in a purely theatrical and nonliterary manner; and it enabled him to justify his use of visual communication through hieroglyphic symbols, which is the method by which dream communication takes place. It was through the use of the dream technique, too, that Artaud could present the apparitions, effigies, and other "shocks and surprises" which could bring the audience into the desired mystic union with one another, with the action, and with the cruel, primeval, juggernautlike forces governing the world.

ARTHUR ADAMOV
The Way Out of the Void

ARTHUR ADAMOV's early plays illustrate in their purest form the principles of the avant-garde drama. In all the dramas of the current avant-garde the purpose is protest against the hopelessness of the human condition and against the strictures imposed on the individual by society. The method by which this protest is conveyed is the method of paradox, in which a truth is presented by an exaggerated emphasis on its opposite.

Like most modern dramatists, Adamov has a thoroughly pessimistic outlook on life. His themes are the tyranny of parental love; the innate cruelty of the society in which we are forced to live; and the meaninglessness, futility, and confusion of everyday life.

The tyranny of parental love, which the avant-gardists consider one of the oppressions inherent in human existence, is treated by Adamov in *Les Retrouvailles* (The Recoveries, published 1955) and *Le Sens de la Marche* (this title cannot be translated as it contains two double meanings in the French— The Direction of the March, The Meaning of the Way). These two plays deal with, respectively, an amorphous mother image that literally forces the son back to a state of physical infancy; and with a son who rebels against a father and a father-substitute, finally killing the latter. *Les Retrouvailles* is a play of hopelessness whose final scene is strongly reminiscent of the scene in Strindberg's *The Father* in which the Captain reverts to an infantile state under the pressure of his nurse-mother. Beyond this grotesquely powerful final curtain scene, however, there is little of interest in *Les Retrouvailles*. *Le Sens de la Marche* is more in the mainstream of the modern avant-garde movement as a play of rebellion. In this often incoherent and badly constructed play the son carries on a rebellion against society, the army, love, and finally his father, a crotchety, demanding old man who, in all but actual physical appearance, is the traditional Xanthippo-Oedipal stage mother. The son finally purges himself of the poisonous parental influence by strangling his father's companion and alter ego in a fit of uncontrollable, instinctive, self-purifying rebellion.

Even in these thematically fragmentary plays Adamov follows the pattern of protest, which is the chief characteristic of the modern avant-garde drama.[1] He protests against the merciless cruelty of the world—a cruelty that is at once inhuman and superhuman, omnipresent in the external and immanent in the individual's inner world, an almost tangible entity in itself and at the same time an emanation of a greater, instinctively malicious entity. The purpose of the protest, as Camus has shown us in *The Rebel*, is to curtail the cruel power *by rebelling against it*. The power against which the protest is made is thwarted to an extent directly in proportion to the violence of the protest. The reason for this is the postulated theory that all power, whether temporal or metaphysical, is based upon an imbalance of strength and weakness which can never reach perfect equilibrium; but the delicately poised scale adjusts instantly to any change, so that a gain on one side automatically involves a corresponding loss on the other. Thus if the violence of the protest is sufficiently radical, as in the son's murder of the father-substitute in *Le Sens de la Marche*, the scale tips over entirely, and one particular aspect of the universal, all-pervading cruelty is triumphantly vanquished. In *Les Retrouvailles*, on the other hand, the son's protest is unsuccessful, and the play ends with the sudden and complete triumph of the forces of cruelty as the mother wheels her full-grown son off in a baby carriage.

The sense of cosmic cruelty that appears in Adamov's work is accompanied and balanced in most cases by a narrower, spe-

1. The best piece of scholarship on Adamov to appear in English so far is Martin Esslin's "Arthur Adamov: The Curable and the Incurable" in *The Theatre of the Absurd* (Garden City, N. Y.: Doubleday & Company, Inc., 1961), pp. 47–78.

cifically human type of cruelty. The sense of helplessness that
man experiences when confronted by the metaphysical world is
intensified by his confrontation with the same helplessness and
thwarted desire when he turns to his fellow men. Man becomes
a dumb animal frustratedly bellowing back and forth across a
crowded space that seems to him a void. Adamov has recorded
for us how an ordinary street incident first made him aware of
the dramatic possibilities of mutual solitude. He saw one day
two young girls passing a blind beggar on the street. As they
passed arm-in-arm, oblivious of the beggar, they sang a popular
song of the day, the words of which went, "*J'ai fermé les yeux,
c'était merveilleux*" (I closed my eyes; it was wonderful). As
soon as he saw this, Adamov tells us, he said to himself, "That's
theatre, that's what I want to do." [2] It is significant that this
particular incident should have stimulated a modern dramatist,
for it is exactly the opposite of what has always been thought
dramatic. Here we have the absence of communication, the
absence of human sympathy and emotion, and above all the
absence of conflict. Adamov concentrates in his early plays
(*La Parodie, L'Invasion, La grande et la petite Manoeuvre,
Tous contre Tous*) on this impersonal type of drama in which
the characters have no psychological individuality. These plays
are a sort of mystic ritual dance between two magnets with
the like poles constantly turned towards each other. Nothing
decisive ever happens, except the inevitable, meaningless and
reasonless death at the end, which represents the remerging of
the human with the greater impersonal controlling power. During the play the characters move aimlessly in mutually exclusive spheres running on courses unfathomable to their occupants.

The theme of cruelty within the social system shows up in
Tous contre Tous (All Against All, 1953) and *Paolo Paoli*
(1957). In the earlier play the theme is treated in general
symbolic terms; in the later one in specific, individual terms.
Tous contre Tous is undoubtedly Adamov's best play. It is
about the instinctive mutual enmity human beings display

2. Arthur Adamov, *Théâtre* (Paris: Gallimard, 1955), II, p. 8.

toward each other. The play is not so much an indictment of a social system which forces human beings to act in their habitual dog-eat-dog manner as an implication that the social system is a result of human nature. A social system, Adamov is saying, is no more than a conglomeration of individuals and their traits. The only rule the individual respects is the rule of self; therefore, the society in which he lives is an impersonal one where the law of self-preservation is the only guiding principle and treachery the accepted mode of conduct.

Briefly, *Tous contre Tous* concerns the persecution of a particular group of people within the society. These people are distinguished from the rest of their fellows by having a limp. They are used as scapegoats whenever a scapegoat is needed. Between these persecutions they are tolerated and even respected, since many of them show an ability to be even more unscrupulous than their straight-walking compatriots and are therefore more successful. The ironic thing is that the trait that supposedly distinguishes them from the rest of the populace—their limp—is by no means confined to them. There are plenty of people who limp but are not *réfugiés*, and plenty who do not limp but are *réfugiés*. Naturally the people who limp but are not really *réfugiés* are the ones who are the most rabid enemies of the *réfugiés*. The play as a whole may be described as a microcosmic view of treachery, hate, and double-dealing. The characters are driven to deceive each other and injure or betray each other by the impersonal, blandly mischievous power represented by the radio, whose announcements at the beginning of each scene determine the characters' actions. The characters are skeletal puppets, stripped bare of all dignity and feeling—obsessed only by their desire to survive at any cost.

As in all plays of rebellion, death is the great enemy. Here, though, the inevitably futile struggle against the onslaught of death does not produce the heroic protester, but a small, sneaking, sniveling, shameless schemer who tries to subvert death, to slide unnoticed away from it, to shove someone else into its jaws instead of defying it. As one reads the play, one feels only disgust and revulsion at such a picture of the human race.

But it is a true picture; there is no doubt of that. Adamov explicitly states in his introduction to the play that it is an allegory of the Central European persecution of the Jews and of the attempt of many of those Jews to continue living their old lives at whatever price to their personal dignity.[3] The play ends—necessarily—with the brutal, violent and, above all, *senseless* death of all the main characters.

In *Paolo Paoli* Adamov again took up the theme of social cruelty he began in *Tous contre Tous*. This time, however, he has treated the matter in terms of specific individuals rather than in generalized terms.

Paolo Paoli shows the development in France of a state of mind that made World War I possible. In order to present this story Adamov has taken over a stage technique perfected by Bertolt Brecht in *Der Aufhaltsame Aufstieg des Arturo Ui* (The Preventable Rise of Arturo Ui). Each of the twelve scenes is preceded by a short "movie show" of pictures and extracts from newspapers, magazines, and speeches of the pre-World War I period. These provide an ironic contrast with the action that follows and serve to put that action into its proper historical focus. Adamov himself states that the purpose of the technique is to remind the audience how war was slowly but inevitably being prepared underneath the veneer of carefree and euphoric living.[4] The tragedy of the political events described in the screen projections is underlined by an accompaniment of contemporary popular songs, which slowly change to military marches as the play progresses. The idea is excellent, but the actual story of Paolo Paoli is simply dull. In turning from the general to the specific, Adamov has paradoxically lost the knack of telling a story in dramatic terms. The specific petty chicaneries of Paolo Paoli as he trades in butterfly bodies may be symbolic of a materialism that sacrifices esthetic values for commercial considerations, but they are not interesting in

3. *Ibid.*, p. 14.
4. This remark does not appear in the French edition (Paris: Gallimard, 1957) but shows up in the prefatory note to Pierre Aron's German translation (Arthur Adamov, *Theaterstücke* [Darmstadt: Hermann Luchterhand Verlag, 1959], pp. [187]–320).

themselves. The continuous vacillation from faithfulness to adultery of Paoli's half-Catholic, half-Protestant, Franco-German wife may be symbolic of a moral degeneration which, when raised to the social level, leads inevitably to war, but it is merely dull in itself. In *Tous contre Tous*, on the other hand, the generalized actions of the frankly symbolic characters are far more interesting because the audience is able to transfer them to its own specific experiences and observations.

Adamov's first two plays, *La Parodie* (The Parody, written 1947, performed 1952) and *L'Invasion* (The Invasion, written 1949, performed 1950), deal with the mutual isolation of human beings. The world depicted in these plays resembles the one envisioned by Leibnitz, who saw an endless rain of self-contained monads floating blindly down through space, accidentally bumping into each other now and then. However, since these monads are "windowless," the occupants have no more real contact with each other than the yolks of two eggs lying side by side with the shells touching. Whenever two of these drifting cells bump into one another, the persons inside are jarred, but they have no idea what has disturbed them. Consequently their reactions have absolutely nothing to do with the real facts of the situation. Even more often some undefined but malicious and invisible power reaches out and casually crushes a monad, so that the person inside is either killed or maimed.

La Parodie is, as the title indicates, a parody of human existence. There is no plot to speak of. The two leading characters, identified only as N and The Employee, represent, respectively, rejection and acceptance of life as it is. Both are destroyed in the end, so that Adamov appears to be saying that it does not matter what one's attitude to life is—that it is pointless indeed to bother having any attiude at all—since it all comes to the same thing in the end.

In his second play, *L'Invasion*, Adamov changed his method but not his theme. Instead of using type chracters in an undefined setting, as in *La Parodie*, he used specific people in a specific, realistic setting. But the idea remains the same: nobody listens to anybody else. Everyone lives wrapped up in the cocoon of his own personal absorptions. The title of the play refers to the "invasion" that human beings suffer through social obligations; through the presence of other people, who are in their turn absorbed in and weighed down by their own preoccupations; and through the constant pressure of inanimate external forces that can only with great difficulty be brought into harmony with the individual's inner life. All these influences work upon the individual like an insidious, creeping paralysis until he is completely stripped of his own character.

In *L'Invasion* the victim of this assault is a scholar who has decided to devote his whole existence to the endless task of editing and publishing the papers of his dead friend. In the opening scene he is eagerly attacking the piles of paper lying all over the room in utter confusion. As the play progresses, the piles of paper slowly become sorted and stacked away so that, at the end, the room is as neat as a business office. As this external tidying process advances, the victim's internal tidiness decreases in direct proportion. At the end, the scholar stands in the middle of his room, utterly confused among all the apparent neatness and order. He tears up all the papers, which constitute his life's work, and kills himself. Life has simply been too much for him, and so he leaves it. Instead of being permitted to cope with what interests him most in life, he is forced to take into account his mother, his wife, and her lover, a rival scholar who disagrees with his method of editing, and others. The solution is, of course, needlessly drastic, but Adamov has always been of the opinion that the solution to any human problem when it is presented in dramatic terms must be the ultimate solution. In Adamov the climax of a human event must always involve the relentless destruction of the hero. *L'Invasion*, then, is simply the drama of each person's isolation within himself and the impossibility of mutual adjustment.

La grande et la petite Manoeuvre (The Great and the Small Manoeuvre, 1950) and *Le Professeur Taranne* (Professor Taranne, 1953) are two dream plays in which, by means of a breakthrough into the subconscious world, the individual gains a momentary (and horrifying) glimpse of the world outside his monad. The inevitable result is that he is destroyed. The basic emotion running through both these plays is fear: the protagonist becomes gradually more and more conscious of the fact that every time he comes into contact with the outside world he will be hurt. In *La grande et la petite Manoeuvre* we have the picture of a harmless, terrified person caught between the active opposing factions of the modern world: between the rebels and the oppressors. This eternal victim, called "Le Mutilé," is constantly controlled by invisible voices, audible only to him, which tell him what to do and where to go. Every time he hears these voices he begins to tremble violently and feels impelled to go away. Whenever he comes back after obeying one of these mysterious orders, we find that he has lost a limb. At the end of the play he is an armless and legless cripple in a wheelchair. His gradual destruction has no reason: he is simply a victim of more powerful forces.

La grande et la petite Manoeuvre is an intensely bizarre allegorical dream about the cruelty of life; *Le Professeur Taranne* is an equally bizarre personal nightmare. Like its companion play, *Le Professeur Taranne* is about a man's amazed horror on discovering the obverse side of the world, the unseen one outside his cocoon. Professor Taranne is the epitome of self-centered harmlessness set down in the midst of an amorphous nightmare world inexplicably crystallized into reality. Both he and The Mutilated One undergo a long, slow, symbolic castration at the end of which they simply give up— human flies caught on the cosmic flypaper.

Professor Taranne's dream is that he, a famous savant, has been arrested because some children have accused him of walking around nude on the beach. The professor's explanation is essentially only an ineffective excuse for repeating assertions of his eminence in the scholarly world. But he finds that the things on which he has based his life mean absolutely nothing to anyone else. In the police station he goes up to several persons he knows well but is recognized by none of them. One person even mistakes him for his archrival, Professor Ménard. Immediately after his second encounter with the police, the professor is accused of scribbling obscenities on the walls of the bathing huts. As before, his bewildered explanation is cut short by the abrupt departure of the policemen, who suddenly lose interest in him. After this the professor receives an enormous map of a ship's dining room that shows him placed next to the captain in the seat of honor. While he is poring over this, he receives a letter from the foreign university where he has been a guest lecturer telling him that he will not be invited back because he has plagiarized Professor Ménard and because no one ever paid any attention to his lectures anyway. As the play ends, Professor Taranne hangs the map of the ship's dining room on the wall. It is seen to be a blank sheet of paper. Contemplating this sight with the ruminative attention of a scholar unhurriedly and carefully digesting a new discovery, the professor begins slowly to undress himself.

In *Le Ping-Pong* (Ping-Pong, 1955) the point of view is entirely changed. Adamov has abandoned the deterministic play for a more flexible, psychological drama. The characters are no longer helpless automatons but human beings endowed with free will. The people of *Ping-Pong* choose their own destiny and only they are to blame if, incapable of rebelling, they become the victims of superior *manmade* powers. Instead of a cosmic power to rebel against, the characters in *Ping-Pong* are given only a modest socioeconomic power to fight. The play is concerned with the reactions of two young students Arthur and Victor and the people around them to a pinball machine. The machine, which symbolizes money and prestige, can, of course, simply be left alone; one can play it or not, as one pleases. Nevertheless it has an absolutely irresistible attraction for the two young men and their friends. The flashing lights, the glistening steel balls, the jerking flippers, and the implacable bumpers draw them on like a magnet. They hang over the monstrous machine like degenerates over an opium pipe. The machine replaces religion; and the corporation, with "the Old Man" at the top, replaces the celestial hierarchy. The lust for money and the ephemeral prestige that comes with it has stifled all the formerly powerful spiritual values, Adamov is saying. But at the same time there is a choice in Adamov's philosophy now: one does not have to play. All the characters, however, devote the best part of their lives to the corporation.

At the end of the play comes the scene which gives it its name. In this scene, which Adamov wrote first and which he admits has no organic connection with the rest of the play,[5] Arthur and Victor, both old men now, play ping-pong. They begin to quarrel over the rules of the game, as they did in their younger days over the operation of the pinball machine, and finally wind up playing ping-pong without net or paddles. As Victor tries to leap in the air to bat the ball down with his bare hand, he falls dead.

Le Ping-Pong and Paolo Paoli mark an interesting evolution in the work of a typical avant-garde playwright. Like Ionesco, Adamov has abandoned the doctrinaire determinism of Antonin Artaud's faithful followers. Both Ionesco (The Killer and Rhinoceros) and Adamov have come around to the view that man, despite his admitted feebleness, can still struggle to some effect and therefore has moral responsibility. From here it is a direct step to the complete absorption with social responsibility that Adamov has shown in the anti-Gaullist sketches he published in 1958 [6] and in his latest play, Le Printemps 71 (Springtime '71, 1960). In the preface to this play about the Paris Commune, modeled partly on Brecht, whom Adamov has taken as his new mentor,[7] and partly on Büchner, Adamov states that by writing a historical play, "I was at last able to escape from those 'interiors' where I was suffocating, and to speak not only of the bourgeoisie, but of everyone, of those who make up the majority of people—that is to say, whether one likes it or not, of the proletariat." [8] With this step Adamov leaves the death-oriented hopelessness that is the avant-garde drama's chief philosophical standpoint and returns to a belief in the temporal hopes that exist in the illusion-laden world of social humanity.

5. Adamov, Théâtre, II, p. 17.
6. Arthur Adamov, Guy Demoy, and Maurice Regnaut, Théâtre de Société (scènes d'actualité) (Paris: Petite bibliothèque républicaine, 1958), pp. 9–52.
7. The old one was obviously Antonin Artaud despite Adamov's doubts about his influence on himself and on the subsequent theater in general. Cf. Arthur Adamov, "Parce que je l'ai beaucoup aimé . . . ," Cahiers de la Compagnie Madeleine Renaud - Jean-Louis Barrault, Nos. 22 and 23 (May, 1958), pp. 128–29.
8. Arthur Adamov, Le Printemps 71 (Paris: Gallimard, 1961), p. [5].

SAMUEL BECKETT
Life in the Void

SAMUEL BECKETT first came to the attention of the
American public with the Broadway production of *Waiting for
Godot* (En Attendant Godot, 1953) in 1956. The play received
a sort of perverse notoriety because nobody was quite sure
what it was all about. The public went to see it because Bert
Lahr was in it (as Estragon) and because some cunning pub-
licity work based largely on intellectual snob appeal had convinced them that going to see *Waiting for Godot* was the thing
to do. The play thus received a longer run on Broadway than
it had any right to expect, and Beckett's name suddenly became
a well-known one in the American theater. Since then *Endgame*
(Fin de Partie, 1957) and *Krapp's Last Tape* (1958) have been
successful off Broadway, and Beckett's novels have been published by Grove Press. None of Beckett's works conforms to the
orthodox literary form of its genre; none of them is easy to
understand. One thing is obvious about them, however: they
all appear to throw off a stark pessimism about human affairs
that has rarely, if ever, been equaled in literature.

Naturally enough, a great deal of critical writing about
Beckett has quickly appeared. This writing is disturbing, to say
the least. Confronted with a writer who takes as uncomprisingly
uncomfortable a viewpoint as Beckett, the critics have frantically tried to justify his existence by seeing signs of their own
views in his works. The main point of the criticism is that
Beckett could not possibly mean what he appears to mean
because that would be very unpleasant indeed. In short, what
is happening to Beckett is very much like what happened to
Shaw: unable to face up to him, the critics have attempted to
snuff him out by hailing him as a Member of the Establishment.

Perhaps the most curiously uncomprehending view of Beckett comes from Frederick Lumley. Lumley represents the reactions of the "pillar-of-society" theatergoer, who goes to plays
to be entertained and to have his beliefs reaffirmed. It is surprising to see how outmoded this point of view has become in the

few years since the first productions of Beckett, Ionesco, and
the rest of the avant-garde dramatists. There is something amus-
ingly anachronistic about Lumley's plaint: this is criticism from
the vantage point of the English country garden satirized in
Wilde:

> Even at the risk of sounding like a second Clement Scott
> writing on a new *Ghosts*, it seems to this writer that this
> play is more akin to a cesspool of the degradations of hu-
> man souls than a tragedy of misfortune. Is there no limit
> to the depths to which man may descend and is there so
> little faith left in man that he must lie here forgotten? Will
> he never be given a resurrection, will we never again have
> new horizons opened to us through the nobility of man,
> and be able to enter a world not altogether unlike our own
> where there is no exploitation of facile optimism or morbid
> despair? [1]

Lumley's desire to run away from this world to a new stage
world where man will be comfortably exalted is in itself a subconscious recognition of the truth of Mephistopheles's remark
in Marlowe's *Dr. Faustus*, "Why this is hell, nor am I out of it."
Lumley and the daily-newspaper reviewers are aware, at least,
that the world of Beckett, even if it is a true world, is not
the world they want to see. To the extent that they condemn
it, they are honest critics. Honest also, if naïve and unrealistic,
is the criticism of Bonamy Dobrée, the historian of eighteenth-
century literature, who, in writing about *Waiting for Godot*,
informs us that "it is time to affirm that anything that can be
called art must ultimately be in praise of life, or must at least
promote acceptance of life, thus indicating some values." [2] Less
honest are the "romantic" critics. By romantic criticism I mean
the quality of seeing what one would like to see rather than
what is really there. An example of starry-eyed romanticism at
its most extreme would be Kenneth Rexroth's reading of a

1. Frederick Lumley, *Trends in Twentieth Century Drama* (London:
Barrie & Rockliff, 1960), p. 142.
2. Bonamy Dobrée, "The London Theatre, 1957," *Sewanee Review*,
LXVI (Winter, 1958), p. 152.

plea for universal brotherhood into *Waiting for Godot:* "the comradeship of men, whether verminous tramps with unmanageable pants or Jim and Huck Finn drifting through all the universe on their raft—the comradeship of men in work, in art, or simply in waiting, in the utterly unacquisitive act of waiting—is an ultimate value, so ultimate that it gives life sufficient dignity and satisfaction." [3] According to Rexroth, Beckett is writing about only the last two hundred years when he writes about the sickness of society. His point is the same as Homer's—that we must accept the world on secular terms and believe in the brotherhood of man, represented by Vladimir and Estragon.[4] Leonard Pronko also emphasizes this quality of "togetherness" when he says that *Waiting for Godot* shows that the quality of friendship is the only solace human beings have on this earth.[5] Pronko sees *Endgame* as a picture of the disintegration of a human universe,[6] but he can still somehow conclude that Beckett's view of life is basically religious.[7] Following the same line of thought, Edith Kern sees *Waiting for Godot* as glorifying "the all-surpassing power of human tenderness," which, she feels, is a substitute for the real redeemer, who never comes and for whom men wait with forlorn hope.[8]

Worst of all, perhaps, is the attribution of Christian principles to Beckett. *Waiting for Godot* is particularly fertile ground for the symbol-seeker, and since there are undeniable references to God, Christianity, and the Bible in the play, it is quite easy to give it a religious interpretation with some judicious out-of-context quoting. Charles S. McCoy, Professor of Religion in Higher Education at the Pacific School of Religion, points out that "each interpreter runs the risk of merely reading into the

3. Kenneth Rexroth, "The Point is Irrelevance," *The Nation* (April 14, 1956), p. 328.
4. *Ibid.*
5. Leonard Pronko, *Avant-Garde* (Berkeley, Cal.: University of California Press, 1962), p. 39.
6. *Ibid.*, p. 47.
7. *Ibid.*, p. 54.
8. Edith Kern, "Drama Stripped for Inaction: Beckett's *Godot*," *Yale French Studies*, No. 14 (Winter, 1954–1955), p. 47.

play his own point of view." [9] Having pointed out the trap,
he disregards it. He concludes, for example, that Godot *does*
come because the tree sprouts leaves in the second act, and a
tree is a symbol of the Cross and of life.[10] God(ot) is thus
immanent throughout the second act, but mankind is too willfully blind to see him. This is an ingenious interpretation, but
it ignores the overwhelming evidence of Beckett's lack of faith
to be found in his other plays and in his novels, as well as in
Waiting for Godot itself when looked at as a whole. The tree
is again plucked out by another Christian critic, who sees it
as the Tree of the Knowledge of Good and Evil, the Tree of
Life, the Cross, and the Tree of Judas. He concludes that *Waiting for Godot* is a "modern morality play on permanent Christian themes" and represents the "tension and uncertainty in
which the average Christian must live in this world." [11]

Another dangerous pitfall when dealing with a writer as
objective as Beckett is the biographical approach. Horace Gregory compares Beckett's characters to ancient Roman gladiators
because they live outside the conventions of society. Their
martyrdoms are not tragic, but anonymous. He attributes this
view to the effect on Beckett of being brought up as a Protestant
in southern Ireland, which gave him a feeling of alienation from
society.[12] The trouble with this interpretation is that it puts
the cart before the horse. Gregory starts out with a fact of
Beckett's life and concludes from this that certain attitudes
must be found in his works. But it is not true that Beckett's
characters must be social outsiders simply because he was
brought up as a social outsider. Beckett's men are not, as a
matter fact, outside the conventions of society: their actions
depict the inner reality of men in society. This biographical
method is taken one step further by Lionel Abel, who, noting
that Beckett used to be Joyce's secretary, postulates that Pozzo

9. Charles S. McCoy, *"Waiting for Godot:* A Biblical Appraisal,"
Religion in Life, XXVIII (Autumn, 1959), p. 595.
10. *Ibid.,* p. 602.
11. *Times Literary Supplement,* February 10, 1956, p. 84.
12. Horace Gregory, "Beckett's Dying Gladiators," *Commonweal*
(October 26, 1956), pp. 88–89.

in *Waiting for Godot* is a portrait of James Joyce and that Hamm in *Endgame* is a portrait of Joyce satirizing himself.[13]

All this is not to say that Beckett criticism, which is extremely voluminous by now, is uniformly on the wrong track. Ruby Cohn, in the best critical study of Beckett to appear so far, points out that Beckett's man lives in "a world that he did not make and that resists his efforts to make sense of it." [14] Charles Glicksberg agrees that pessimism and unrelieved meaninglessness are the main themes in Beckett's work.[15] And Rosette Lamont has said that "his theatre will remain as the ultimate expression of the despair of the atomic generation." [16]

Beckett's philosophical system, like that of so many of the current avant-garde writers, is based on a paradox. It is the concept that Thought (by which is meant logical thought, philosophical contemplation) is useless. Thought, says Beckett, can reveal nothing to us in the final analysis. All ultimate truth is forever beyond the compass of the human mind; and therefore truth does not, in effect, exist. It is this hopelessness and helplessness in an alien and incomprehensible universe that lead Beckett to the savage purity of his pessimism. Beckett makes Schopenhauer look like a gay optimist and Nietzsche like a devout believer.

The key passage for an understanding of Beckett's intellectual nihilism is the conversation about the four evangelists in *Waiting for Godot*. This passage has been inexplicably cited by at least one critic as proof of Beckett's Christianity. Vladimir tells Estragon that one of the two thieves crucified with Jesus was saved—according to one of the evangelists. Two of them say nothing about the matter, and the fourth says that both thieves cursed him. Vladimir becomes obsessed by the fact that although all four evangelists were there—"or thereabouts"—

13. Lionel Abel, *Metatheatre* (New York: Hill & Wang, Inc., 1963), pp. 135–36.
14. Ruby Cohn, *Samuel Beckett: The Comic Gamut* (New Brunswick, N. J.: Rutgers University Press, 1962), p. 225.
15. Charles I. Glicksberg, "Samuel Beckett's World of Fiction," *Arizona Quarterly*, XVIII (Spring, 1962), pp. 32–47.
16. Rosette C. Lamont, "The Metaphysical Farce: Beckett and Ionesco," *French Review*, XXXII (February, 1959), p. 328.

only one says that one of the thieves was saved. Why should
the evangelist who says that one of the thieves was saved be
believed rather than one of the others?

"Who believes him?" asks Estragon. "Everybody," answers
Vladimir. "It's the only version they know."

And then we have Estragon's, and, I think, Beckett's verdict: "People are bloody ignorant apes."

Beckett is saying here that a precise and analytical discussion of religious problems leads only to confusion. All we find
out is that the "ultimate truths" upon which we base the
conduct of our lives and on which we rely as a source of moral
justification for our actions are based on the flimsiest evidence
and are often mutually contradictory. As the incident of the
four evangelists shows, we cannot even begin to approach an
understanding of the truths of religion—assuming that there
are any such truths. If, then, we can know nothing about religion, which deals with such things as the origin of the world
and the existence of human beings, it follows that we cannot
really know anything about the world and the people on it
either. The powers of the human mind are an illusion since
they can tell us nothing about matters on which those things
it apparently does understand ultimately depend. In short, all
knowledge is an illusion and all things are pointless—in so far
as the human mind is concerned.

The uselessness of thought and the consequent pointlessness of all human action appears again and again as a theme in
Beckett's work. This is the crucial point upon which all of
Beckett's thought rests: if the ultimate is meaningless, then the
immediate is meaningless as well. The clearest statement of
Beckett's belief in the uselessness of thought is in the tremendously effective scene of Lucky's tirade in *Waiting for Godot*.
Beckett here implies that it is only in modern times that man
has become impotent in thought and action. Man's increased
"knowledge" has only served to make him aware of the uselessness of knowledge, the impossibility of certainty. Thus all that
he has learned degenerates into a confused babble. Lucky's
speech is a long, garbled stream-of-consciousness monologue
which is a parody of logically connected utterance and scientific

discourse. Just before his speech, Lucky goes through a weird dance called "The Net" which is expressive of bewilderment and impotence. Pozzo, Lucky's master, tells Vladimir and Estragon that Lucky used to dance farandoles, flings, brawls, jigs, fandangos, and hornpipes, but now he only dances this eerie, sinuous, tortured movement called "The Net." Similarly, Lucky "used to think very prettily once," but now he can only chatter away incoherently. Now there is only the numb impotence implied in Lucky's dance, his monologue, and his condition (he is a yoked beast of burden for his domineering master, Pozzo, the man who thinks he is created in God's image).

Beckett's belief in the uselessness of any attempt to arrive at a conclusion about anything can also be seen in the chess-game allegory in *Endgame* and *Murphy* (1938). Chess, the most logical of games, almost a symbol of logic itself, is made to look ridiculous in both works. The pure logic of the game is subverted, and the game becomes instead a blind, stupidly willful negation of logic. *Endgame*—the title may mean the playing out of the lives of the characters, the playing out of human existence, or the final moves of a fantastically perverted chess game—is a static ballet of two immovable pawns, a helpless king, and an aimlessly roving knight playing themselves into a hopeless stalemate. The climax of *Murphy* comes when Murphy plays a game of chess with a madman while working as an attendant in a lunatic asylum. In this game, which Beckett gives move by move in the text, every logical chess move is avoided. Only those moves that avoid an attack are used, and after about twenty moves the two players are back where they started, having moved all their pieces back (except the pawns, of course).

Beckett's early novel *Watt* (1953) is completely taken up with useless mental convolutions. Watt's interior monologues reduce the process of logical thinking to an absurdity. Watt is a servant in the house of a Mr. Knott and spends all his time worrying about the nature of his duties. How he ever gets anything done is a mystery, for his time seems to be wholly taken up with compulsively working out various combinations of ways in which he could do things. Everything that happens to Watt or to anyone he knows is minutely analyzed from all angles with obsessive diligence. Thus Watt figures out twelve ways in which Mr. Knott may have arrived at his peculiar method of eating; and we are given no less than thirty-six ways in which Mr. Knott can move around his room, the furniture of which can be arranged in twenty different ways—all of them described in detail.

Watt's thinking seems to be a way of passing time—not in the sense of amusing oneself, but in the sense of getting rid of life. It is a substitute for thought rather than thought itself. For Beckett this substitute makes as much (or as little) sense as the thing itself: "You would do better, or at least no worse," Molloy says, "to obliterate texts than to blacken margins, to fill in the holes of words till all is blank and flat and the whole ghastly business looks like what it is, senseless, speechless, issueless misery." Beckett looks at human knowledge *sub specie aeternitatis* and finds that it makes no sense when set beside the permanent incomprehensibles. His view of life is similar to the one expressed in Conrad's *Heart of Darkness*: "Droll thing life is—that mysterious arrangement of merciless logic for a futile purpose." The Beckettian man has achieved the degree of insight where all temporal concerns crumble, and nothing— or *Nothing*—is seen through the breach.

The force or forces that control the universe cannot be comprehended and appear to be unconcerned about humanity (Godot never comes; the *Endgame* players are alone). Therefore the concerns and actions of human beings are meaningless because they can have no ultimate goal. Occasionally Beckett seems to derive some sort of perverse comfort from this, as when he has the Unnamable say, "Nothing to do but stretch out comfortably on the rack in the blissful knowledge you are nobody for all eternity." Usually, however, Beckett's pessimism is intensified by his perception of the dreariness and pointlessness of life. The events of human existence have a monotonous sameness. Time is a succession of meaningless events that merge into each other so imperceptibly that they are indistinguishable. The whole world from the beginning of time to the present seems to Beckett like Tennyson's Land of the Lotos-Eaters—"a land where all things always seemed the same." Life goes on—and on—and on: infinite monotony, infinite torture. Everything is gray, as Clov tells Hamm in *Endgame*. The sun riseth no more—Beckett cannot even see the pitiful variety granted us by the Bible's supreme pessimist.

Endgame and *Waiting for Godot* are the best examples of Beckett's views on the monotony of life. The chief characters of both these plays—Vladimir and Estragon in *Waiting for Godot*; Hamm and Clov in *Endgame*—give one the idea that they are alive because they have to be. Objectively, they would like to die, but they are unable to kill themselves because the will to live (over which they have no control) is stronger than the will to die. And so they wearily occupy themselves with spinning out the skein of life, never daring to hope that some merciful Atropos will cut the thread for them. They play out the moves in their endless, aimless game with robotlike submissiveness.

"We're getting on," Hamm says with morbid self-satisfaction every time he and Clov complete another one of the eternally recurring episodes in their eternal farce.

"All life long, the same questions, the same answers," says Clov.

Only nature's cycles distinguish one period from another in Beckett's continuum of time. When Estragon and Vladimir return in the second act, the only difference in the dreary landscape is that the tree has flowered. It may be the next day, as they think. It may, however, also be the next month, or the next year, or it may be a thousand years later—it is always the same. The treadmill goes on, and Time turns upon itself like Vladimir's meaningless song about the dog that keeps eating and dying endlessly:

> A dog came in the kitchen
> And stole a crust of bread.
> Then cook up with a ladle
> And beat him till he was dead.
> Then all the dogs came running

And dug the dog a tomb
And wrote upon the tombstone
For the eyes of dogs to come:
A dog came in the kitchen
And stole a crust of bread.
Then cook up with a ladle
And beat him till he was dead.
Then all the dogs came running
And dug the dog a tomb (etc.)

Vladimir and Estragon just go on and on doggedly. They are faceless humanity slogging on through the dreary landscape with its blasted tree. They are always disappointed by Godot, whom they never see and whom they know only through his bland emissary, the boy. This boy always looks the same, but is always different. He brings reassurance of Godot's existence, although he himself really knows nothing about his supposed master and simply agrees that the image that the two tramps have built up for themselves is real. The allegory is inescapable —the boy might just as well appear in skullcap and cassock. Because there is "nothing to be done" in this world, Vladimir and Estragon arrive every day and numbly wait. Occasionally they hear a "terrible cry" and a "menace" from which they "cringe." This way they know that whether or not it is ever coming to them, whether it is GOD-ot or not, there is some superior and terrible power over them. The deterministic philosophy that underlies all of Beckett's work is most clearly exemplified in his drama.

In this colorless world where nothing significant happens, it is only natural that the people should be indistinguishable from each other as well. Beckett's characters are forever in search of the identity that will set them off from others, and of course they never find it. Molloy and Moran merge into one another and so do Mahood, Worm, and the pathetic Unnamable, who has not even got so much as a formal label to distinguish him. Beckett's five novels deal with five men who are trying to solve the problem of their own identity. In *Murphy*, the earliest, easiest to understand, and best of the novels, the "hero" ("antihero" would be a better term for Beckett's chief characters) is an expatriate Irish mystic whose peculiar custom it is to tie himself naked into a rocking chair with seven scarves and thus try to approach Nirvana. Murphy finally finds peace from pursuit in a job as a male nurse in a mental home. It is here that Murphy plays the chess game previously referred to with a mental patient significantly named Mr. Endon. At the end of the game Murphy peers into Mr. Endon's eyes and finds that the madman no longer sees him: the eyes are perfectly blank. In other words, Murphy discovers that he has ceased to exist in Mr. Endon's mind.

At the same time he forgets all his other acquaintances. He no longer exists in Mr. Endon's mind, and the people he knows no longer exist in his mind. His ceasing to exist in actual fact is therefore only a formality. Murphy goes to his room, ties himself into his rocking chair, and is annihilated by a gas explosion. Beckett's point is that if we exist in any sense at all, we exist in the minds of others and in our relationships with and effect on them. At some point in our lives however, we realize that we are unseen by others. Communication ceases. Each person is absorbed in himself, but he cannot exist unless he exists in someone else's mind. Ergo, he does not really exist. The reasoning is circular and therefore meaningless—like everything else.

Beckett's second novel *Watt* is about a compulsive manservant who feels impelled to build up an edifice of complicated reasoning about each trivial event in his life in order to prove to himself that he exists. Watt turns Descartes' straightforward logic into a paradox: "I think, therefore I am" becomes "I think, but do I exist?"

Beckett's later trilogy, *Molloy* (1951), *Malone Dies* (1951), and *The Unnamable* (1953), is composed of books written in the first person by men who are reminiscing at the end of their lives, trying to fasten upon some significant event so as to prove to themselves it was not all in vain. This is also Krapp's purpose in *Krapp's Last Tape*. None of them succeed. Molloy, Malone, and the Unnamable are essentially the same person. They are completely negative beings who have accomplished nothing.

C

This is not a condemnation of ineffective persons—Beckett's point is that no one has accomplished anything. Molloy, indeed, loses himself so completely that some omniscient force sends out a private detective to track him down and bring him back alive. The detective, Moran, does not find Molloy: he becomes him instead. Moran's possessions drop away from him, he loses contact with his comfortable, bourgeois home, his son deserts him; and then, when he is completely adrift in the middle of the forest, his legs become paralyzed. Like Molloy, Moran then has to drag himself hand over hand, inch by inch through the muck to his destination.

Malone is nothing and never was anything. He is writing down his reminiscences before dying, with a sort of sardonic self-satisfaction at his failure to turn up anything significant or even a little self-assertive in his vegetablelike past. Krapp does the same thing, but Beckett turns it into a touching piece of drama by making him lose his self-satisfaction. Instead of writing down his reminiscences, Krapp listens to them. Every year on his birthday he makes a tape recording of his thoughts about the past year. Now on his sixty-ninth birthday he listens to the tape he made exactly thirty years ago. On it he speaks of his one attempt to make love to a woman in a manner above the strictly animal level. He listens to the short, idyllic passage over and over as he realizes that it represents the one moment, in his otherwise meaningless and wasted life, that had some status as a true and significant experience. As the play ends, Krapp sits staring before him, listening once more to the inadequate description of his one love affair, overcome with helpless nostalgia for the one chance of genuine feeling he lightly tossed aside in the cynicism of thirty years before. The Unnamable, as we shall see, is hardly an individual even in the purely physical sense. He has no name for himself and constantly floats back and forth between Mahood and Worm, two characters that exist in his mind only.

Since no actions can mean anything, everything that man does is merely so much absurd pretension. The chief example of this is Hamm, the petty despot of *Endgame*, who rules not only over the bare-walled room which represents our accessible world but over the two garbage cans filled with the human refuse that created him. The inference, of course, is the vanity of human pomp and circumstance. Hamm's preoccupation with being in the center of the room is another instance of this, as is his grandiose self-pity when he wakes up at the beginning of the play ("Can there be misery loftier than mine?"). But the most marvelous example of all is the superbly ironic scene in which Hamm issues commands to his stuffed toy dog. The dog is not finished yet and has only three legs. Hamm, who is blind, asks Clov whether the dog is standing before him, "imploring" him. Clov assures him that it is, although the dog is, of course, lying on its side and is incapable of begging anyway. In the second act of *Waiting for Godot*, Pozzo's reappearance blind and helpless, after his domineering behaviour in the first act, is another case in point. Pozzo represents the masters of the earth, the omnipotent, in Act I, and his fall in Act II symbolizes the illusion inherent in even the greatest apparent power.

What all these things—the sameness of the human beings and their actions, the vanity of human ambition, the uselessness of thought—amount to is a pessimism deeper than any that has ever been put into words before. Throughout Beckett's work we can find evidence of his conviction that everything is hopeless, meaningless, purposeless, and, above all, agonizing to endure. Beckett's people are leveled off and merged into each other by being all more or less physically disabled—as if this were really the common condition of men on earth. In *Endgame* Nagg and Nell (Hamm's parents) are old and crippled and unable to climb out of their garbage cans. Hamm is blind and cannot stand. Clov cannot sit and, like Vladimir and Estragon in *Waiting for Godot*, has a constant nagging feeling of being unwell. Pozzo becomes blind and helpless and Lucky is dumb (during his one speech he is "thinking"). Molloy and his alter ego Moran both become paralyzed from the waist down. Malone is dying and cannot get up. Mrs. Rooney, in *All That Fall* (1957), is fat, senile, and dropsical, and her husband is blind. The Unnamable is an armless, legless hulk observing the world over the rim of a jar which hangs outside a restaurant, the proprietress of which feeds him and changes his

sawdust once a week. Winnie in *Happy Days* (1961) is im-
mobilized in a mound of sand, buried up to the waist in the
first act, up to the neck in the second. And yet, like all of us,
she still blithely and unconsciously goes through all the motions
of living as best she can. And finally in *Watt* we have an account of the Lynch family, all twenty-eight members of which
are crippled in one way or another.

As one plows through the catalog of the Lynches and their
ailments, all minutely described, one feels that this is Beckett's
view of the condition of all people: lameness is the natural
state of man. Speaking of his mother, Molloy gives perhaps the
most bitter and despairing of all Beckett's statements: "I know
she did all she could not to have me, except of course the one
thing, and if she never succeeded in getting me unstuck, it was
that fate had earmarked me for less compassionate sewers."
Surely disgust and loathing can get no further. Beckett's view
of existence is summed up in Hamm's question, "Did you ever
have an instant of happiness?" and Clov's answer, "Not to my
knowledge"; and later in Hamm's despairing cry, "Use your
head, can't you, use your head—you're on earth, there's no cure
for that." Even in the comparatively cheerful early novels there
are passages full of a biting misanthropy. The garden at the
back of Mr. Knott's house in *Watt* is an example. Here Watt
and Sam savagely kill the larks and robins, born and unborn,
but affectionately feed the black rats with frogs, birds, or the
rats' and frogs' own baby offspring. Sam states that he and
Watt felt "closest to God" when they were feeding live baby
rats to the voracious parent rats.

Beckett has come around by quite another path to Blaise
Pascal's conclusion that the condition of man is *"inconstance,
ennui, inquiétude."* He sees man as a ridiculous mechanical
puppet who, like the two figures in *Act Without Words, No. 2*
(published 1960), responds to some persistent, merciless, and
impersonal goad by going through the motions of everyday living, either morosely and lackadaisically or with the anesthetizing
briskness and efficiency which leave no time for thought. Beckett has drawn one of the two possible conclusions from the
perception that the universe is unknowable. The other conclu-

sion—that the world as it is, is worthwhile for the simple reason
that it is all that there is (that Being in any form is better than
Nonbeing, in other words)—is Camus'. Beckett is the prophet
of negation and sterility. He holds out no hope to humanity,
only a picture of unrelieved blackness; and those who profess
to see in Beckett signs of a Christian approach or signs of compassion are simply refusing to see what is there.

EUGENE IONESCO
The Absurd as Warning

WITH THE exception of Samuel Beckett, no present-
day dramatist has caused such a varied spray of critical interpretations as Eugene Ionesco. The meaning of his plays is never
explicit. His work is characterized, instead, by what may be
termed a purposeful vagueness. His plays, in other words, are
full of possible meanings, but void both of specific polemic
purposes and of solutions. Ionesco is not committed to a point
of view because he realizes that all points of view are useless.
His plays are demonstrations of the incongruity between the
human condition and the human being's desires. As such, they
are true tragedies, for tragedy, as Ionesco himself points out,
lies in the unbearable.[1] His plays are "demystifications." They
strip the veils off man's everyday actions and expose the unbearable, tragic impasse beneath. Reality is tragic, Ionesco tells
us, and it will always remain so, no matter what form the masks
take. Committed playwrights, such as Arthur Miller or Bertolt
Brecht (Ionesco's particular bête noire), are merely attempting
the contemptibly superficial task of changing the masks.

It is this iconoclastic attitude that has caused Ionesco the
greatest trouble with his critics. Unable to reconcile themselves
to the idea of a generalized protest against the human condition or to a criticism of society that holds out no hope for
improvement, the critics have produced all sorts of bizarre

1. Eugène Ionesco, *Notes et contre-notes* (Paris: Gallimard, 1962),
p. 7.

explanations. Richard Coe, in his excellent critical study, gives a run-down of some of the more *outré* of these. *The Lesson* is an allegory of national revolt against dictatorship, or it is an attack on the philistinism of female college students. *Victims of Duty* can be taken either as a Freudian dream-play, a satire on the Oedipus complex, or as a working-out of Hegelian dialectic. The killer's knife can mean death, or the impossibility of communication, or the perversion of logic, or the frustration of bourgeois society, or the corruption of the police force. *Rhinoceros* can be taken as a satire on fascism, communism, trade unionism, or big business.[2]

The most virulent and typical critical outburst against Ionesco was that initiated by Kenneth Tynan in *The Observer* of June 22, 1958. After having fought for Ionesco's acceptance in England, Tynan suddenly had doubts about the value of plays that were not committed to some specific political point of view. His dissatisfaction stemmed from the fact that Ionesco no longer conformed to the left-wing social rebellion Tynan had championed in the works of Osborne, Wesker, Kops, and the rest of the "angry young men." Ionesco, of course, had never conformed to it, but Tynan may well have been misled into associating him with it by the use of the swastika armband in *The Lesson* and by the apparent specific satire of English bourgeois society in *The Bald Soprano.* Ionesco replied that a work of art has nothing to do with doctrines.[3] He maintained that the function of criticism is not to tell the author what he *should* have said but to explicate and criticize what he *did* say.[4] The Ionesco-Tynan controversy was not, as Martin Esslin would have us believe, "brilliantly conducted on both sides." [5] It was a brilliant vindication by Ionesco of the artist's right to be judged on his own terms; and an attack on that right, uncomfortably reminiscent of the doctrinaire pronunciamentos of totalitarian state critics, by Tynan. Tynan seems to understand

2. Richard Coe, *Eugene Ionesco* (New York: Grove Press, Inc., 1961), p. 108.
3. *Notes et contre-notes*, p. 72.
4. *Ibid.*, p. 75.
5. Martin Esslin, *The Theatre of the Absurd* (Garden City, N. Y.: Doubleday & Company, Inc., 1961), pp. 83–84.

Ionesco as little as does Thomas Barbour, who sees him simply as a purveyor of telling stage effects and places him closer to Oscar Hammerstein II and Joshua Logan, intellectually speaking, than to Beckett.[6]

Ionesco's plays fall easily into three subdivisions: the representative avant-garde, "theater of the absurd" plays; the "social warning" plays (*The Killer* and *Rhinoceros*); and the confessional plays (*The King Dies* and *The Aerial Pedestrian*). Like Beckett, Genet, Adamov, and the other authors of the French dramatic avant-garde, Ionesco bases his plays on the twin pillars of protest and paradox. The purpose of all of the plays of the dramatic avant-garde in general and of Ionesco's plays in particular is protest against the social order and the human condition. This protest does not take the form of a dispassionate rational criticism as in the traditional didactic drama with its implied attitude of aloof superiority; it is far more a chaotic and frenzied scream, the scream of a person who is trapped and knows it but who is determined to strain against his bonds to the last. The apparent absurdity of all of Ionesco's plays is actually an attempt to break through the confining borders of reality to a *beyond-reality* that, by its very existence, renders the everyday reality it protests against ridiculous by contrast. In other words, the seeming irrationality of the avant-garde drama is caused by the use of a technique that may be described as the selective exaggeration of reality in order to point up the ridiculousness of certain aspects of everyday reality, the *essential* ridiculousness of which usually passes unnoticed.

The technique of exaggerating selected aspects of everyday reality in order to demonstrate its pointlessness is the technique of paradox. Ionesco and the other avant-garde dramatists always show their truths by presenting their audiences with situations that conflict so strongly with commonly held ideas of the reasonable as to seem at first (or even second) glance senseless and absurd. The point is made all the stronger, once it has sunk in, by having initially masqueraded as apparent nonsense.

6. Thomas Barbour, "Beckett and Ionesco," *Hudson Review*, XI (Summer, 1958), p. 276.

Ionesco's first play, *The Bald Soprano* (La Cantatrice Chauve, 1950), was the ground-breaker for the current avant-garde tradition on the stage. It illustrates, first of all, the dramatic technique which the avant-garde derived from Antonin Artaud; but, more important still, it illustrates the basic philosophical premise on which the whole avant-garde drama is based. This philosophical premise, the importance of which cannot be overestimated in a study of the avant-garde drama, is the concept of the absurd in human affairs. First appearing in a more or less unconscious form in the works of Alfred Jarry, it was continued in an equally instinctive and unreflecting vein by the surrealists and the Dadaists; but it was not until the appearance of Albert Camus' *The Myth of Sisyphus* that the "philosophy of the absurd" received a conscious and rational formulation.

Briefly stated, Camus' "philosophy of the absurd" says that human existence is unintelligible. Man lives in the world but understands neither it nor his own function in it. He is a displaced alien in what must ultimately appear an incomprehensible void to him. Man functions in this wilderness by anesthetizing himself to reality with various specious, artificial beliefs; by immersing himself in a comforting routine that gives him the illusion of having some significance; and by deluding himself into believing that he is not alone. It is the self-appointed task of the avant-garde dramatists to debunk these beliefs and to shock people into a realization of the *absurdity* of their position.

Ionesco concentrates mainly on showing his audiences the mutual isolation of human beings and the meaninglessness of the daily actions which constitute the major portion of their existence on earth.

The story of *The Bald Soprano* is unimportant in itself. We see an English living room in which an English couple are carrying on a parody of an English after-dinner conversation. They are visited by another English married couple, who cannot make up their minds whether they know each other or not, and by an incongruously but unmistakably Gallic fire chief. The action of the play consists simply of the characters sitting there and talking what appears to be utter nonsense. Ionesco has himself stated that the play's English setting is purely coincidental. He happened to be studying the language and the ridiculousness of the expressions in his Assimil-method phrase book struck him so forcibly that he was inspired to write the play.[7]

Ionesco uses the device of nonsense speech as a means of showing one aspect of the absurdity of everyday life through the breakdown of semantics. Since everyday life, whether absurd or not, depends for its coherence entirely on the coherence of speech patterns, it follows that if our speech patterns are absurd, everyday life in general is absurd *as far as we are concerned* (it is possible that to an individual the world does not appear absurd, but since he has no means of communication with other people except through intrinsically senseless speech patterns, it follows that his view is actually nonexistent in practice). Even if the world appears ordered and coherent to *everyone*, Ionesco is saying, it is still absurd because each person is trapped inside his own individual cell by the inadequacies of his means of communication. The only possible type of communication is the indirect method of paradox.[8]

Ionesco begins his attack on linguistic meaning right at the beginning of the play in the first stage direction. Here, in the description of the Smiths' living room, the word "English" is used seventeen times in a passage of seventy-five words—an average of once every four and a half words. Here we see (Plato, Wittgenstein, and Cassirer notwithstanding) that no word can retain its meaning under the stress of constant irrelevant usage. As soon as the curtain rises, Ionesco's point is made clearer by the "conversation" between Mrs. Smith and her husband, in which the truisms of everyday speech are repeated until they

7. Coe, *op. cit.*, pp. 45–47.
8. Wallace Fowlie, *Dionysus in Paris* (New York: Meridian Books, 1960), pp. 230–31, suggests that the theme of *The Bald Soprano* is the guilt of the aged couple, who have made a failure of marriage. This may well be the theme, or one of the themes, of *The Chairs* and of *Amédée*, but in *The Bald Soprano* the relationship of the Smiths is not described thoroughly enough for us to make an assertion one way or the other about their happiness. They seem quite content with their existence.

become ludicrous. When Mr. Smith finally does consent to join the conversation, it is only to comment on the death and burial of one Bobby Watson. This whole passage is a hilarious indictment of the illusion of human identity. The Bobby Watsons in the story proliferate until everyone seems to be called Bobby Watson. The individual's pride in his own uniqueness is vain: to other persons he is just another manifestation of each person's projected self.

Following this dialogue between the Smiths we have an apparently equally meaningless dialogue between their guests, the Martins. The Martins's problem is that, even though they have been introduced to us as man and wife, they don't know each other. During the course of their conversation they discover that they both come from Manchester, that they came up to London at the same time in the same compartment of the same train, and that they are staying on the same floor in the same hotel and, in fact, are occupying the same room and sleeping in the same bed. All these coincidences fail to convince them that they know each other and it is only when they discover that they each have a daughter with one white eye and one red one that they decide that they are probably man and wife. From a purely farcical standpoint the whole scene irresistibly reminds one of the recognition scene in *Cox and Box*. From a more serious standpoint, however, we see a typical couple, married for some years, who do not know each other. What Ionesco is saying—once more—is that people are isolated, people never *really* know each other, even when they are living together in the closest possible relationship. We always know only our illusions of each other. Cast-iron as the Martins's reasoning seems, it is instantly destroyed by the maid, who tells the audience that the Martins are not really man and wife because his child has a white right eye and a red left eye and hers has a red right eye and a white left eye. The point of the maid's interpolation seems to be that even the most closely knit chain of reasoning is futile. This perception that reason is essentially inadequate and at the same time the only form of thought available to us is the original basis for the philosophy of the absurd. The passage discussed here is analogous to

Lucky's speech in *Waiting for Godot*, which is a parody of logic and scientific speech. Lucky's tirade is a long and confused jumble of tag ends of scientific discourse that gradually degenerates into an utterly incoherent babble. The enormously involved chains of reasoning made up for the most trivial purposes by the protagonist of Beckett's *Watt* are another example of this comment on the inadequacy of human thought processes. *The Bald Soprano* also breaks up into an incoherent nonsense babble at the end as all the characters scream snatches of familiar sayings and quotations at each other. As this shouting match fades away, the lights come up again on the same scene as at the beginning of the play. The meaningless monotony continues ad infinitum and ad nauseam.

Ionesco's next play was *The Lesson* (La Leçon, 1951). Here he shows us a private lesson given by an elderly professor to a young girl preparing, somewhat intrepidly, for her "total doctorate." At first the professor is the typical absent-minded pedagogue and the young girl is the confident and glib pupil. Gradually the roles reverse: the professor becomes confident, positive, overbearing; the girl timid, uncertain, and mentally paralyzed. Finally, the professor, enraged at the girl's stupidity, stabs her. When he realizes that the girl is dead, the frightened professor calls his maid to help him. Totally undisturbed by the dead body, which, as she casually remarks, is the fortieth that day, the maid calms the professor down. When he suggests that forty coffins might cause comment, she tells him that nobody will make awkward enquiries: the people are used to such sights. The professor, who has now reverted to the childlike timidity he displayed at the beginning of the play, is finally reassured when the maid pins "an armband with an insignia, possibly the Nazi swastika" on him. As the two accomplices carry the body out, the doorbell rings again, announcing the day's forty-first luckless visitor.

The interesting thing about *The Lesson* is the complete reversal of viewpoint as the play progresses. At the beginning, the play is purely realistic: a new pupil visits her tutor for her first lesson. The language is perfectly ordinary and intelligible. In fact, except for an occasional momentary hop into the

facetious, like the business about studying for all the doctor-
ates at once and the professor practically tying himself into
knots with amazed delight when the pupil gives Paris as the
capital of France, the first part of the play is so natural as to
be almost banal. The play thus follows the regular formula of
most of Ionesco's plays: an opening scene of everyday banality
succeeded by a breakthrough into the fantastic by emphasizing
the banality, as if Ionesco were a dentist probing a nerve inces-
santly until a transition to a new realm of pain occurs. In *The
Bald Soprano* he accomplished this by the cumulative illogicality of the dialogue; in *The New Tenant*, by the endless piling
on of the furniture; in *Jack*, by the bridegroom's demand for
more and more grotesqueness in his bride; and here, in *The
Lesson*, by reversing the personalities of professor and pupil as
the former becomes carried away by his meaningless lecture.

What Ionesco is saying, by the professor working himself
up into a homicidal frenzy as he gabbles his hysterical tirade
on Neo-Spanish and its related identical tongues, is that the
more wild, senseless, illogical, inane, and irrational words become, the more powerful—and, of course, the more dangerous
—they become. As the professor raves about Neo-Spanish and
Sardanapolitan, his power over his pupil increases until finally
he kills her. The allegory is obvious: the insidious deadliness of
the professor's speech is precisely analogous to the equally
insidious deadliness of the rhetoric used by the Nazis—and
nothing was more appalling about the Nazi era than the extent
to which the German intellectuals (the teachers, the artists,
all those, in short, whose task it is to guard the truth) willingly
used their powers to pervert the truth, to give falsehood the
appearance of truth.[9] Ionesco's professor perverts language,
which, as he himself says, is more important than anything else,
for it is the medium through which truth is expressed. As the
words lose meaning, they become deadlier: the professor's

9. Esslin (in *The Theatre of the Absurd*, p. 96) suggests that *The
Lesson* deals with the sexual nature of all power and with the interdepend-
ence of language and power. This is true up to a point, but the most obvious examples available to Ionesco of sadism—sexual or otherwise—and of
corruption through misuse of language cannot be ignored as a specific
source of inspiration.

frenzied gabble and Hitler's hysterical ravings—which were not only meaningless but unintelligible as well—are one and the same. Semantic anarchy equals moral anarchy.

After the production of *The Chairs* (Les Chaises) in 1952 Ionesco began to be more widely known. It is in this play that he is most successful in achieving that abstract quality, that breaking-up of conventional theatrical forms, which he states he was striving for in his drama. *The Chairs* is the story of a very old couple who have invited a large crowd to the island on which they live so that the husband may impart the wisdom he has accumulated during ninety-five years. His plan for saving the world is to be communicated by a professional orator. The guests, all invisible, keep arriving, until finally the stage is filled with chairs. The old man announces that the orator will present his messianic secret to the audience; then he and his wife commit suicide by throwing themselves out of the window. As soon as they are gone, the orator indicates that he is deaf and dumb.

Ionesco's point here is the impossibility of communication between human beings. By his own definition of tragedy ("For the unbearable there is no solution, and only the unbearable is true [i.e., tragic] theater") *The Chairs* is Ionesco's most tragic play. Nothing could be more "unbearable" and at the same time finely ironic, than the orator's impotence. The vague, incomprehensible maunderings of the two old people are suddenly knitted together by the superbly dramatic device of the vaunted orator's desperate attempt to speak. Life, Ionesco is saying, is a hell in which each person is imprisoned in his own separate soundproof cubicle, invisible and inaudible to everyone else. All so-called communication is illusory: the only person we really communicate with all the time is ourself.

Victims of Duty (Victimes du Devoir), first produced in 1953, is a satire on conventionality, particularly conventionality in the theater. The play, subtitled a "pseudo-drama," begins, as is usual with Ionesco, in that citadel of banality, a *petit bourgeois* home. Choubert and his wife, a perfectly ordinary middle-class couple, are discussing the news. Suddenly, apropos of nothing, Choubert begins a Socratic disquisition on the modern drama. The classification of all drama that has ever been written under the heading of "thriller" is at least refreshing:

> CHOUBERT: What do you think of the modern theatre: What are your ideas on the drama?
>
> MADELEINE: You and your theatre! It's an obsession, you'll soon be a pathological case.
>
> CHOUBERT: Do you really think something new can be done in the theatre?
>
> MADELEINE: I've just told you there's nothing new under the sun. Even when there isn't any.
>
> CHOUBERT: You're right. Yes, you're right. All the plays that have ever been written, from Ancient Greece to the present day, have never really been anything but thrillers. Drama's always been realistic and there's always been a detective about. Every play's an investigation brought to a successful conclusion. There's a riddle, and it's solved in the final scene. Sometimes earlier. You seek, and then you find. Might as well give the game away at the start.
>
> MADELEINE: You ought to quote examples, you know.
>
> CHOUBERT: I was thinking of the Miracle Play about the woman Our Lady saved from being burned alive. If you can forget that bit of divine intervention, which really has nothing to do with it, what's left is a newspaper story about a woman who has her son-in-law murdered by a couple of stray killers for reasons that are unmentioned . . .
>
> MADELEINE: And unmentionable.
>
> CHOUBERT: The police arrive, there's an investigation and the criminal is unmasked. It's a thriller. A naturalistic drama, fit for the theatre of Antoine . . . Come to think of it, there's never been much evolution in the theatre.
>
> MADELEINE: Pity.
>
> CHOUBERT: You see, the theatre's a riddle, and the riddle's a thriller. It's always that way.
>
> MADELEINE: What about the classics?

CHOUBERT: Refined detective drama. Just like naturalism.[10]

At this point a detective actually does appear. The rest of the play is concerned with his frantic attempt to force Choubert to give him some entirely nonsensical information. It all ends as the detective, who is forcing Choubert to swallow chunks of stale bread in order to "plug the gaps in his memory," is killed by a huge, black-bearded character named Nicholas d'Eu. This d'Eu sounds off with a few more of Ionesco's opinions on the theatre:

D'EU: The theatre of my dreams would be irrationalist . . . Inspiring me with a different logic and a different psychology, I should introduce contradiction where there is no contradiction, and no contradiction where there is what common-sense usually calls contradiction. We'll get rid of the principle of identity and unity of character and let movement and dynamic psychology take its place. We are not ourselves. Personality doesn't exist. Within us there are only forces that are either contradictory or not contradictory . . . The characters lose their form in the formlessness of becoming. Each character is not so much himself as another . . . As for plot and motivation, let's not mention them. We ought to ignore them completely, at least in their old form, which was too clumsy, too obvious—too phony, like anything that's too obvious—No more drama, no more tragedy: the tragic's turning comic, the comic is tragic, and life's getting more cheerful.[11]

In Choubert's statements we have a perfectly explicit account of Ionesco's view of all drama other than his own; in d'Eu's statement, we have his account of what he feels drama ought to be. *Victims of Duty* is, however, not merely an academic discussion of the drama. It is also a horrifyingly nightmarish picture of the ordinary man's unthinking subservience to the

10. Eugène Ionesco, *Three Plays: Amédée, The New Tenant, Victims of Duty*, translated by Donald Watson. Copyright © 1958 by the Grove Press, Inc. (New York: Grove Press, Inc., 1958), pp. 119–20.
11. *Ibid.*, pp. 157–59.

conventions of society. All of us are victims of duty: Choubert and Madeleine, victims of the detective's official authority; the detective, victim of a higher level in the official pecking order; and even Nicholas d'Eu, the intellectual rebel, falls victim to "duty" the moment he has eliminated the detective. He takes over the dead man's functions, and poor Choubert has to get on the treadmill again.

Victims of Duty was first produced in February, 1953. Almost exactly a year later, Ionesco's next play, *Amédée, or How to Get Rid Of It* (Amédée, ou Comment s'en Débarrasser), was performed. Amédée is a mousey little playwright who never seems to get anywhere—his average output is in the vicinity of one line every few years. Fifteen years before the play starts, a young man visited Amédée and his wife, Madeleine. He never left the apartment alive—Amédée can't quite remember whether he killed him in a fit of jealousy or whether the young man just died—and his body, perfectly preserved, has been reposing in the best bedroom ever since. The trouble with the body is that it is more than perfectly preserved: not content merely to ward off putrefaction, it is actually growing all the time. In short, the body is suffering from "Geometrical Progression, the incurable disease of the dead." During the play the disease switches from the chronic stage to the acute, and we have the spectacle of the body steadily advancing across the stage until it fills practically the whole playing area, and Amédée and his wife are squeezed uncomfortably into a corner.

Amédée finally makes up his mind to get rid of the body, and late at night Madeleine lowers it down to him through the window, much as one might lower an enormously long, soggily limp salami. Amédée drags the body through the deserted streets leading to the river. Before he gets there, however, he meets an American soldier and from that point on everything goes wrong. The whole town wakes up: dogs start barking, windows open, whistles blow, trains start rolling, the police show up, fireworks are detonated, comets and shooting stars appear in the sky. Amédée, panic-stricken, rolls the body around his waist for more convenient carrying. Soon he is

completely wrapped up in this coil of flesh, and then, "a surprising thing happens. The body wound round Amédée's waist
seems to have opened out like a sail or a huge parachute; the
dead man's head has become a sort of flowing banner . . .
Amédée is flying up out of reach of the policeman. The banner
is like a huge scarf, on which the head of the dead man is
drawn, recognizable by the long beard, etc." [12] Slowly Amédée
and the dead man float into the celestial regions, thoughtfully
scattering such earthly dross as shoes and cigarettes as they go.

The rolling up and carrying away of the body, accompanied
as it is in its later stages by fireworks, shooting stars, comets,
police whistles, and so forth, is a hilarious parody of the funeral
procession with all the empty pomp and circumstance reduced
to flippant ribaldry. The ascent of Amédée with the body is,
of course, a burlesque of the traditional ascent to Paradise. One
is irresistibly reminded of Little Eva and her more sublime
though no less ridiculous *Himmelfahrt*.

Amédée is the most allusive and obscure of Ionesco's works.
The meaning, of course, hinges on the central symbol of the
growing body. Is it a symbol of the ever greater and greater
encroachment of death on our lives? As the body grows, our
span of life becomes smaller (Amédée's living space shrinks),
and decay sets in as we grow older (toadstools sprout in the
apartment). Or is it a symbol of the unsuccessful and now
dead love of Amédée and Madeleine, the forever doomed "love"
of the poet and dreamer for the hard, acquisitive, unsentimental
woman? [13] My own feeling is that this play foreshadows
Ionesco's feelings about death, which he was to treat in his
two intensely subjective and confessional plays *The King Dies*
and *The Aerial Pedestrian*.

Ionesco's next play, *Jack, or Submission* (Jacques, ou la
Soumission, 1955), is purely a study in dramatic surrealism.
Stylistically it is a throwback to *The Chairs*. The story of a
young man who has to submit to the conventions of family
and society by confessing that he likes roast potatoes, it is
Ionesco's demonstration of the evils of *not* rebelling. The ac-

12. *Ibid.*, p. 73.
13. Esslin, *op. cit.*, p. 108.

tions we go through in submitting to *our* social conventions, Ionesco is saying, are as ridiculous as the ones Jack is made to go through; and very possibly he is right. Once Jack has submitted, he is introduced to his future bride, a young lady with two noses, whom he refuses on the rather bizarre ground that she is not ugly enough. He is then offered one with three noses, whom he finally accepts, though not without some preliminary grumbling about her inadequate repulsiveness.

In *The New Tenant* (Le Nouveau Locataire, 1957), a man hires a room on the top floor of a house. His furniture is delivered, and two moving men bring it up. They bring up a great deal of furniture and then they bring up more—and more —and more—and more. When they can't fit any more in, they leave it on the stairs and finally on the street in front of the house. Then reports pour in that the gentleman's furniture is blocking traffic, stopping up the subway, damming up the Seine: the whole country becomes paralyzed. Meanwhile the gentleman has ensconced himself in a little cubbyhole just large enough to hold him. Walled in on all sides by furniture, he disappears from view; and as the play ends we hear his muffled voice ordering the movers to put out the light. The room is plunged into darkness, and the gentleman has indeed gone back as far as he can go.

The nameless tenant is another Mr. Zero. He constructs a mechanistic womb for himself in terms of everyday banality and creeps into it. He is back in the cocoon; nothing will trouble him anymore. Similarly, the furniture chokes off all traffic and totally engulfs the country. In other words, not only is the tenant insulated against the necessary troubles of the world, but everyone else as well. The paralyzing flood of furniture is a symbol of the deliberately created wall of banality (television, movies, pulp magazines, picnics, cocktail parties, etc.) with which modern man desperately seeks to shut himself off from the necessity of thinking.

In *The Killer* (Tueur sans Gages, 1959) and *Rhinoceros* (1960) Ionesco emerges more and more concretely as a playwright of rebellion against social conformity. The abstract and seemingly frivolous qualities of his earlier plays are gone and we see an Ionesco who has become more topical, more socially conscious, more polemic—in short, more *worried*. It is as if he had suddenly realized that his pleas for the independence of the human spirit, his condemnations of slavishness and conformity to the artificially created and tyrannically imposed "ideals" of society were not coming across and that there was no time to lose.

The Killer gives us a picture of a termite-infested society about to collapse of its own rot. Everything is drab and lusterless in this modern society, mildewed from the "moral damp" that seeps in everywhere. It has not always been this way, however. Bérenger, the timid, ineffectual little Everyman who is the protagonist of the play, can vaguely remember a time when things were different: "once upon a time there was a blazing fire inside me. The cold could do nothing against it, a youthfulness, a spring no autumn could touch; a source of light, glowing wells of joy that seemed inexhaustible. Not happiness, I mean joy, felicity, which made it possible for me to live. . . . Must be centuries ago . . . or perhaps only a few years, perhaps it was yesterday." [14] And now he thinks he has suddenly recovered this wonderful period of his youth, of humanity's youth. Within the cold, unfriendly city in which he lives he has found a "radiant city" where the sun always shines and where it never rains (no "moral damp") and where everything is always in bloom. This "radiant city" has been designed and built by the Architect, one of those omniscient puppeteer-bureaucrats so frequently encountered in the modern avant-garde drama. The "radiant city," however, is beautiful only on the surface. Ionesco seems to be contrasting the hopefulness and energy—above all, the individuality—of people before the present with the bureaucratic age, symbolized by the Architect and his flawed, machine-made, preplanned (and therefore essentially drab) "radiant city." For this city is rotten at the core. It is haunted by a ruthless killer who murders two or three persons every day. These killings, the Architect explains to the horrified and disillusioned Bérenger, are always accom-

14. Eugène Ionesco, *The Killer and Other Plays*, translated by Donald Watson (New York: Grove Press, Inc., 1960), p. 20.

plished in the same way: the killer, dressed as a beggar, pursues his victim until they come to an ornamental pool in the middle of the radiant area. Here the killer offers to show his victim the "picture of the colonel." For some reason this is always irresistible, and the victim is pushed into the pool while he is absorbed in the picture. Men, women, and children meet death in this way; only members of the civil service are immune.

After making this shattering discovery, Bérenger hurries home. As he does so, he goes from illusion to reality: the scene in the "radiant city" is played on a brightly lit bare stage, but Bérenger's house is reproduced with deliberately ponderous realism. When he gets home, Bérenger finds Eduard, a tubercular and deformed friend of his, waiting for him. This Eduard, it turns out, has a briefcase full of pictures of the colonel. His explanation is that someone once sent them to him and that he had forgotten all about them—not being the nosey type, he has not looked into his briefcase lately. Bérenger immediately urges Eduard to rush off with him to the police. Eduard, however, leaves the briefcase in the room. The next scene is devoted principally to Bérenger's frantic search for the missing briefcase. Eduard, who is totally unconcerned about the murders, offers no help at all. This is played against a background of a fantastic political harangue given by "Mother Peep" to her "geese." Mother Peep's speech, like the Professor's in *The Lesson*, is an example of the perversion of words. It is a parody of a totalitarian campaign speech and is wildly applauded by the listeners. The point is that a goose-stepping society like the one Mother Peep is trying to create doesn't think—it permits insidious influences like the killer to operate.

At the end of the play Bérenger finally meets the killer, who turns out to be a puny, deformed, one-eyed dwarf. Bérenger, in a long speech to the killer, who never says a word, tries to find some ground for condemning him. But every time he brings up an argument against the killer, he finds some specious justification for the other side. Next he tries to exhort the killer to lead a better life, and finally he tries to exterminate him. But he is helpless: "how weak my strength is against your cold determination, your ruthlessness! And what good are bullets

against the resistance of an infinitely stubborn will!" [15] He lets
his pistols drop as the killer slowly advances on him, knife in
hand.

Ionesco's theme is the moral spinelessness of society, personified in men like Bérenger, the perfect types of Eliot's "hollow men." Bérenger's powerlessness against the killer is, as
Ionesco says, due to his own "rather commonplace morality."
Bérenger has nothing to stand on; in spite of himself he keeps
finding arguments to justify the killer's actions. Having no
belief of his own, he represents a society that no longer has
any right to defend itself against evil because it is not convinced
that it is better than the evil opposing it. And the canker that
has been rotting society, according to Ionesco and all the other
playwrights of protest in the dramatic avant-garde, is the dein-
dividualizing caused by the Mother Peeps and their gospel of
the "disalienation of mankind" and the "mystification of the
demystifiers"—of the suppression of the individual and the
exaltation of the lie.

Bérenger endures another Calvary in Ionesco's next play,
Rhinoceros, which is philosophically a continuation of *The
Killer.* Once more Ionesco is concerned with the problem of
the suppression of individuality in modern society. Mother
Peep's geese are simply changed into rhinoceroses. But where
Mother Peep's geese play a purely complementary part, providing a sort of ironic background mood music to Bérenger's
doomed quest for justice, the animals of *Rhinoceros* are the
main feature. *The Killer* is a generalized protest against complacency about the ever-present elements of evil that pervade
society. *Rhinoceros,* like *The Lesson,* is an obvious commentary
on the disintegration of reason and morality under a totalitarian
state. Only those unfamiliar with the history of Nazism will
be at all puzzled by its allegory.

Unlike *The Killer, Rhinoceros* has no moral: it is a simple
horror story. A rhinoceros (or man in a brown shirt with a No!
bizarre-looking insignia on his right arm) appears and kills a
cat. Everyone is horrified. No one does anything about it. Soon

objective

15. *Ibid.,* p. 108.

more and more rhinoceroses begin to appear on the streets, roaring discordantly and trampling on things. Bérenger's best friend suddenly turns green, develops a leathery skin, and grows a horn above his nose. "We must rebuild the foundations of our existence. We must return to primordial integrity," the new party member tells Bérenger. Soon Bérenger's other associates join up. A fellow worker comes to tell him that their boss has become a rhinoceros: " 'We must move with the times.' Those were his last human words." Then the fellow worker joins up too: "My duty requires me to follow the example of my superiors and fellow workers for better or for worse." The discordant roaring of the rhinoceroses turns into a barbarically rhythmic marching song; their undisciplined rampaging turns into the measured tramp of the goose step. Finally Bérenger is left alone with his fiancée. Then she too leaves him. Alone, he wavers. But then, as the rhinoceroses advance on him, he pulls himself together, and, realizing that only he is left of all the humans in his town, he screams "*Je ne capitule pas!*" as the curtain falls. Bérenger's willful, stubborn (even, from a certain point of view, unreasonable and stupid) defiance raises him, congenital nonentity though he is, to a level of selfless heroism given to few men to attain. With that magnificent cry, at once a defiance and a curse, which he utters at the end, Bérenger pulls himself up to the level of the universal rebel described by Camus. For the sake of justice, humanity, and decency—above all, for the sake of the highest virtue of all, the virtue of moderation—Bérenger sacrifices himself despite all the specious dictates of reason. His act of symbolic rebellion is useless on the immediate, primary level, but it is nonetheless an act of faith in the independence of the human spirit and as such serves to testify against and undermine the tyranny that kills him.

The parallel between the situations of *Rhinoceros* and the gradual acceptance, through complacency and expediency, of the Nazi hooliganism as the ordinary and correct way of life by the German *petite bourgeoisie* is obvious. Ionesco's play is both a warning and a castigation; with regard to the former, it is probably no coincidence that the play is set in France.

In his two latest plays, *The King Dies* (Le Roi se meurt, 1962) and *The Aerial Pedestrian* (Le Piéton de l'air, 1963), Ionesco turns to a frankly confessional style of writing. In his excellent article, "The Inner and the Outer Reality," Richard Schechner points out that all of Ionesco's plays are autobiographical and confessional.[16] His early plays are externalizations of deeply personal obsessions, which, "like Kafka's, . . . are public coin, at least for this moment in history." [17] His success and growing importance brought him a measure of self-confidence and personal security, which in turn led to a greater involvement in immediately temporal affairs.[18] This led to the *engagé* plays, *The Killer* and *Rhinoceros*. As a result of his success he has come to have a sense of satisfaction with life and a love of all its aspects, without at the same time relinquishing his deeply rooted pessimism. He eats, he sleeps, he loves; and whereas before he did these things automatically, he now wallows in sensuous enjoyment of them. Like Camus, he has come to realize that life is all that there is; that death is the only real enemy. His two latest plays are an expression of his fear of death. It would not be too rash to predict that Ionesco has reached his final phase—that all his future work will be concerned with this obsession. Like all great artists, he has at last come to grips with the only true reality and with the most unbearable and insoluble—and therefore the most tragic —subject.

The King Dies is a long, completely static one-act play. Donald Watson has pointed out that the characteristic aspect of Ionesco's art is the inflation of situation into the source of dramatic action.[19] The static situation viewed from every angle thus replaces plot. *The King Dies* takes place in a mythical kingdom, ruled over by King Bérenger I. Bérenger, the worried Everyman with whom Ionesco identifies in *The Killer* and *Rhinoceros*, is thus exalted and made the king of his own

16. Richard Schechner, "The Inner and the Outer Reality," *Tulane Drama Review*, VII (Spring, 1963), p. 187.
17. *Ibid.*
18. *Ibid.*, p. 206.
19. Donald Watson, "The Plays of Ionesco," *Tulane Drama Review*, III (Fall, 1958), p. 53.

shadow world, just as each man is the king, the supreme figure, in his own personal world. Bérenger has not made much of a success of his reign. Under his heedless mismanagement his kingdom has shrunk to the point where it can be traversed from one end to the other in a few paces. It is inhabited exclusively by old men, congenital cretins, mongoloid idiots, and hydrocephalics. His palace is ghostly and run-down, somewhat like the palace in Ghelderode's *Escurial.* Bérenger himself is quite unaware of all this. He comes on full of vigor, greets his two wives, and prepares to bumble through another day. This is the day when at last he becomes aware of his life, by being made aware of his death. Marguerite, his embittered first wife, and the court physician (who is also the court executioner, bacteriologist, and astrologer) inform him that he will die in one-and-a-half hours, "at the end of the play." The rest of the play is taken up with Bérenger's gradual realization that he will in fact die, his desperate fight against that realization, and his progressive physical and mental deterioration. At the end he is only an incoherently babbling hulk of flesh, whose transition into total annihilation is barely noticeable.

The play is full of allusive touches. Ionesco plays with the concept of time: Bérenger has lived hundreds of years and he has lived only a few minutes. When one thinks of death and eternity, all time is the same. Marguerite seems at times like one of the implacable Fates. At others, she seems to be the hate that complements the intense love of Marie, the second wife. The real power of the play, however, resides in the poignancy of the emotion and the intensity of the repulsion with which Bérenger faces the prospect of his own annihilation. Like Ionesco, like modern man generally, Bérenger does not have the consolations of religion. Death means oblivion to him. Total disintegration of all that exists, as far as he is concerned. The thought that all will be as if he had never been is unbearable to King Bérenger. Like every man, Bérenger is his own universe, and the thought of its destruction fills him with horror:

Without me, without me. They'll laugh, they'll joke, they'll dance on my grave. I will never have existed. Ah, let them remember me. Let them weep, let them despair. Let them perpetuate my memory in all the history books. Let everyone know my life by heart. Let everyone re-live it. Let the students and the scholars have no other subject of study but me, my kingdom, my exploits. Let them burn every other book, let them destroy all the statues, let them put mine in all the public places. My image in all the ministries, all the police stations, all the internal revenue offices, all the hospitals. Let them name all the airplanes, all the ships, all the motor cars, and all the push-carts after me. Let all the other kings, warriors, poets, tenors, and philosophers be forgotten and let there be no one but me in everyone's mind. One single baptismal name, one single family name for everyone. Let them learn to read by spelling out my name: B-é-Bé, Bérenger. Let me be on the images and on all the millions of crosses in all the churches. Let them say Masses for me, let me be the Host. . . . Let them call on me for ever and ever, let them pray to me, let them implore me.[20]

In *The Aerial Pedestrian* Bérenger has recognizably become Ionesco again. He is a French dramatist who has given up writing for the theater because, as he reluctantly explains to an importunate newspaper reporter, "I am paralyzed since I know I must die." [21] As he leaves his house, a German bomber left over from the war blows it to bits.[22] Bérenger then demonstrates his ability to fly, an ability that everyone has, though its use has been forgotten. Schechner suggests that flying may be a metaphor for the creative act itself.[23] I incline to the view that it is a metaphor for the act of living with full awareness. Bérenger's flight gives him a panoramic view of the earth. When he lands, he describes a landscape ravaged by bombs, by fire, and by ice. It is a vision of the earth as it might be after

20. Eugène Ionesco, *Le Roi se meurt* (Paris: Gallimard, 1963), pp. 79–80.
21. Eugène Ionesco, *Théâtre* (Paris: Gallimard, 1963), III, p. 128.
22. Compare Mme. Rosepettle's speech in Arthur Kopit's *Oh Dad, Poor Dad . . .*, *infra.*, p. 291.
23. Schechner, *op. cit.*, p. 216.

Armageddon, a writhing mass of fiercely striving, dismembered bodies, overcome by the implacable forces of Nature. Schechner suggests that this vision may be the postnuclear landscape.[24] More probably it is Ionesco's view of the inner reality of the earth and the people on it here and now.

We can see from this examination of Ionesco's plays that the main themes of his early plays (1950–1953) are (i) the paradox of the isolation of the individual in the midst of his fellows; and (ii) the paradox of the ultimate meaninglessness of the actions, which, taken together, constitute the sum of human existence. In the plays of his second period (*The Killer* and *Rhinoceros*) Ionesco abandoned the view of pessimistic fatalism in which man is a helpless puppet futilely and despairingly hammering against incomprehensible forces that always overwhelm him. Instead of the doctrinaire determinism which he derived from Antonin Artaud, Ionesco gave man a certain amount of free choice within the context of his temporal life. He thus made man morally responsible for his actions. With moral responsibility human existence once more took on meaning. Human actions once again became significant because they could be shown to have foreseeable results. Ionesco made the transition from preoccupation with ultimates, which is so characteristic of absolutists such as Artaud, to a concern for immediate, if relative, results—in other words, to the limited rebellion of Albert Camus, which concentrates on an individual ethical protest designed to bring about a relative alleviation of the human condition within the foreseeable future. In his latest (and probably last) phase, Ionesco has openly become an intensely personal writer. *The King Dies* and *The Aerial Pedestrian* are about Ionesco's preoccupation with his own finiteness. Here again the influence of Camus can be discerned. In the future Ionesco must either find some sort of peace in philosophical speculation, as Camus did, or (as he has threatened in *The Aerial Pedestrian*) stop writing altogether.

24. *Ibid.*, p. 217.

JACQUES AUDIBERTI
The Drama of the Savage God

ONE OF THE marks of a great critic is his ability to grasp
the significance of a particular work of art. To understand the
meaning of a work is sufficiently difficult in itself; but to be
able to place a work of art into its historical perspective upon
first seeing it is a gift granted to few. The fact that he was
totally unable to understand the work makes Yeats's remark
about Jarry's *Ubu roi* all the more impressive. Most people
dismissed Jarry as either a hoaxer or a psychopath, but Yeats
had the critical perceptiveness to see that his play changed the
whole course of creative thought in the theatre. "After us," he
wrote, "the Savage God!" [1] More than twenty years later
Antonin Artaud was to prove the truth of Yeats's prophecy;
and more than twenty years after Artaud wrote *Le Théâtre et
son Double* Jacques Audiberti was to write a series of plays
with the Savage God—the malignant power of the cosmos—as
protagonist.[2]

Awareness of and protest against the power of the Savage
God is a characteristic of all current avant-garde drama. A sense
of the twisted malignity of the universe hovers over all the
plays of Ionesco, Beckett, Genet, and Adamov, but only in certain of the plays of Jacques Audiberti does this presence attain
the stature of an invisible protagonist permeating the work.

Jacques Audiberti does not belong wholeheartedly to the
avant-garde school of drama, and his plays look a little strange
in the company of Ionesco, Genet, et al. With most avant-garde
dramas, as soon as the curtain rises there is an instant assault
on form and language which shocks the audience and forces it

1. William Butler Yeats, *Autobiography* (Garden City, N. Y.: Doubleday & Company, Inc., 1958), pp. 233–34. I am indebted to Professor Roger
Shattuck's *The Banquet Years* for leading me to this reference.
2. Jacques Audiberti was born at Antibes in 1899 and is known in
France primarily as a poet and novelist. He has published several volumes
of poetry (e.g., *La beauté de l'amour, La pluie sur les boulevards, Race des
hommes, Rempart, Des tonnes de semence, Toujours, Vive guitare*) and
fifteen novels, the best known of which is probably *La Nâ*.

out of the conventional dramatic frame of reference. Audiberti
does not operate in this way. His plays look superficially like
perfectly ordinary plays in an unusual or exotic setting. All of
these plays, however, have some peculiar, even fantastic, twist
in the story that renders them unintelligible as ordinary melodrama. The whole secret of understanding Audiberti's drama
—and, indeed, most avant-garde drama—is not to expect to
understand the plot as such. Ordinarily, the plot of a play is a
carefully planned, logical, incident-by-incident account of what
the play is about; and a discussion of the "meaning" of the
play is identical with a discussion of the "meaning" of the plot.
In the avant-garde drama, on the contrary, the plot is either a
seemingly haphazard conglomeration of illogically connected
incidents or a perfectly ordinary story with one or two unexpected insertions which suddenly make it unintelligible in
the context of ordinary dramatic conventions. The point of all
this is that in the avant-garde drama the plot is unimportant
per se. The avant-gardist never tries to tell a story. Instead, he
uses incidents to illustrate a theme. When Ionesco, for example,
has the hero of *Jack* browbeaten into asserting that he likes
roast potatoes, he is not writing a story about a young man being browbeaten into asserting that he likes roast potatoes, which
would be senseless. He is writing about a young man being
forced to submit to ridiculous and arbitrary conventions (hence
the use of the fantastic example of eating roast potatoes) by
family pressure. Similarly, Beckett is not writing about the
activities of two aimless vagrants in *Waiting for Godot*: their
aimless meanderings are illustrative of the pointlessness and
hopelessness of human existence. Precisely *what* Vladimir and
Estragon do is not important at all. Precisely *what* Jack is
forced to submit to is not important either. What is important
is that the incidents serve to clarify some general theme. In
the avant-garde drama, plot is relegated to a position of literally
no importance whatsoever; only the theme matters. It is necessary, therefore, when studying the avant-garde drama to *disregard* the actual incidents of the play and apprehend instead
the general theme of the author. Then one can observe how
the incidents of the play, which may at first have seemed to be
willfully meaningless, serve to illustrate the theme.

The two principal themes that Audiberti derives from
Antonin Artaud are (i) the conflict between paganism and
Christianity and (ii) the presence of a primordial spirit of
evil in human affairs.

In Audiberti's eyes, as in Artaud's, paganism represents a
purer state of mind than Christianity. Paganism was the first
religion. It was a result of man's spontaneous, unsophisticated,
unreasoned reaction to the powers of Nature. It was therefore
far more real than the artificial, civilized, reasoned religion that
Christianity represents. Paganism was a natural, instinctive reaction; Christianity is merely a patchwork of afterthoughts
laid over the reality of human nature, which it stifles for the
sake of social convenience. Anything that takes the human
being away from his inborn reality is evil; and since in Audiberti's eyes the human being is evil to begin with, it follows
that all artificial religions represent greater gradations of evil.
The simplicity of instinctive human nature represents the best
of all possible worlds in a universe where all possible worlds are
bad.

Audiberti's second point—the pervading presence of evil in
all human affairs—is usually expressed through his obsession
with the idea of the controlling power of sex. He feels that in
his sexual activities the human being comes closest to being
an animal. With this emphasis on sex Audiberti pares all men
down to one common level and gets rid of the artificial social
distinctions that serve to differentiate people from each other
in the traditional drama. All of Audiberti's characters are animalistic (with the exception of the myth characters in *Pucelle*
and *Opéra parlé*); and there are no good animals in Audiberti's
world. All of them are stained with the mark of an evil spirit.
There is another, less obvious, reason for the emphasis Audiberti places on sex and that is the assumption that the act of
intercourse merges us with Nature and therefore brings us
nearer to the primordial evil. This view leads him to a sort of
Manichean dichotomy between flesh and spirit with the flesh
always conquering and leading inevitably to disaster.[3]

3. Leonard C. Pronko (in *Avant-Garde* [Berkeley, Cal.: University of
California Press, 1962], p. 188) sees Audiberti's plays as pantheistic: man
is pure only when he remerges with nature.

The conflict between paganism and Christianity, which runs through all of Audiberti's plays, is treated overtly only in *Quoat-Quoat* (1946) and *Opéra parlé* (Spoken Opera, published 1956). In *Quoat-Quoat*, for example, Audiberti is talking about the latent power in the primeval myths that formed the human character far back in prehistoric times, long before the advent of the skin-deep, artificially superimposed pseudomyths by which we live now. To illustrate this theme he sets his story on a ship bound from France to Mexico about one hundred years ago. Amédée has come on board in the guise of a young scholar in search of Mexican archaeological antiquities. But the captain informs him that he is aware that Amédée is really a French spy sent to discover the whereabouts of the late Emperor Maximilian's hidden treasure. He reads him the pertinent section from the law of the high seas which provides that any accredited espionage agent found entering into a relationship with a woman on board ship must be shot. Immediately afterwards, Amédée is caught making love to the captain's daughter and is sentenced to be shot by the overjoyed captain, who gets a bonus for each corpse. While he is awaiting the dawn, Amédée is visited by a wild-looking Mexican woman who offers to rescue him by means of a magic stone belonging to the ancient Mexican god Quoat-Quoat. Amédée refuses and insists on accepting the fate to which his actions have delivered him. He hands the woman and her magic stone over to the captain. Finally a third woman, a rather bedraggled, gypsylike hag, shows up and announces that she is the real spy and that Amédée was just an innocent decoy to divert suspicion from her. Amédée is now free since he is no longer subject to laws governing the behavior of spies on the high seas. He refuses, however, to avoid the fate to which he sincerely thought his actions had led him. Locking the captain and the real spy into the cabin, he rushes on deck and has himself shot by the firing squad. As the curtain falls, the captain raises the stone of Quoat-Quoat preparatory to annihilating the ship.

The important point in this apparently extremely confused plot is that Audiberti undoubtedly wishes us to believe that as the curtain falls the captain destroys his ship and everyone on it with the stone of the ancient god Quoat-Quoat. This does not mean that Audiberti literally believes in the existence of a childish black magic, but rather that he feels that the modern world represented by the ship, with its weblike overlay of arbitrary legal minutiae, is still basically at the mercy of the turbulent atavistic forces that originally molded the human spirit. To both Artaud and Audiberti the true expression of human nature is the phenomenon of the Malay native running amok, slashing without regard through the gradually woven net of "civilized" conventions. Only Amédée in a sense escapes. Although he too dies, he dies by his own choice, by making an existential decision and declining any longer to be bound up and batted back and forth by directions that do not concern him as a separate individual. Amédée is the rebel-hero of whom Camus speaks. He finds his death—and, paradoxically, his freedom at the same time—by taking his stand and saying thus far will he permit himself to be driven and no further. At some point one must rebel against the net of convention, and if the rebellion results in death, *tant pis.*

In *Opéra parlé* Audiberti again writes of his belief in the latent power of paganism. Here he describes the eclipse of paganism by Christianity as being a voluntary and temporary one. Set in the ninth century, A.D., the play tells of the cutting of a straight highway through the depths of a forest in eastern France. This straight road symbolizes the ascendancy of Christianity, with its mute promise of a definite destination at the end, over the mysterious tangled forest of druidic paganism. It is the triumph of the ordered over the arcane, of the highway over the labyrinth. The builder of the highway has under his care a young girl who had been entrusted to him by the Grand Master of the Pagan order. As the play opens, the Grand Master appears again and takes "a stone both visible and invisible" from between the girl's eyes:

> THE MASTER: Give back to me the stone both visible and invisible which shimmers between your eyes. . . . Little by little you will lose your power. You will become weak. You will become mild. You will become a woman.[4]

4. Jacques Audiberti, *Théâtre* (Paris: Gallimard, 1956), III, p. 110.

This act deprives her of her powers as a pagan goddess. She is now no longer free to merge with the woods and the waters and to communicate with the animals, for she must marry a Christian and subjugate herself and all that she represents to him. The holy oracles have spoken, the Grand Master tells her: for a time the people will wish to live according to the laws of the clerics:

> After the forest, the highway. After the star, the church. After the girl, the woman. . . . For a time the Gascons and the Saxons and all the nations will live according to the law clerical, canonical, episcopal, pontifical.[5]

But the Church of Christ will fall in its turn as well and then the pagan gods will come back from their eclipse. Meanwhile the young goddess must marry a Christian. She obeys and marries Baron Massacre, who embodies the bloody, vengeful, unnatural aspects of Christianity; but the pagan spirit cannot be entirely subjugated. While the girl loses her powers and becomes the wife of the baron, her real lover, a previously exemplary military officer, turns his back on Christianity in disgust at this unjust and incongruous union and becomes a sort of Robin Hoodlike outlaw specializing in the destruction and plunder of churches and monasteries. At the end all three protagonists are killed, as befits the conventions of the tragic melodrama that Audiberti uses as his framework for this story on the theme of the immortality of the pagan spirit.

Audiberti's plays about the latent force of the pagan spirit in the modern world do not mean that he himself believes in paganism. His point is that the essence of paganism is freedom from arbitrary, socially initiated coercion and that it is therefore closer to the Nature from which man originally sprang and from which he derives his true being. Paganism is not good in itself: it is merely *natural* and therefore inevitable. There is no absolute good in Audiberti's cosmos—only absolute evil and the comparative good that is to be found in not attempting to act against one's nature. In so far as men drift away from their origins, they become progressively more evil. This is the basis

5. *Ibid.*, p. 113.

of the series of plays Audiberti has written about the problem
of evil in society.

His first play of this type, and probably his best-known play,
is *Le Mal court* (The Evil Runs, 1947). As usual, the plot is
unimportant in itself, serving only to illustrate the theme,
which is that of the omnipresence and inexorable force of evil.
Audiberti uses a conventional fairy-tale plot: beautiful young
princess, daughter of an impoverished king, goes to marry rich
young king; wicked cardinal intervenes and prevents marriage
for political reasons; beautiful young princess heartbroken, etc.,
etc. Audiberti carries his classic fairy-tale formula only up to a
point: the rich young king does not throw the wicked cardinal
into an oubliette so that he can marry the beautiful young
princess at the end. Instead, the princess, Alarica, finds as the
play proceeds that she is, and always has been, ringed around
with evil and deceit. Her illusions about the goodness of life
and the decency and trustworthiness of people drop from her
one by one in a series of painful shocks. She discovers that her
projected marriage had been secretly abandoned a long time
ago and that she is being used as a decoy so that the young king
can make a politically more advantageous match. Even her
old and faithful nurse is in the plot. There is absolutely nobody
she can trust. Everyone is self-seeking, corruptible, and dishonest because everyone is living and ordering his existence
within the context of an artificial and corrupt society. As the
series of shocks she is obliged to undergo bludgeon her into an
awareness of the true nature of the world, Alarica realizes that
she must make her compromise with it if she is to survive
as something other than a pawn. She determines to fight evil
with evil—to let "the evil run." She deposes her amiable,
bumbling old father, disregarding his pleas for filial respect, and
resolves to rule with complete ruthlessness. If everything is
evil, then the most evil wins.

If evil in *Le Mal court* takes the form of personal deceit, in
La Fête noire, *La Logeuse*, and *Les Naturels du Bordelais* Audiberti links it with sex. Sex is for Audiberti a manifestation of
elemental Nature. As such it is evil in itself, but evil also arises
from its repression, from its transformation in society to some-

D

thing artificial and therefore perverted. This state of affairs brings about a paradox: evil is implicit in repression and perversion, and evil also comes when the long repressed force of sex inevitably breaks out with cyclonic savagery. In this latter form, Audiberti's sex is analogous to Artaud's plague—the heedless emotional whirlwind that takes the human being back into the long-abandoned racial subconsciousness, his only true reality.

Audiberti's most explicit statement of this theme and at the same time far and away his best play is *La Fête noire* (The Black Feast, 1948), which is also the most successful and faithful dramatization of the theories of Antonin Artaud. *La Fête noire* takes place in a wild and mountainous region of southern France, where Felicien, the hero of the piece, is the local doctor. Felicien's one desire is to win the love of a woman. But this is precisely the one thing that always eludes him. As the unnatural repression builds up in him, Felicien becomes a sort of perverted superman figure, a symbol of the masculine drive, the motor force behind men's actions, hemmed in by the restrictions imposed on its free outpouring by the laws of civilized society. Audiberti sees Felicien as Superman Bound—and bound so effectively that his ineluctable force can emerge only in a horribly twisted form, maliciously revenging itself on the culture that has fettered it. Felicien's pent-up fury escapes from him and, like an angry genie at last released from his bottle, takes the form of an evil beast that roams the country literally ripping open any woman it meets. At first this ecstatic and elemental fury spends itself on the women who have rejected Felicien, but gradually it eludes his control and becomes an independent scourge to punish all women for their disavowal of sex. This Jack the Ripper-like scourge is not to be taken literally, of course: it is the embodiment of Artaud's "plague," the instinctive force that the drama should express.

The second act of the play is a semifarcical parable about the killing of the beast. The whole countryside is up in arms as a result of the outrages committed, and Felicien is appointed leader of the hunt. The "beast" is cornered in a small square in front of a mountain-side shrine. Hundreds of people have turned out to watch the slaughter, which is to be blessed by a

high-ranking prelate. The "beast" is driven on and turns out
to be only a broken-down old goat. The goat is then cere-
moniously killed with much blowing of trumpets and sprinkling
of holy water, and the only person who recognizes the "beast"
for what it is and has the courage to say so is driven off by
the soldiers. Just as the bells are beginning to toll in celebration
of the death of the "beast," word comes that another girl has
been ripped apart in a neighboring village, but nobody takes
any notice of this: the "beast" has been officially killed; therefore, any further evidence of its presence is to be ignored.

Audiberti's parable here concerns the gradual suppression
by the Church of the natural human sex drives. Through its
ritual and liturgy the Church has tried to stifle the natural
human impulses and mold the human spirit to an artificial ideal.
But this molding process has inevitably been as unsuccessful as
the killing of the "beast" in the play. The continual repetition
of the forms and rituals, as well as the living repression of Nature in the celibacy of the clergy, has had the effect of numb-
ing the senses of the arbiters of civilized behavior; and, having
officially decreed the beast dead, they can afford to take no
notice of its continued depredations beyond the range of their
comforting incense.

At the end of the play Audiberti changes the atmosphere
of his parable from farce to irony. Felicien has become world-
famous as the slayer of the beast. All the governments of the
world have decorated him, learned societies consult him, graduate students write theses on the habits of the Black Beast.
Felicien has grown rich by selling relics of the beast: he is just
about to dispose of the beast's eleven thousandth tooth. In
short, the beast has become a sort of religious cult. Alleged
pieces of the beast are revered in all the royal courts of the
world and are solemnly preserved and studied in all the great
universities. The priests eagerly abet Felicien's sale of dogs'
and cows' teeth as relics of the True Beast. But the beast has
in fact now become real and out of its creator's control: at the
end it destroys Felicien himself.

La Fête noire is important in the history of the modern
avant-garde drama because it is the most perfect realization of

Artaud's theories. Not only does Audiberti use the "plague" (in the form of the destructive beast) as his binding theme, but he also follows Artaud's specifications for involving the spectators in the vortex of emotion. Just before the "beast" is led in to be killed, Audiberti has the following stage direction:

> Brouhaha. The ground shakes under the audience's seats. Green leaves fly through the auditorium. At the back of the stage a hairy, sallow face floats by. It will be quite easy to bring about this rapid apparition.[6]

Here Audiberti directly follows Artaud's suggestions for encircling the audience and involving it in the action:

> Every spectacle will contain a physical and objective element, perceptible to all. Cries, groans, apparitions, surprises, theatricalities of all kinds, . . . concrete appearances of new and surprising objects, masks, effigies yards high, . . . A direct communication will be re-established between the spectator and the spectacle, between the actor and the spectator, from the fact that the spectator, placed in the middle of the action, is engulfed and physically affected by it. . . . The hall will be enclosed by four walls, without any kind of ornament, and the public will be seated in the middle of the room, on the ground floor, on mobile chairs which will allow them to follow the spectacle which will take place all around them.[7]

Audiberti continues his "actualization" of myths in *La Logeuse* (The Landlady, written 1954) and *Les Naturels du Bordelais*,[8] the only other two plays he has written which have any significance as avant-garde dramas. In *La Logeuse* Audiberti uses the Circe myth as the basis for a story about matriarchal domination. In modern life Circe becomes Mme. Cirqué, the

6. Jacques Audiberti, *Théâtre* (Paris: Gallimard, 1952), II, p. 73.
7. Antonin Artaud, *The Theater and its Double*, translated by Mary C. Richards. Copyright © 1958 by the Grove Press, Inc. (New York: Grove Press, Inc., 1958), pp. 93–96.
8. The several punning implications of this title are untranslatable. The literal translation would be *The Natives of the Bordelais* (the area around Bordeaux); it was first published in 1952.

owner of a rooming house, who transforms her male lodgers
into slaves. Her husband, for example, was formerly a high-
ranking government official, but now he spends all his time at
home making ladies' hats. During the play Mme. Cirqué is
arrested for hiding a fugitive from justice (her daughter's fiancé,
whom she had egged on to commit a robbery). While she is
away, all her men return to their former lives and live together
in happy comradeship, their one fear that she will return. And
return she does, having put her spell on the police inspector
who had originally trapped her by pretending to be hypnotized
by her charm. Now he is hypnotized in reality and helplessly
joins the other swine in Mme. Cirqué's female-dominated
household-world.

Les Naturels du Bordelais is easily Audiberti's most con-
fusing play. Here he takes the theme of the destructiveness of
sex one step further. Under Mme. Cirqué the men are figura-
tively turned into swine by the sexual force that radiates from
her. In Les Naturels the characters are literally turned into
animals. Just as surrender of the mind turns the characters of
Ionesco's Rhinoceros into rampaging horned beasts, so a constant preoccupation with sex, a surrender of the mind to the
animalism of the body, turns the characters of Audiberti's
play into insects. Audiberti is, of course, referring here not to
natural, unrepressed sex, but to the sickly, perverted, sexual
preoccupation of modern society.

Audiberti has written several other plays, notably Pucelle
(1950) and L'Effet Glapion (The Glapion Effect, 1959), but
they are not significant in the history of the avant-garde movement. Both Pucelle and L'Effet Glapion, which has been mentioned for Broadway production, are about Audiberti's belief
that true reality lies in the fantasies and not in the actual everyday experiences of people. More recently Audiberti has concentrated on writing radio plays.

It is extremely difficult to form any judgment of Audiberti's
work. Some of his plays exemplify more perfectly than any
others the theories of the twentieth-century avant-garde drama.
However, Audiberti is primarily a poet, and he frequently goes
off into lyric flights that are there for their own sake rather

than for the play's. As a playwright he is distinctly out of his element. His plays are written as if he had carefully read Artaud and had deliberately followed his method in constructing them. They are like textbook examples of the avant-garde drama—lifeless, dry, dispassionate, carefully dovetailed, and laboriously planed. Yet despite his lucid approach, Audiberti is difficult to understand, perhaps more difficult than any other avant-garde dramatist. Writers like Ionesco and Beckett are difficult to understand because their meaning is implied rather than stated. Audiberti's obscurity is caused not by his meaning being implied, but by its being abstruse. Like most poets whose minds work easiest in the channels of symbolist verse, Audiberti is essentially a mystic; and mysticism on the stage is hopelessly out of place. The essence of stage writing is clarity, while the essence of mystical writing is its arcane quality. The apparent obscurity of Ionesco, Beckett, and Genet can instantly be made clear by good stage production: the obscurity of mysticism cannot.

JEAN TARDIEU
The Art of the One-Act Play

"THE PROBLEM, in my opinion, does not lie in knowing whether the theatre of the future will be 'realistic' or not, but rather in the discovery of new forms and in the unceasing search for new ways of expression." [1] These words by Jean Tardieu help to explain the remarkable series of one-act plays that he has published in the last few years.

The one-act play has always been a sort of theatrical lame dog. After the seventeenth century *entremés*, its most popular period was during the nineteenth century, when almost every full-length play was preceded by a one-act play and often followed by one as well. These short plays were usually farces. They were never taken very seriously by anyone, neither by the

1. I am indebted to M. Tardieu for this definition of his work.

managers, nor by the players, nor by the audiences, nor (consequently) by the ill-paid hacks who wrote them. It was generally understood that the prologue served merely to give "fashionable" latecomers the satisfaction of creating a disturbance without at the same time missing any part of the main attraction. The epilogue, similarly, let the world of fashion serenely sweep out during a play instead of shuffling out with the crowd at the end and at the same time gave the glassy-eyed die-hards in the low-priced seats the illusion of having had their money's worth. Since those days the prestige of the one-act play has not risen appreciably. During the twentieth century it has usually been either a children's play or an adolescents' play or a play by someone too lazy to write a full-length play. The annual anthologies are carefully avoided by all theater people except high-school drama directors.

Tardieu has given the one-act form new meaning by realizing that it is inadequate for the treatment of any one theme. To take a theme or to preplan a story and then to try and squeeze it into the confines of the one-act form results inevitably in failure. The one-act play must be a self-contained entity. Instead of treating a "subject" (i.e., a theme or a planned story), it should treat an "object" (i.e., a thing, a given problem, or situation). In other words, instead of writing drama *de*ductively (by starting with a theme or philosophical concept and working in toward a specific plot situation designed to illustrate it), Tardieu writes *in*ductively (by starting with a specific plot situation and letting it effloresce at will until the ramifications of the action touch upon some larger theme, even if only allusively). Tardieu confines himself to the given situation or concrete object about which he has decided to write, never once bringing in any subsidiary motifs. In this way he has given new life to the one-act form and hopes to complete a "well-tempered clavichord" of the one-act experimental drama.[2]

Tardieu's plays may be divided into two classes: the serious and the experimental-linguistic. The first class consists of miniature expositions of the principles of the avant-garde drama.

2. Interview with the author.

They deal with the chief philosophical preoccupations of the avant-garde school: man's state as a powerless atom in a reasonless void, and, on a temporal level, the enslavement of the human mind, such as it is, by social pressure.

Tardieu's early plays are a strange combination of his interest in poetic language, his instinctive and natural faith in life, and his rationalized philosophy of despair. His characters seem to float in a mysterious and hostile immensity, in a void pulsating with implied menace, where they can feel "the stillness of an implacable force brooding over an inscrutable intention." And yet, unlike the other avant-garde dramatists, Tardieu sometimes holds out hope. There is hope for man if he can forget his cosmic context and concentrate on love: at certain moments Tardieu seems to be that paradoxical hybrid, a pessimistic romantic. This attitude can be seen most clearly in the early play *Le Sacre de la Nuit* (The Rite of Night, written 1948), in which two young people observe the depth of the sky and the night and fasten upon each other in the immensity:

> THE MAN: . . . The demons and the gods are in flight. You have merged with the immensity of the night, you have entered into communion with the innocence of the world. Be happy in this shower of light and honey and freshness. Be reborn, pure and adorned for love, carried on the wings of motionless time, weightless in my adoring night. Come!
> *(The man rises. He and the woman slowly advance towards each other. When they reach the middle of the stage, they take each other's hands and go slowly towards the right.)*
> THE WOMAN: I will go with you along the road without an ending.[3]

All of these early plays of Tardieu's are little more than pastiches, exercises in the creation of a *mood* (as distinct from a situation or an action) on the stage. His first play, *Qui est là?* (Who Is There?, written 1947, performed 1949), perfectly

3. Jean Tardieu, *Théâtre de Chambre I* (Paris: Gallimard, 1955), p. 31.

compresses into the one-act form all the principles of the avant-garde drama, as set forth by Antonin Artaud. Artaud decreed that drama should strip man of the façade of illusion that society erects around him and show him in his *real* context—a helpless and insignificant being in an immense and hostile nothingness. Artaud describes this nothingness through his twin symbols of cruelty and the plague. The void is evil and preys on men; and man's consciousness of it drives him into a sort of atavistic delirium, symbolized in the drama by irrational behaviour and "unexpected happenings." Thus, in *Qui est là?* we have an ordinary family—father, mother, and son—who sit in a harshly lit, almost bare room. The trappings of "civilization" are deliberately avoided. The members of the family are not identified by name: they are thoroughly depersonalized so that they could be anybody. This is in accordance with Artaud's idea that what we call individual personality is merely a superficial gloss and the drama should seek to portray the elemental quality common to all men. In Tardieu's play the members of the family are sitting around their dinner table when a woman suddenly materializes, and, like one of the mythic Norns, gives vague warnings of danger. Immediately afterwards the father is strangled by a "hired murderer" (hired by whom? The malign cosmic forces, presumably); and the mother and son, looking out of the window, see a landscape covered with dead. It is as if they were looking out on a scene by Hieronymus Bosch. The father emerges from this blanket of cadavers, which stifles the earth from above instead of fertilizing it from below, but he is not alive. He tells us that the man in all of us is dead but that one day he *will be*. As he makes this prediction, light floods the scene, and Tardieu ends his play on the "hollow man" theme with an expression of hope.

La Politesse Inutile (Useless Courtesy, written 1947, performed 1950), Tardieu's second play, has the same theme as *Qui est là?* but in a more restricted form. Again Tardieu is talking about the invisible, unsuspected line that separates man from reality. Within the magic circle of his illusions man feels secure, comfortable, self-respecting. He never understands that he is in a circle until he inadvertently steps across the incredibly thin line of its circumference or until some external influence invades his territory. When this happens man feels like a goldfish who has flipped out of his bowl or like one whose bowl is suddenly disturbed by a groping human hand. In *La Politesse Inutile* a respected professor, self-satisfied, a symbol of comfortable security, is visited by a sinister, shabby character who slaps him and leaves, threatening to return. The professor's habitual self-assurance can never again be the same, for he now knows he is as vulnerable as a toy balloon in a maze of capriciously moving spikes.[4]

Tardieu's most successful effort so far to depict the relationship between man and the universe is *L'A.B.C. de notre vie* (The A.B.C. of Our Life, 1959). In this long one-act play we see an ordinary man go through the motions of a typical day while a chorus of men and women provide a muted accompaniment of everyday sounds. The stage is divided into two parts, the young man on one side, the chorus on the other. While the young man—Tardieu calls him the "protagonist"— describes the various emotions he feels as he goes through his day, the chorus provides an undertone of murmured words which can be understood only occasionally and which fades away into a vox humana obbligato during the protagonist's speeches. In addition to these two forces, which complement each other like the scales of a balance, there are two characters named Monsieur Mot and Madame Parole who stand in the middle, so to speak, and comment on the action. Their comments consist mostly of strings of consecutive polysyllabic words from the dictionary, and they have the double function of providing comic relief and giving us Tardieu's own tongue-in-cheek view of the action. The play's purpose, and, indeed, the purpose of Tardieu's work as a whole, is summed up in the prologue's speech:

Here begins the symphony of the great city,/A symphony

4. The professor figure as a symbol of self-assurance and comfortable respectability has also been used by Arthur Adamov in *Le Professeur Taranne*. Taranne suddenly finds that his academic reputation is gone and that nobody recognizes him. There is also a close thematic relationship between *La Politesse Inutile* and Edward Albee's *The Zoo Story*.

without music, composed of murmurs, words, and cries,/
Here, before the break of day,/The sleeping citizens play
out their churning dreams./One man among many slowly
awakes./He wants to find again his childhood dream: his
freedom in the wind, the trees, the sea . . . /But the vast
murmur of the city/Will not let him escape. See him
there/Caught up by the relentless multitude,/Bound to
History and to the immediate event,/To something of which
he is unaware, which happens far away from him./Love
alone can be reborn, ever virginal and ever new/As on the
first day of the world . . . / . . . No, Man cannot escape
his fellow man,/For he is all he knows/And the murmur
which lulls him to sleep/After so much trouble and tor-
ment/Is his own—the ocean of words,/Monotonous and
devoid of sense/Like the sound of the wind among the
trees.[5]

Most of Tardieu's plays are a satiric protest against the
enslavement of the human mind by social pressure. We see
this idea running through play after play and growing automatically and unconsciously out of Tardieu's "given situation."
It is seen most clearly in *Le Guichet* (translated as The Information Bureau, 1955), the simplest and dramatically most
effective of Tardieu's plays. Here Tardieu deals with the supreme position that bureaucracy has blandly assumed in modern
society. Faced with the bureaucratic official, the ordinary individual automatically adopts the condition of a cocoon on a
roller coaster. In Tardieu's cosmos the filing cabinet is God
and the filing clerk is its prophet. The frightening aspect is that
the ordinary man makes no attempt to fight. On the contrary,
he has complete faith, and, once he feels himself en rapport
with the official, he curls up with relief and allows himself to
be rushed into the dark, comfortable maw that awaits him.
There are only two characters in *Le Guichet*: the information-
bureau official and the inquirer. The latter comes in to inquire
about train departures and is instantly enmeshed in the bureaucratic net. He is given a tag numbered 3640 and told to

5. Jean Tardieu, *Poèmes à Jouer* (Paris: Gallimard, 1960), pp. [17]–18.

wait, although he is the only person there. When the official has got through scratching himself and listening to the weather report, he calls the little man and asks him his name, his place and date of birth, profession and marital state. Then he examines his tongue and the palms of his hands. All this goes down on a file card before the inquirer can get a word out of his mouth. Finally it becomes the client's turn to ask some questions. It turns out that he has come to the information office much as an ancient Greek might have come to the Delphic oracle. Not only does he want to know when his train leaves —he also wants to know which train he should take. At first the official refuses to advise the man on the ground that it is not his business to do so. The inquirer is crushed by this unexpected rebuff:"And I wanted so much to get some advice, to find out what I should do . . . what I should do . . . what direction I should take . . . ! Yes, I would so much like to know what direction I should take . . . in life . . . and above all . . ." [6] This speech is ominously interrupted by the loudspeaker saying, *in a far-away and dreamlike voice,* "Passengers for all directions, get ready, please . . . Attention, all passengers . . . your train is leaving . . . your train, your automobile, your horse is leaving in a few minutes . . . Attention! . . . Attention! . . . Get ready!" [7] The official, thawed by the man's pitiful state, decides to help him. He gets the little man to admit that he is really seeking *"Une femme du genre 'femme de ma vie.'* " The omniscient filing system steps in:

THE OFFICIAL: Wait a moment while I consult my files. Let's see, your name begins with M and ends with T . . . good . . . (*He leafs through his cards*) Here we are. A brunette answering to the name of Rita Caraquilla crossed the street at 3:45 p.m. heading in a south-westerly direction. Is that the one?

THE MAN: I don't think so. The woman of my life would be more blonde . . . blonde shading to chestnut . . . Between the two, in short.

6. Jean Tardieu, *Théâtre de Chambre I*, pp. 77–78.
7. *Ibid.*, p. 77.

THE OFFICIAL: All right, perhaps it's this one then:
Miss Rose Plouvier, modest . . . No, sorry: Modiste, will
cross the porch of the building across the street tomorrow
at 9 a.m. She will be going to visit a customer, Mrs. Cou-
chois, who . . .[8]

But this isn't the right one either. The little man's "femme
de ma vie" does not appear to exist. He then progresses to more
complex questions: What does the official think of his way
of living (he is advised to give up newspapers and black coffee);
what will be his destiny in life (he is told he doesn't have one);
and, finally, when will he die? The official takes his horoscope
and then amiably tells him he will die in a few minutes—in
fact, as soon as he leaves the office. Hopelessly, the man leaves.
We hear a terrific crash and a scream. The official listens at-
tentively. There is neither satisfaction nor regret in his attitude:
only the quiet assurance of a mechanic who knows a car will
stop if someone steps on the brake. He returns calmly to his
file cards. I have treated *Le Guichet* at some length because I
feel that it is the best example of Tardieu's theories of playwriting in practice, because it is a perfect example of what a
one-act play ought to be, and because it deals with a dramatic
theme that is constantly becoming more important.

In *Le Guichet* Tardieu has taken a simple, objective everyday situation, that of a man making inquiries in an information
office. Everyday situations are not in themselves dramatic. The
only thing that is dramatic is the *special* situation, the unusual
twist in the everyday situation, the sudden entrance of the
bizarre or ironic into the humdrum milieu. The introduction
of the unusual and unexpected into the ordinary situation
sharpens it, gives a point to what was pointless, and directs that
point at the jarred consciousness of the audience. In other
words, realistic situations can only be made dramatic by inserting unrealistic elements. There never has been a "realistic
drama." Every so-called "realistic drama" has been rendered
dramatic by internal contrast with the unrealistic (that which
does not constitute an element of ordinary everyday life). There

8. *Ibid.*, pp. 79–80.

is no such thing as a *tranche de vie* play. Any slice or sliver of anyone's life may be very interesting, as Thornton Wilder tells us, but no play purporting to present an ordinary, unadorned, unadulterated slice of life has ever been read seriously all the way through. M. Tardieu flavors his slice of life with a type of urbane irony and perverse humour commonly and erroneously attributed to his countrymen as a class by critics who rely on time-honored generalizations as a substitute for thought. Actually this quality is peculiar to M. Tardieu and a select international group of other highly gifted thinkers. Tardieu's twist is that the client seeks information about his destiny, and his bombshell is that the information bureau is fully informed about his destiny—indeed, even appears to control it.

Tardieu sees the human race as pressed down flat by the weight of the social institutions that it has itself built up. Mentally, man has no initiative any more: he has been mangled and pounded by his mechanistic masters until his mind resembles nothing so much as a piece of very gelatinous head cheese. Physically, man is a neurotic, timid, ulcer-ridden mouse with a ring through his nose. The tragedy is that he has been brought to a state where his one wish is not to break the ring but to hook it to something—anything. The official is no better off, of course: he is merely a robot without knowing it. He is not seeking to hook his ring on to a machine: he has already been wholly fused into one.

The theme of human helplessness against authority occurs again and again in Tardieu's works. In *La Société Apollon* (The Apollo Society, 1955) he satirizes, on the surface at least, the gushy enthusiasm of the more ridiculous type of art worshipper. An amateur art-lovers' club pays a visit to a sculptor's studio. The sculptor is not at home, so the club leader, a bony, bucktoothed lady with a voice like an off-key English horn, proceeds to explain the various freshly created objets d'art scattered around the studio. An imposing arrangement of wires, cranks, and hooks in the middle of the studio attracts her attention, and she points out its "beauties" to her gawking acolytes. The object's marvelous form, ethos, and various other *"un je ne sais quoi"* attributes are faithfully admired and com-

mented upon with the required knowledgeable air. The bubble
has to be burst, of course; and pretty soon the sculptor enters
and explains. The much-admired centerpiece is his "great invention, the universal kitchen machine." All one need do is
dump the raw material into the hopper, turn the crank, and
the finished product is spewed out at the bottom. His eyes
aglint at the prospect of making a sale, the "master" passes
out investment brochures to his now outraged visitors. One
after another they dodge out of the door. Finally the "master"
is alone, but he is so enraptured with the sacred fire that he
fails to notice it. As the lights fade out, he stands before a
jumble of squiggles on the wall and explains that it is an ear-
washing machine for dogs.

La Société Apollon is more than just a cheap laugh at the
poor defenseless incompetents who moon around Bohemian
neighborhoods. Tardieu is trying to tell us (what is obvious
enough but cannot be repeated too often) that the sheeplike
stupidity of the art club members in following their donkey
of a cicerone, though harmless and amusing in itself, is sympto-
matic of an unhealthy condition of the modern mind. In
Tardieu the modern mind—the mind, that is, of the ordinary
man-in-the-street—craves irresponsibility and therefore willingly
and uncritically, almost by now instinctively, abases itself before the first vague semblance of authority that it encounters.

In Conversation-Sinfonietta (1951) Tardieu's effect, though
less immediate, is none the less powerful. The scene is a
broadcasting studio. The orchestra members have no instruments. Instead, they speak the phrases of ordinary everyday
life as the conductor's baton directs them. The baton comes
down, points, and "Good morning, good morning, good morning," the bassos mumble. "How do you do? How do you
do? How do you do? You're looking well today," the tenor
chimes in. The soprano simpers, "Oh, do you really think so?"
And so on, and so on, and so on. The "orchestra" runs through
all the petty phrases of an ordinary day at the conductor's command. That is all there is to it; but as the play goes on the
speakers become more and more the puppets of authority and
the conductor's baton looms ever larger as a symbol of the

omnipotent cosmic meaninglessness that jiggles them into motion and stills them at will.

In *Un Geste pour un autre* (One Way For Another, 1951) Tardieu satirizes the ordinary conventions of behavior in polite society. He exposes the basic meaninglessness of the little automatic gestures required by society simply by inventing a society the same as ours in all respects except that these gestures are reversed. Admiral Sepulchre has discovered the Nameless Archipelago. He describes it as a place where there are many beautiful cities newly built in the most modern styles thanks to their previous destruction in bombing attacks; where there are completely free citizens protected by an omnipresent police force; where there are peaceful customs defended by a militia armed to the teeth; and where there is a stable parliament founded upon constantly unstable opinions. In short, as he puts it, all the trappings of Progress are there. But this country, so much like ours from a political standpoint, has completely different social customs. The point, of course, is that one set of customs will do as well as another, and therefore both are pointless. In the Nameless Archipelago, when a guest arrives at a party, he puts a hat on and takes his shoes and socks off, making the hostess a present of the latter. Then he kisses her foot. During the party the guests amuse themselves by coughing and spitting and insulting each other. The fact that this latter habit is becoming more prevalent at parties in our own society is one proof of the validity of M. Tardieu's theme. Perhaps we will soon be coughing and spitting and doing gymnastics at our parties too.

The essence of Tardieu's formula for the one-act play is that the selected situation must be carried to its logical conclusion. Thus in *Le Guichet* he takes the situation of a man making inquiries as far as it can go; in *Le Meuble* (The Piece of Furniture, 1954), a play about an answering machine that shoots its questioners if they catch it making mistakes, he takes the situation of an "infallible" machine as far as it can go; and in *La Serrure* (The Keyhole, 1955) he takes that good old French institution, the strip tease, as far as *it* can go. *La Serrure* is a sophisticated *grand guignol* skit shot through with a macabre humour. A timid little pervert comes to a whorehouse in order to see a woman undress. He is strictly a voyeur—personal contact with the woman does not interest him. The madam arranges matters so that he can watch one of her girls undress through a huge keyhole. We are given to understand that this occasion is the culminating point of the man's life—something he has been looking forward to and working for since an early age. Ecstatically the man watches the woman strip naked, but she does not stop. She takes out her eyes, pulls off her lips, peels off her flesh. Finally, when only a skeleton is left, the man drops dead. The madam appears again in the darkened room, looks down at the body, and says, *à voix très basse, presque en chuchotant* (in a very low voice, almost a whisper), "Je pense . . . que le monsieur . . . est satisfait." ("I trust . . . the gentleman . . . has no complaints.")

Tardieu's satires on mechanistic society are counterbalanced by another group of plays dealing with the peculiarities of meaning. This subject appears to fascinate Tardieu, and he has written a nondramatic book, *Un Mot pour un autre* (One Word for Another, 1951) on it as well. In *La Sonate* (The Sonata, written 1952, performed 1955), probably his best-known play, three men sit on stools on a bare stage and talk dreamily, rhythmically, meaninglessly. Tardieu tries to imitate the musical sonata form in this play, using words as sounds. *Eux seuls le savent* (They Alone Know It, 1952) is a satire on obscure drama. A group of highly nervous and intensely vague characters drifts in and out of a drawing room and discusses the advisability of choosing the "first possibility" rather than the "second possibility." *Il y avait Foule au Manoir, ou Les Monologues* (Party at the Manor, or The Monologues, 1951) satirizes, rather belatedly, the conventions of nineteenth-century melodrama. Since there is never more than one person on the stage, the whole play consists of a succession of asides. The best and most significant of Tardieu's "linguistic" plays is undoubtedly *Les Amants du Métro* (The Lovers in the Métro, 1952). In this play Tardieu brings together the two subjects that chiefly preoccupy him when he is not concerned with the avant-garde leitmotiv of human helplessness in the void. The two subjects are romantic love and the linguistic basis of communication.

In *La Sonate, Eux seuls le savent,* and *Les Monologues* Tardieu
has tried to show that the perversities of language render it inadequate as a means of communication. This is even more
clearly demonstrated in *Oswald et Zénaide, ou Les Apartés* (Oswald and Zénaide, or The Asides, 1951), where the characters
relate to each other purely by means of formal clichés while
they tell their real thoughts in asides. In *Les Amants du Métro*
we see two young lovers meeting on a bustling Paris Metro plat-
form. Their exuberance and joy in each other is expressed as
they waltz around the stage to their own word-music,[9] *"Un,
deux, trois, amour. Un, deux, trois, toujours."* The roar of the
trains and the conversation of the other travelers, oblivious, for
the most part, of the lovers, provide the orchestral obbligato.
The speeches of the lovers do not make any particular sense
("You are?" "I am." "I was nothing. You came. I am." "We
are." "We will be." "I want to be you." "You are me."), but
they understand each other completely. Their words, which
would be meaningless or silly to anyone else, make sense to the
lovers because they are emotionally en rapport. But they quarrel,
of course; and as soon as they do, they are unable to communicate. Each goes off into his own one-track-minded self-justifica-
tions, and the power of language, the only means we have to
transmit meaning, becomes an absurdity: "It's you who is no
longer you!" "Oh, that's too much! It's you who is no longer
me!" "But what? But why? But what is it?" "You know very
well that!" "That what?" Tardieu's point is that language, i.e.,
communication, is only possible through *feeling.* When two
people feel for each other, they understand each other. Mutual
trust and feeling bridge the gap between people: language
merely carries the messages across the bridge. Rational meaning
in language is not the important thing, since each person's
reason is subjective: the important thing is that the language
beat the *dreivierteltakt* between the two dancers. When the
lovers lose each other completely, they become totally incoherent, each one struggling against the barrier that language has

9. A term that might be applied to all of Tardieu's attempts to demonstrate the rhythmic quality of language, e.g., in *Conversation-Sinfonietta,
La Sonate, Rythme à trois temps,* and *Ce que parler veut dire.*

now become between them: "Yes, I you!" "I you never, me!"
"Yes, you me!" "It's you who!" "Me who what?" "When
then?" "Nowhere!" "Where then?" "Never!" In the second
scene, which takes place in a crowded Metro car, the lovers are
reunited after he has fought his way to her through a row of
passengers, and the play ends to the sound of their verbal
waltz tune.

Tardieu's experiments with drama purely as language are
carried to their furthest point in *Rythme à trois temps* (Rhythm
in Threes, 1958) and *Une Voix sans personne* (A Disembodied
Voice, 1958). These are "skeletal" plays in which Tardieu has
trimmed off all the appurtenances of the ordinary play and left
only the bare essentials. He shows us in these plays that effective drama can exist without action—with sight and sound
alone. In *Rythme à trois temps, ou Le Temple de Ségeste*
(Rhythm in Threes, or The Temple of Segestus), Tardieu attempts to give the *atmosphere* of a deserted Greek ruin in Sicily
by having an off-stage voice give a poetic description of the
scene while six young women, representing the six columns at
the front of the temple, execute a slow, stately ballet. As they
move together they speak lines that merge with the off-stage
commentator's to give the impression of "a countryside motion-
less as if fixed in eternity." [10] In *Une Voix sans personne* Tardieu
has cut the scope of the drama even further. There are no
actors—only an off-stage voice and a room. The room is fully
furnished, and the voice describes the life that has gone on in
it as the light gradually fades away.

These "linguistic" plays are not in themselves (that is, with
respect to their content) as important as the plays I have discussed previously, but they do illustrate equally well the technique Tardieu has developed for the one-act play. Tardieu uses
the one-act play to present a single situation. What Tardieu
has shown us is that we must not try to squeeze a full Aristotelian action into the short play form. The one-act play with a
complete plot is as unwieldy as a bagatelle in sonata form.

10. Tardieu, *Poèmes à Jouer*, p. [85].

MICHEL DE GHELDERODE
The Theater of the Grotesque

AMONG MODERN dramatists Michel de Ghelderode stands by himself. If we must have a classification for him, then he can most nearly be compared to that group of novelists who have concentrated on the creation of a fictional world of their own, a microcosm in which to reflect their view of human behavior in the world as a whole. Like William Faulkner with his Yoknapatawpha County, Charles Dickens with his nineteenth century London, or James Joyce with his Dublin, Ghelderode has created an enclosed world that reflects and comments upon the larger world outside. Ghelderode's world is medieval Flanders, and his view of the world can best be described as savagely grotesque. His plays are sadistic caricatures shot through with a ribald scatological humor which reminds one of the pictures of his countrymen Hieronymus Bosch and Pieter Breughel and of the anonymous woodcuts of the danse macabre. Indeed, Ghelderode has specifically set some of his plays in a fictitious "Breughellande" where the painter's grotesque and ribald creations come to life. In all of his plays, with the exception of those written on specifically Biblical themes and set in the Holy Land, there is this quality of the painted, frozen grimace suddenly animated. Several of Ghelderode's plays are actually written for marionettes, and in these the sense of moment-to-moment transformation from still picture to moving picture is intensified. The marionettelike quality is retained in Ghelderode's plays for actors, which give the impression less of continuous movement than of a series of static tableaux in which the characters switch from one bizarre position to another, their faces seemingly permanently stretched into a sort of hysterical frozen rictus, their bodies reminding us more of Bosch's semihuman, basilisklike creatures than of human beings. Figures based upon a concentrated exaggeration of one particular physical trait recur constantly. His characters, like spitefully caricatured puppets, are all lopsided in one direction: either enormously fat or unbelievably cadaverous, shriveled into de-

formed lumps of scabrous flesh (Ghelderode is particularly fond
of inserting fiendish dwarfs into his plays) or stretched into
lanky, stilt-supported scarecrows, saintlike guileless fools (a rare
type in Ghelderode), or exaggeratedly sinister figures like the
danse-macabre personifications of Death that he uses so frequently.

No better introduction to the atmosphere of the "Ghelderode country" could be given than this typical stage direction
from *Marie la Misérable,* a modern miracle play that Ghelderode
wrote in 1952 to be performed before the Church of St. Lam-
bert in Woluwe, near Brussels:

> . . . enter an extraordinary procession to the sound of ca-
> cophonous music which is at the same time arhythmic and
> infinitely nostalgic—the music of some other, barbaric world,
> played upon baroque instruments. . . . This musical dragon
> (actually a camouflaged automobile with its headlights on
> containing a jazz band whose instruments have been altered
> to appear as if they did not belong to any particular period
> and whose Negro players have been disguised to look un-
> real) . . . pulls a ship, a sort of fourteenth century vessel
> —the Ship of Fools of the medieval moralists—with a raised
> forecastle and quarter-deck constituting practicable plat-
> forms. The mast, in the center, has only shreds of sail at-
> tached to it. Grim-looking black pavilions ornament the
> mast and poop. The quarterdeck is surmounted by a sort
> of arched ruin in which can be seen an admiral's skeleton.
> It is drinking and holding on its knees a woman covered
> with leprous sores. She has no nose and is naked under a
> shroud. Several scrawny and spastic couples are dancing to-
> gether in front of the ship with signs of mutual disgust, as
> if they were fighting a merciless combat: a savage frolic, with
> the women's hair hanging down to their waists and flying
> round their rigid, sallow faces and the young men dressed
> in shrouds, their jaws bound shut with strips of cloth, danc-
> ing like robots to the hypnotic music. Their faces express
> disgust and dread, their dance shows the battle of the sexes.
> The middle of the ship is occupied by people wearing devil

masks, pigs' snouts, animal muzzles, elephant trunks, asses' ears—a swarming menagerie, clucking, bellowing, whistling . . .[1]

Here we have a typical scene from the world of Ghelderode—fantastic, grotesque, bizarre, hypnotic: a subtle combination of the danse macabre with the lusty vulgarity of a Flemish peasants' kermess.

We can find this curious combination of demonism with ribaldry in all of Ghelderode's Flemish plays. As in the painting of Breughel, the world is seen as a place where the Devil is in control and moral perversity reigns. As in Breughel, this perversity takes the form of aimlessness and distraction in idle pursuits. Only the very few, like Marie la Misérable, see the purpose of life clearly and accomplish it through faith. Ghelderode's plays are almost all preoccupied, directly or indirectly, with Catholicism. However, their Rabelaisian attitude toward religion is not so much derisive of holy matters as a demonstration of his belief that sin has overcome the earth and that man's energies, instead of being concentrated on religion itself, are scattered and misdirected to the diabolic perversions of religion.

Several of Ghelderode's plays are taken *directly* from Breughel's paintings. Among these are *Les Aveugles* (The Blind Men, written 1933), *La Pie sur le Gibet* (The Magpie on the Gallows, written 1935), and *Le Cavalier Bizarre* (The Strange Rider, written 1920). The first of these is a short sketch inspired by Breughel's painting "The Parable of the Blind," now in the Museo Nazionale, Naples. Breughel's picture shows six blind men walking along one behind the other and about to tumble into the ditch into which their leader has already fallen. Breughel based his picture on the Biblical proverb, "they be blind leaders of the blind. And if the blind lead the blind both shall fall into the ditch." [2] In Breughel's picture, as in Ghelderode's world, the blind men are the helpless victims of a system perverted by the Devil's ascendancy. If the Devil were not in

1. Michel de Ghelderode, *Théâtre*. Copyright © Editions Gallimard (Paris: Gallimard, 1955), IV, pp. 288–89.
2. Matthew, XV:14.

control of the world, the men would not be blind, there would
be no treacherously placed ditch for them to fall into, and they
would not be instinctively led to disaster anyway, but rather to
the church in the background of the picture. The literal presence of the Devil and his cohorts was a real concept to
Breughel, as it undoubtedly is to Ghelderode as well. But
Ghelderode makes the plan of the picture somewhat harsher.
In Ghelderode's world the Devil makes men perverse: they are
the victims not of their alien surroundings but of their own
twisted and willful natures. The characteristic of the damned
in religion, after all, is that they heed the promptings of the
Devil instead of the voice of God. Ghelderode's blind men (reduced to three, presumably for convenience of staging) are pil-
grims on the way to Rome, where they believe they have now
arrived, although they have actually been wandering around in
circles for weeks and are still in Flanders. A one-eyed man warns
them that they are in dangerous country and offers to lead
them to a monastery where they will be safe. The blind men
refuse to believe him and scornfully reject his help. They trudge
off and are swallowed up in a bog. Breughel's blind men are
merely comically ducked in a ditch, but Ghelderode's deliberately turn down an offer of salvation and die.

In *La Pie sur le Gibet* Ghelderode has again dramatized a
Breughel painting. "The Merry Way to the Gallows," now in
the Darmstadt Museum, simply shows a gallows on a hill over-
looking a countryside of extraordinary beauty. A magpie sits
perched on top of the gallows, and a group of holidaying peasants is heedlessly dancing up the hill. Breughel here effects a
double comment on the unfeeling stupidity of mankind, first
in placing the gallows against a background of such idyllic tranquillity and secondly in having the peasants ignore both the
beauty and the ugliness in the throes of their loutish dance.
Ghelderode changes all this into a rollicking yet savagely contemptuous farce. The magpie becomes a sort of cynical croaking
commentator on the action which here concerns a real execution. The peasants come dancing up to the gibbet and then are
replaced by a group of pompous officials (Ghelderode's professional men are invariably caricatured) who have come to hang

Tyl Ulenspiegel. The strange location of the gibbet is now explained. The new ruler, wishing to temper justice with mercy, has decreed that death is to be made as pleasant as humanly possible for the condemned. They are to be hanged only after being permitted to get drunk on the best vintage wine. The ceremony is to be performed on a pink gibbet with a golden rope, and as the condemned man's eyeballs are extruded from his head by the force of strangulation his last view is to be of the most beautiful piece of countryside in Flanders. The condemned man drops dead just before he is to be hanged, and when the officials examine the body they find it is not Tyl Ulenspiegel at all. As the magpie croaks derisively, the carousing peasants return and the curtain falls.

Le Cavalier Bizarre is another short play and, if not directly taken from a Breughel painting like the two preceding ones, is inspired by the Flemish master's art. In his preface to the play Ghelderode states that his characters are taken from the brush of Breughel or the burin of Jacques Callot. A group of old people are living together in a large, dormitorylike room at a medieval Flemish hospice. They hear ghostly bells where none are supposed to be heard; one of them looks out of the window and sees a huge knight with large bells on his horse's bridle approaching. He says the horseman is Death, and the old people, believing him, go into a wild, kermesslike dance—their "last fling"—and then babble out their sins. They look like peaceful and innocent grandparents, and it is hard to imagine them once young and lusty and straight-backed. But the shriveled and bent old woman had sold her body when she was a beautiful young girl, one of the men had stolen, another fornicated tremendously, another had committed sacrilege, and still another had sinned so much that he feels only the pope in person could absolve him. After getting their sins off their chests, the ancients cease resigning themselves to their fate: "We want to live, no matter how—sick, suffering, covered with sores and vermin— but living!" [3] The whole thing ends with the watcher's revelation that Death has not come for them at all but has carried off

3. Michel de Ghelderode, Théâtre (Paris: Gallimard, 1952), II, p. 21.

a newborn child from another part of the hospice; and the audience is left in doubt as to whether the whole story proceeded from the watcher's imagination or not. The play ends with "a spasmodic dance of ancients, their mouths open, their fists clenched, like rigid marionettes." [4] After a moment's self-realization Ghelderode's ancients, teetering on the brink of death, fall back into the distraction from reality that is so typical of his people.

Demonism and Rabelaisianism are undoubtedly the two keynotes of Ghelderode's work: his plays combine the perversion of religious or political functions with scatological farce. Although the scatology often seems to be dragged in with willful vulgarity, it is really an extremely effective (because shocking) way of showing the author's disgust with the manner in which the world and the people in it have worked out. This element, too, Ghelderode seems to have got from Breughel, whose pictures, even the most idyllic ones, are full of hidden little scenes of defecation, urination, and animalistic fornication.

Two of Ghelderode's best plays, as yet unpublished in English, are La Balade du Grand Macabre (The Grand Macabre's Stroll, written 1934) and Magie Rouge (Red Magic, written 1931). In both of these ribald and unrestrained farces the demonism which suffuses Ghelderode's world takes the form of the primal satanic sin of belief in one's own divinity. In Ghelderode's view this leads to the creation of what may, literally, be described as monsters—persons who have become so obsessed by one of the more perverse possible phases of human character that they become in fact dehumanized personifications of it. This is, of course, essentially the same philosophy of dramatic construction as Ben Jonson's "humor" theory, except that Jonson uses it with satiric intent (i.e., he laughs at it from a position of superiority, thus implying that improvement is possible), while Ghelderode presents it as a literal picture of the world gone mad. Ghelderode's world is not populated by a few fools, as Jonson's is, but is collectively foolish.

In Magie Rouge Ghelderode has been influenced in about

4. Ibid., p. 25.

equal parts by Molière's *L'Avare* and Jonson's *The Alchemist*. Hieronymus is Sir Epicure Mammon taken seriously. He is avarice personified. He has the primary characteristic of the true obsessive in that he will not hesitate to sacrifice his own comfort to feed his obsession. For example, although he has a young and attractive wife (he himself being a filthy and unattractive old man in the best Molière tradition) he has kept her a virgin so that he will not be enchained by her and have to spend money on her. Naturally his wife can take just so much of this. She enters into a plot with one Armador, a sleight-of-hand artist, and two others to get all of Hieronymus's money. Armador is introduced to Hieronymus as one of the world's greatest alchemists. He promises to find the elixir of gold for Hieronymus and retires to the cellar with his paramour, ostensibly to begin his experiments. Meanwhile, Hieronymus sits upstairs in his counting-house planning, among other things, to buy the pope and the Holy Trinity once he has all the money in the world. On one of his trips up for air, Armador, pretending to be drunk, lets Hieronymus take a black stone off him which he says grants immortality to the wearer. Armador and his mistress escape after murdering their two fellow conspirators and leave Hieronymus with the bodies and a coffer full of counterfeit money. Arrested and led out to torture and execution, Hieronymus remains wrapped up in his grandiose self-delusion:

> I don't understand! What did you say? . . . The gallows?
> . . . The executioner? . . . (*He tears himself away*) It's
> enough to make one laugh! . . . (*He laughs*) Ho, ho! . . .
> You've been nicely tricked. I am the leader of the living.
> Bah! I'm every bit as good as the Emperor! . . . Me die?
> . . . I'll buy up Justice, ho . . . ho . . . ho! . . . Listen to
> me! . . . I'm the same as God. Yes! Don't you realize yet
> that I'm immortal? . . . (*He laughs at the top of his voice.
> They drag him out to the hooting of the crowd.*) [5]

La Balade du Grand Macabre is a thoroughly unbridled farce that takes place in Ghelderode's Breughellande. Here the delu-

5. Michel de Ghelderode, *Théâtre* (Paris: Gallimard, 1950), I, p. 179.

sion of godhead is assumed by a strange, pilgrimlike figure calling himself Nekrotozar who thinks he is one of the archangels
sent down to earth to announce the imminent end of the world
—or at least of Breughellande. In Breughellande, or Brugelmonde as it is called in another play, the people have been
twisted body and soul by the workings of the Devil and are
taken up with the practice of one or another of the seven deadly
sins.

The play opens with an idyllic and passionate love scene
between two young lovers, the play's only innocents. They retire into an abandoned tomb to make love and are followed by
a hollow laugh and chattering voice coming from "the clouds
perhaps." The voice sardonically and gleefully predicts that the
lovers' bones "will be dispersed in the folds of the earth among
the rotting weeds and the clefts of the rocks. The passionate
gestures will be imprinted in the oozing slime." [6] The voice turns
out to be Nekrotozar's. He climbs down from the tree and pro-
claims that Breughellande will cease to exist at midnight. The
rest of the play is taken up with the exploits of Nekrotozar as
he goes around whipping everyone up into a frenzy with his
news until the night ends in a tremendous drunken orgy. He is
assisted in his efforts by Porprenaz, the town's chief drunkard,
and Videbolle, the henpecked state philosopher of Breughellande, whose job it is to reflect, a habit which the other citizens
are unable to contract, to declare (like Pangloss) that everything
is good and could not be better, and to make agreeable fore-
casts exclusively while giving agreeable explanations for any dis-
agreeable occurrences that may take place instead. The play
ends as Nekrotozar expires of an excess of drink and exertion,
and the lovers emerge from the tomb still totally wrapped up in
each other and completely oblivious of all that has happened.
They represent, presumably, the hope of better things for
Breughellande.

The fortunes of Brugelmonde, as it is called this time, are
continued in *D'un Diable qui prêcha Merveilles* (Of A Devil
Who Preached Wonders, written 1934). Here the sins com-

6. *Théâtre*, II, p. 32.

mitted in this northern Gomorrah are revealed in a series of
scenes in which all the leading citizens enter one after the other
and confess their failings to each other. The occasion for this
attack of communal breast-beating is not repentance but fear.
The town has just received word that news of its dissoluteness
has reached Rome and that a well-known hell-fire–and–brim-
stone preacher has been sent to clean the place up. And there is
certainly plenty of cleaning up to be done: the bishop uses the
poor-box money to finance his sybaritic banquets; the abbess is
pregnant by her confessor, a young Italian of great ingenuity at
thinking up new forms of erotica; the sheriff has embezzled the
town funds so his wife can finance her orgies; and other prominent citizens all display an equal reluctance to earn an honest
penny. Even the town's resident devil has grown neglectful of
his duties and is just reading a letter from the infernal regions
warning him that he will be turned into a hermit monk if he
doesn't get cracking and produce some really first-class sinners.
Capricant is in despair since he is old and no longer has any
taste for devil's work. But Fergerite, the local sorceress, advises
him to dress-up as the preacher and deliver the sermon in his
place while she sees to it that the real preacher is led astray. The
sermon is an enormous success since the devil simply advises
everyone to go on living in sin—with the Church's blessing. At
the end the devil and the preacher meet and go off to Rome
together, the preacher believing that the devil-monk is the only
just man he has met in Brugelmonde.

The tangible presence of death is always a very real concept
to Ghelderode and several of his plays contain scenes in which
either a personified Death is the protagonist or a character returns from the dead. *Le Cavalier Bizarre* has already been mentioned as a play in which Death is personified. *Mademoiselle
Jaïre* (written 1934) tells the story of a girl who dies and is resus-
citated by a sorcerer who is later crucified. The girl remains
alive only until the following spring, when a root-covered corpse
named Lazarus, who comes to visit her and whom she has
apparently known in the world beyond, bursts into flower. The
point of the play seems to be the paradox that death, even when
it takes the form of the mildew-and-damp-earth–covered putrefy-

ing flesh of Lazarus, is purer than life. Lazarus, for all of his repellent appearance, is embraced by Jaïre and speaks lyrically of the beauties of death that will be theirs when his flesh bears fruit and flower in the spring. In dying, in passing out of the world as Ghelderode sees it, one is translated from chaos to order, from impurity to purity, from the Devil to God.

Although Ghelderode's genuinely religious feelings may be somewhat obscured by his emphasis on the reverse side of the coin—the diabolic aspects of religion—in such works as *Fastes d'Enfer* (Chronicles of Hell, written 1929) and *D'un Diable qui prêcha Merveilles*, they are expressed most explicitly in *Marie La Misérable*. In this play Ghelderode is entirely on the side of the angels, although the diabolic element is by no means absent.[7] The play tells the story of Marie la Cluse, a saintly and very beautiful young recluse who lives in the church precincts and devotes herself to good works. A young nobleman, Eglon d'Arken, is overcome by lust for her; but when she rejects him with the proper amount of scorn, he accuses her of witchcraft and with the help of his deformed, dwarfish servant makes her appear guilty of theft. Marie is martyred and the true source of the machinations against her is revealed when the dwarf is killed and "revolting fumes, as if Hell were coming out of his carcass" rise up from his body.[8]

What happens when the powers of hell gain the upper hand over religion may be seen in Ghelderode's most notorious play, *Fastes d'Enfer*. This work caused a minor sensation when it was first produced by Jean-Louis Barrault in Paris in 1949—and no wonder. The main character is the Bishop of Lapideopolis, a titular see somewhere in Flanders. He is lying in state in an adjoining room, having just passed away to the great relief of every member of his staff. John of the Desert, as the bishop is called, is not even an ordained priest. Years before, he was washed up on the shore during a great plague, which was devastating the city. His appearance bearing a huge cross coincided with the end of the plague and he was elected bishop by acclamation, an act later confirmed by the Holy See, which knows

7. Cf. *supra*, pp. 99–100.
8. *Théâtre*, IV, p. 264.

a *fait accompli* when it sees one. As the priests, all of them grotesque, misshapen creatures, celebrate his passing, John suddenly appears in the doorway, apparently as alive as ever. It turns out he was unable to swallow the Host which he was given before dying and it is choking him. After an eerie battle with his successor and chief enemy, Simon Laquedeem, during which the room is wrecked as a tremendous thunderstorm crackles outside, he is finally able to spit out the Host and die. The priests, led by Laquedeem, celebrate his final passing by hopping about the room with their robes trussed up, gleefully breaking wind to express their relief.

Ghelderode turns the theme of the personification of Death into a hilarious farce in *La Farce des Ténébreux* (The Farce of the Shadows, written 1936). This play concerns Fernand d'Abcaude, a ridiculous fool worthy of rating with any of Ben Jonson's most extreme "humor" characters. D'Abcaude's pleasure is to imagine that he is dying of grief for his beloved Azurine. He spends all his time in darkness, starving himself and having his valet describe the extremely elaborate funeral procession he has planned for himself. He cannot wait to die so that the funeral oration he has written can be recited and the biography he has ghost written can be published. To disabuse Fernand of his wish to die in order to join Azurine in a mutually virginal eternity, his doctor hires an actress to play the fiancée's ghost. Failing this, the doctor plans to cure d'Abcaude by giving him a whale-oil enema. The ruse is effective, however, since the actress manages to persuade d'Abcaude that Azurine was not the virginal paragon he believed her to be but rather something little better than the town whore. After all sorts of misadventures in a brothel during a carnival, d'Abcaude finally loses his virginity and joy reigns.

All of the plays mentioned thus far are set in Ghelderode's home grounds—in the special world that he has created out of medieval Flanders and Brabant. Not all of his plays are placed in this setting, however. Some of them combine a Spanish setting with a Flemish setting, like *Escurial* (written 1927) and *Le Soleil se couche . . .* (The Sun Sets . . . , written 1933), which take place in Spain but constantly refer back to the char-

acters' former lives in Flanders; or *L'Ecole des Bouffons* (The
School for Buffoons, written 1937), which reverses the process.
None of these plays is particularly interesting, although *L'Ecole
des Bouffons* has first-class theatrical qualities. *Le Soleil se
couche* . . . is a short play about the last days of the Emperor
Charles V. *Escurial* views the famous Escurial as an old and
dilapidated palace somewhere in Spain. The king, who appears
to be in the last stages of febrile decay, is attended only by
howling dogs, an executioner, a priest, and his Flemish jester.
The play is purely and simply a mood piece—a study in de-
cadence. It is unfortunate that this has been one of the few
Ghelderode plays performed in English because it is one of
his weakest works. *L'Ecole des Bouffons*, on the other hand, is
one of Ghelderode's most successful exercises in grotesquerie.
It is about a school of deformed dwarfs, which supplies jesters
to the courts of Europe after having taught them that the secret
of all buffoonery is cruelty.

Those of Ghelderode's plays which are completely out of his
medieval Flemish world may be divided into two groups: those
having a religious basis and those having a mythic basis.

Ghelderode is probably best-known to American audiences
through his two specifically religious plays, *Barabbas* (written
1928) and *Les Femmes au Tombeau* (The Women at the
Tomb, written 1928). *Barabbas* tells the story of the Passion
and Crucifixion from the point of view of the robber who was
released in Christ's place. Barabbas starts out as a defiant and
unregenerate criminal reveling in his own toughness. He is to
be crucified, but he promises the mob a good show when they
come to see him nailed up. While he is in prison he meets
Jesus, who never says a word and meekly accepts whatever abuse
comes his way. Barabbas is greatly impressed by Jesus's behavior. He does not understand Christ's meekness, since it is
entirely outside the bounds of his previous experience, and mistakes it for stoical courage, which he possesses to a high degree
himself and therefore knows how to appreciate. When he is
released in Jesus's place, not so much by the will of the people
as by the cunning maneuvers of the high priest, he wanders
aimlessly around the town, always stealthily followed by the

high priest's spies, who plan to kill him as soon as they have an opportunity. Finally he comes to rest in an abandoned fairground. Here he listens to a mysterious watcher describe the agony of Jesus and gradually comes to think of himself as one of Christ's followers. At the end he dies just after Jesus, stabbed in the back by the clown:

> BARABBAS: Hey? (*He reels.*) They got me. In the back, eh? Pretty good work! (*He falls to his knees like an ox.*) No, no, they haven't got me yet. Got to do something first . . . (*He gets up painfully and cries, hoarsely:*) Hey there, beggars! Bear up! I'm coming. (*But he falls to his knees again.*) You'll make it all right without me. Yes, they've got me all right. Well, what of it? I was condemned to death anyway . . . It's all the same thing to me. I'm not scared anymore. And I'm bleeding. Hey! Jesus? I'm bleeding too. Sacrificed the same day. . . . (*He collapses and half raises himself again.*) But you, you had something to die for. Me, I'm dying for nothing. It's for you all the same . . . for you . . . Jesus. If you like . . . And if I could . . . I'd give you my hand . . . and see you smile . . . Jesus . . . My brother.[9]

Both *Barabbas* and *Les Femmes au Tombeau* are flawed as theatrical works by being too static. *Barabbas* consists principally of the hero's comments—for the most part melodramatic, overwritten, and not particularly interesting—on the watcher's report of the doings on Calvary. Full of undramatic and awkward devices, *Les Femmes au Tombeau*, in which a group of women meet in a deserted house in Jerusalem to discuss the Crucifixion, is simply a discussion play that lacks the brilliance of dialogue and the intellectual acuity with which Shaw made the discussion play a workable drama. Lacking action, both *Barabbas* and *Les Femmes au Tombeau* are more like radio scripts than stage works.

Ghelderode's mythic plays are all based on well-known and frequently used literary myths. (By myth I mean a story, not

9. Michel de Ghelderode, *Théâtre* (Paris: Gallimard, 1957), V, pp. 172–73.

necessarily untrue, that has been used repeatedly in literature and has attained a conventional form so that it can be used by writers as a commonly understood point of reference.) He uses the Don Juan and Faust myths, which are almost obligatory for any dramatic author with a large body of work to his credit, the guileless-fool myth in *Pantagleize*, and the Judith myth in *Sire Halewyn*.

Both *Don Juan* (written 1928) and *La Mort du Docteur Faust* (The Death of Dr. Faust, written 1925) are written in a semipuppet play style with Ghelderode's penchant for the grotesque very much in evidence. In *La Mort du Docteur Faust* Ghelderode plays with a technique that has consistently fascinated him: the Pirandellian double-exposure technique. In addition to *La Mort du Docteur Faust* he has written two other plays specifically to exemplify this technique—*Trois Acteurs, un Drame* (Three Actors, One Drama, written 1926), a short, melodramatic, and clumsy play about three players trying to solve their real-life entanglements by incorporating them into the play they are acting, the only result being that the author shoots himself, presumably out of exasperation; and *Sortie de l'Acteur* (Exit the Actor, written 1930), an equally melodramatic and oversentimental play commemorating the death at the age of twenty-six of the Flemish actor, Renatus Verheyen, which ends in farce as the dead man escapes from his grave and is recaptured by angelic gendarmes who force him to skip up a golden ladder to Heaven.

La Mort du Docteur Faust, which Ghelderode has called his first important theatrical work (it was written in 1925 when he was twenty-seven), is about the transposition of the real, original Doctor Faust to a modern Flemish town where a carnival is in progress. He meets a modern girl named Marguerite, who fancies herself the Marguerite of the story, and the Devil, who is, of course, ubiquitous in every century. All three watch a performance of the Faust legend in a booth set up in a tavern and become inextricably mixed up with the actors playing their characters. The play is lively but diffuse and pointless, while the technique is based mainly on tricks.

Don Juan, which Ghelderode dedicated to Charlie Chaplin,

E

is probably his weakest play. He attempts to depict Don Juan as an eternal figure with a heritage—the compulsion to make love—handed down from generation to generation. The current Don Juan realizes this when he meets a shriveled up little man —"the little green man," Ghelderode calls him—who tells him that he was the previous Don Juan and reveals that he, like all Don Juans, has retired from the lists because he has been overcome by the ailments which inevitably result from indiscriminate dalliance.

A more appropriate play for Ghelderode to have dedicated to Charlie Chaplin would have been *Pantagleize* (written 1929). In this brilliant retelling of the saga of the guileless fool, Ghelderode tells the story of Pantagleize, a harmless little man who innocently trots around town on May Day telling everyone what a lovely day it is. What he does not know is that the town is seething with social unrest and that the innocuous remark he has chosen to celebrate his joy in the beauty of the day is the password for the beginning of a revolution. Pantagleize continues to amble around the town throughout the day, totally unconscious of the strife he has started. Completely oblivious of danger, he goes from one hair-raising situation to another until at the end of the day he meets the fate of all innocents in a world governed by the Devil—that of being massacred. As he dies, still unaware of what is going on, he brings out for the last time the innocent phrase, which remains innocent only in the minds of those who have not lost their innocence: "What . . . a . . . lovely . . . day!"

Ghelderode has recorded that the character of Pantagleize was inspired by an anonymous inhabitant of the Rhineland whom Ghelderode observed reading a book while walking across a public square swept by heavy machine-gun fire during the Spartacist revolt of 1919. In the middle of the square he stopped, looked at the sky, opened an umbrella, and then went on his way, still reading.[10] Ghelderode's profound pessimism can be seen in the description of the character which the sight of the oblivious reader inspired him to create:

10. Michel de Ghelderode, *Seven Plays*, translated by George Hauger (New York: Hill & Wang, Inc., 1960), p. 147.

. . . a fellow like Pantagleize remains an archetype, an exemplary man, and a fine example who has nothing to do with that dangerous thing, intelligence, and a great deal to do with that saviour, instinct. He is human in an age when all is becoming dehumanized. He is the last poet, and the poet is he who believes in heavenly voices, in revelation, in our divine origin. He is the man who has kept the treasure of his childhood in his heart, and who passes through catastrophes in all artlessness. He is bound to Parsifal by purity, and to Don Quixote by courage and holy madness. And if he dies, it is because, particularly in our time, the Innocents must be slaughtered: that has been the law since the time of Jesus. Amen! [11]

Michel de Ghelderode has written several other short plays but none of them contains any significant additions to the main themes of his work. Ghelderode remains primarily the dramatist of his own personally created world of medieval Flanders, which is depicted not as a historical recreation but as a convenient microcosm in which he displays his moral view. It is a world governed by diabolic forces which warp its inhabitants into grotesque, clownish forms as they prance about ignoring the beauties of the world and allowing instead some obsession based on one of the seven deadly sins to corrode and finally damn them. Ghelderode's wildly farcical grotesqueries and unbridled vulgarity is really the expression of a deeply pessimistic but sincere and completely orthodox Christian religious feeling.

JEAN GENET
The Theater of Illusion and Disillusion

EVEN IF HIS plays were not particularly interesting in themselves, even if they were not important examples of a new dramatic technique, Jean Genet would have some of the fascination of a hunchback turned ballet dancer.

11. *Ibid.*, p. 148.

We have very little definite information about Genet's personal background before he began to write. He was abandoned soon after birth and grew up to be a delinquent and later a criminal. In 1943, when he was thirty-three years old, he began writing while serving a prison sentence for theft. In 1948, Genet, after starting to serve a life sentence as a habitual criminal, was granted a pardon by the President of France, who had been petitioned by some of the country's leading writers. Since then Genet seems to have lived peacefully.

Like all the modern avant-garde dramatists, Genet bases his plays on protest and paradox. His paradox is that there is no reality within society. Anyone who acts within the structure of society is literally unreal—nonexistent. What we call reality is only illusion piled on illusion. When all the layers of illusion are stripped away, what is left is emptiness. Another way of looking at Genet's vision of the world is as a diminishing spiral twisting concentrically down to nothingness. "Reality" to Genet is like Peer Gynt's onion. It would perhaps be correct to argue that this view was engendered in Genet by his peculiar role in the world as a person cast out from the "reality" of social living by his thievery and perversion, but the psychological reasons for his attitude toward the commonly accepted realities are not pertinent to a discussion of his views. The views are there and must be dealt with for themselves.

Genet demonstrates his views on the illusion of life by writing plays in which nothing is ever what it appears to be at first glance—or at second glance, for that matter. Jean-Paul Sartre has likened the working of Genet's mind to a whirligig spinning in an ever-increasing tempo.[1] Genet's thought processes are circular and they show us that at the ultimate core of things there is nothing: when Genet starts one of his "whirligig" thought processes, he is like a snake taking its tail into its mouth preparatory to swallowing ad infinitum.

Genet's first play, *The Maids* (Les Bonnes), was written for Louis Jouvet and produced by him at the Théâtre de l'Athénée

1. Jean-Paul Sartre, *Saint Genet: Comédien et Martyr* (Paris: Gallimard, 1952), p. 561.

in 1947.[2] There are only three characters in the play—the two maids and their mistress. Whenever the mistress goes out, the maids take over and play at mistress and maid themselves. Each maid takes a turn at dressing up in Madame's clothes and playing the part of the mistress, while the other serves her. In an effort to add more excitement to their little drama, the maids have denounced Madame's lover to the police with anonymous letters. When they hear that he has been released, they realize that they will be found out, and thus try to poison Madame. Their attempt fails, and instead the younger maid poisons herself, while the other plans to give herself up as her killer.

Here we see that Genet immediately starts the whirligig off with a gentle push by specifying that the three characters of the play be acted by boys.[3] The boys are to be dressed as women, but they must not act well lest the illusion take on the appearance of reality. To guard against this, Genet specifies that throughout the performance the stage must be flanked by large placards proclaiming the fact that the "actresses" are males. The second section of the paradox comes when we see that the maids are playacting at being mistress and maid. *They are not being themselves.* In fact, as we slowly and horrifyingly discover, they have no selves to be—except as illusions, they do not exist! At the same time the whirligig accelerates as we see that the actors are playing women who are acting another role. When we have realized this, we are prepared to follow Genet's next step. The actor playing Solange is playing Solange the maid pretending to be Claire the maid, and the actor playing Claire is playing Claire the maid pretending to be the mistress. By this time the actors' whirligig is spinning merrily: the various shadowy figures on it have merged into each other and become indistinguishable except as fleeting blurs. None of the figures is solid enough to be real, but, on the other hand, they are all that there is. Sartre interprets the flickering individuality of the characters in a more

2. Internal evidence seems to suggest that *Deathwatch* was written before *The Maids*, but the latter was both published and performed first. Furthermore, Sartre (*op. cit.*, p. 564) says that *Deathwatch* is Genet's second play.
3. Jouvet's production used women.

sociopsychological manner when he asserts that the servants have no reality as individuals because when they are in the presence of their masters they have to act the part of the servant—obsequious or dignified, as the case may be; and when they are alone they are trying to ape their masters. Similarly, the masters have to act a part in the presence of their servants—they obviously cannot "be themselves" in front of them; and when they are alone they indulge in grandiosely romantic daydreams (like Madame's desire to follow her lover to Siberia or Devil's Island) engendered by their stagnant existence.[4] If one takes the masters as representative of the members of the social order and the servants as the social outcasts (the thieves, pimps, perverts, murderers—Genet's people), an interesting allegory can be developed. However, I am concerned here less with the sociological than with the philosophical and theatrical aspects of Genet's work. The climax of Genet's demonstration of nonbeing in being comes at the end of the play when Claire, purely as a gesture, commits suicide by drinking the poisoned tea which had been intended for Madame. Having failed to poison her mistress, Claire drinks the poison while pretending to be Madame again. She thus snuffs herself out while pretending to be someone whose individuality rests on equally flimsy foundations. Solange meanwhile steps out on the balcony and grandiosely declaims her own apotheosis as she imagines what will happen when she "confesses" to the murder of Claire. As the play ends, the whirligig slows down and stops; and we see that it is now empty.[5]

Deathwatch (Haute Surveillance), first produced in 1949, takes place in a prison cell. Here again Genet has created a triangular situation, with two of the convicts rivaling each other in their simultaneous love and hate for the third one. As in *The Maids*, there is a considerable element of latent homosexual attraction involved here. Again the play culminates in the violent death of one of the characters: Lefranc strangles the other "maid-convict," Maurice, in an effort to raise himself from a

---

4. Sartre, *op. cit.*, p. 565.
5. A detailed analysis of this play may be found in Oreste F. Pucciani, "Tragedy, Genet, and *The Maids*," *Tulane Drama Review*, VII (Spring, 1963), pp. 42–59.

petty thief to a murderer like Green Eyes, the cell's "mistress-convict." The parallels between *The Maids* and *Deathwatch* are so close that the two plays might be called companion pieces.

The prison cell containing Maurice, Lefranc, and Green Eyes is as much a dead end as the overheated Empire room in Sartre's *No Exit*. The artificial hierarchical society that the three convicts have built up in their cell closely parallels the one set up by the maids in Madame's bedroom. Like Madame, Green Eyes, who occupies the place of honor in this society by virtue of being a murderer while the others are only petty criminals, keeps aloof from the play acting and quarreling of his two cell-mates. Maurice and Lefranc parallel Claire and Solange. Like the two maids, the two convicts both hate (by way of envy) and love their superior and try to imitate him. Lefranc, who is older than Maurice as Solange is older than Claire, kills Maurice at the end, as Solange kills (though not in fact) Claire. *Death-watch* is a little more rooted in reality than is *The Maids:* the whirligig is rotating, but only slowly. Green Eyes is really a murderer and Lefranc actually does kill Maurice. Genet seems to be saying that outside society, where primitive instincts untainted by the artificiality of civilization still prevail, there is more reality, more possibility of achieving the dignity of an existence.[6] Green Eyes *exists*—because he does not *try* to be anything. As he says, he is what he is in spite of himself. He did not seek his distinction as a murderer; he murdered in spite of himself, in-voluntarily, unintentionally: "I didn't want what happened to me to happen. It was all given to me. A gift from God or the devil, but something I didn't want." [7] Green Eyes is passive; he does not act: he reacts. He has achieved a precarious existence by becoming—or never rising above—a human version of Pav-lov's dog. Just as the dog slavers when the bell is rung, so Genet's man murders when he is triggered into action by circumstances: "everything began to move. There was nothing more to be done.

6. Leonard C. Pronko, *Avant-Garde* (Berkeley, Cal.: University of California Press, 1962), p. 143, says that Genet uses the condemned man as a symbol of mankind because he remembers a lost paradise while making the best of it in a cell whose only issue is death.
7. Jean Genet, *The Maids and Deathwatch*, translated by Bernard Frechtman (New York: Grove Press, Inc., 1954), p. 161.

And so I just had to kill someone." [8] Genet seems to be arguing
here—perhaps in his own justification—that the true criminal
is simply being himself. He becomes a criminal by reacting to
the stimuli of society. Maurice and Lefranc, however, are not
content to be themselves: they are obsessed with the true social
being's need of a hierarchy. Maurice, with his fawning, homosexual hero worship, and Lefranc, with his fierce, social climber's
jealousy, admire and envy Green Eyes (and even more so Snow-
ball, the prison's supercriminal). Their quarreling assumes a
deadly seriousness that the conscious playacting of Claire and
Solange never has, and at the end Lefranc actually does strangle
Maurice with his bare hands. Now at last, he thinks, he is the
equal of Green Eyes, who also strangled his victim with his bare
hands. But Green Eyes quickly disillusions him. Lefranc has got
nowhere because he was trying to ape someone else, and there
is no reality in doing things in order to be like someone else.

When we come to *The Balcony* (Le Balcon, 1956), Genet's
best-known play, we find the situation somewhat changed. It is
like stepping off the plain into the forest. The whirligig that
Sartre has suggested as the best image of Genet's works is whirling around madly once again. Genet is once more concentrating
on his favorite paradox that appearance is all the reality there is.
The Balcony is a sort of light-and-shadow optical-illusion puzzle
in which the problem is to find the reality—if any.

"The Balcony" is the name of a fetishist whorehouse, called
a "house of illusions" by its madam. Here insignificant little
men come to play out in "reality" their grandiose fantasies. Each
room in the house is fitted out like a changing stage set so that
to suit the client it can be switched from the setting of one
fantasy to another. The women of the house are chosen as much
for their ability as actresses as for their ability as prostitutes. At
the beginning of the play we see three of these fantasies being
acted out. A gasman dressed in the robes of a bishop gives absolution to a scantily dressed penitent; another client plays a
judge and extracts a "confession" of theft from his girl by alter-

8. *Ibid.*, p. 131.

nately groveling at her feet and ordering his "executioner" to lash her; and finally a timid-looking, puny man dresses as a general and acts out his own hero's funeral à la the Duke of Wellington with the aid of a woman dressed as a horse. All these characters wear enormously padded shoulders and the Greek buskins to make them look bigger than life when they are playing their roles. The interesting thing about these scenes is that not only are the characters unreal (because they find it necessary to be someone else), not only are the figures that they pretend to be unreal (because they are the emanations of unreal minds), but Genet shows us that the figures that these emanations ape (the real bishops, judges, and generals that operate in our society) are unreal as well. This is the condemnation of the artificial structure of society by an outcast from society. Genet maintains that the system that judged and condemned him is dependent upon the free spirits outside it. The law is not an entity in itself (i.e., it is not "real"), since it depends for its existence upon the existence of "crime." Religion exists because "sin" exists. Hero figures exist because tribute is paid to them. The general in the third scene does not get a hero's funeral because he is a hero: he is a "hero" because the pomp and ceremony of the funeral transform him into a heroic symbol. The judge has power only when confronted with lawbreakers and backed up by the elemental savagery of the punishment ritual:

> JUDGE: Look here: you've got to be a model thief if I'm to be a model judge. If you're a fake thief, I become a fake judge. . . . My executioner has hit hard . . . if he didn't hit how could I stop him from hitting? Therefore, he must strike so that I can intervene and demonstrate my authority. . . . My being a judge is an emanation of your being a thief. You need only refuse—but you'd better not!— need only refuse to be who you are—what you are, therefore who you are—for me to cease to be . . . to vanish, evaporated. Burst. Volatized. Denied. . . . But you won't refuse, will you? You won't refuse to be a thief? That would

be wicked. It would be criminal. You'd deprive me of being! [9]

It is for this reason that the judge spends part of the scene
crawling on the floor and licking the feet of the girl playing
the thief. The bishop in the opening scene depends for his
holiness only on being able to forgive sin, which is therefore
primary.

The action of the play turns around a revolution going on
outside in the streets of the city. The Chief of Police, who
protects Mme. Irma's house of illusions, is in charge of stopping
the rebels. He does this by persuading the three clients to assume their roles again and pretend to take the place of the men
they pretended to be in their fantasies—the bishop, whose
severed head is reportedly ornamenting the handle bars of a
bicycle; the Attorney-General, who has died of fright; and the
Generalissimo, who has gone mad. In this way the Chief of
Police and the Court Envoy hope to delude the rebels into
thinking that the heads of the state are still intact. With Mme.
Irma, who is dressed as the Queen, the three step out on the
balcony and show themselves to the populace. Later, after
they have come back from a ride through the city in the state
carriage, the three impostors are still undetected. They are as
completely changed from their former selves as if they had been
transformed by plastic surgery; their sumptuous, glittering robes
of office, shored up with tradition and imprinted as symbols
in the popular consciousness by centuries of habituation, hide
and protect them like the crenellated fortifications of a be-
leaguered city.[10] Not even those who know them well can see
through the appearance to the reality, for in Genet appearance
is reality: "Do you think we were recognized?" asks the judge;
and the bishop answers, "No danger of that. You know whom
I saw . . . with his fat, good-natured mug and pink cheeks . . .

9. Jean Genet, *The Balcony*, translated by Bernard Frechtman. Copyright © 1958 by Bernard Frechtman. (New York: Grove Press Inc., 1958),
pp. 11–15.
10. Pronko (*op. cit.*, p. 148) claims that the impostors do not like the
reality of their roles. I believe rather that they become convinced of the
reality of their pretense and like it.

With his pimples and decayed teeth? and who threw himself on
my hand . . . I thought to bite me, and I was about to pull
away my fingers . . . to kiss my ring? Who? My fruit-and-
vegetable man." [11] Actually, the carriage ride is without danger.
The impostors are accepted by that time. They succeed as
soon as they step onto the balcony, for the balcony is Genet's
supreme symbol of illusion. In modern society the balcony is
the place from which rulers greet the people. For Genet the
ruler on the balcony is the figurehead that gathers into itself
all the falsity inherent in the social system it represents. It is
thus onto the balcony that Mme. Irma and her three clients
step when they wish to embody the illusion of the state and onto the balcony that Solange steps in her final frenzy of deluded
self-glorification. As soon as the three are no longer on the
balcony or in the gilded carriage, the false figures lose their
spurious dignity. To the cynical newspaper photographers who
come to perpetuate their image they are just insignificant little
men (although the photographers never suspect they are not
dealing with the real dignitaries!). These men, accustomed to
falsifying reality and feeding the masses with the pap of symbolism, are again only interested in illusion: "What I want is a
shot of *the* Judge. A good photographer is one who gives a
definitive image." The bishop's photographer tells him, "Get
set for prayer, because the world ought to be bombarded with
the picture of a pious man. . . . Okay, facing both God and
the camera. Hands together. Head up. Eyes down. That's the
classical pose." [12] And then, for a picture of the bishop taking
the Host, the photographer has the judge roll up his sleeve and
place the general's monocle on the prelate's tongue.[13]

11. Genet, *The Balcony*, p. 86. When reports pour into the rebel head-
quarters that the queen, the archbishop and the others have been captured,
and one of the rebels asks what should be done, his leader dryly advises,
"First undress them."

12. Genet, *The Balcony*, p. 89. The photographers' scene was unfortunately left out in Quintero's New York production.

13. Pronko (*op. cit.*, p. 149) says that the "true image, born of a
false spectacle" demonstrated here is probably true of all ritual, whether
theatrical or religious. Shaw touches on the same point in *St. Joan* when
he has the Archbishop of Rheims say that a miracle is any act which in-
duces belief.

If everything inside Mme. Irma's house is unreal, then it would seem that the revolution, which is on the brink of destroying the government and with it the Balcony, would represent the opposite force—namely, reality. But the revolution is as unreal as the government. Starting out as an honest attempt to overthrow the symbol-ridden, illusionary government, it rapidly disintegrates because of the incurable yearning of the human race to be something other than itself. We see this in the contrast between the narcissistic vainglory of the young rebel Armand and the symbol worship of the revolutionary leaders in their use of the escaped whore, Chantal, as a Joan of Arc figure on the one hand, and the matter-of-fact clarity of Roger, the only true rebel, on the other. For people like Armand the serious protest of the revolution is just a joke. His participation is merely an opportunity for him to become the creatures of his daydreams. Like Claire and Solange, Armand never has any reality of his own because, being always engaged in aping someone else, he has no personality of his own:

> ARMAND (*gaily*): . . . it's better than being at the shop. (*He laughs as he looks at himself in the mirror; then, spreading his legs, he plants himself in the middle of the stage.*) Like on the enlistment posters for the Marines: the tanks roll between my legs! (*He strikes another pose.*) Taras Bulba! (*He laughs, takes out his revolver and aims at the bottles.*) Big Chief Buffalo! . . .
>
> ROGER: If ever we had the misfortune of taking pleasure in shooting at men and bottles, it would be good-bye to the revolutionary spirit! As for a red-letter day, this is it! The Law Court's been burned to the ground. The churches have been looted. There are men who are going out to fight in judges' robes and surplices. It's a regular carnival. That ought to please you! [14]

Roger here sees the real purpose of the revolution (and it is Genet's real purpose too): protest against society—burning the law courts, looting the churches, mocking the trappings of

14. Genet, *The Balcony*, pp. 54–55.

authority. The leaders of the revolution are just as bad as Armand in their way. They allow the revolt to congeal, as Mme. Irma aptly puts it in her epilogue speech. They set up Chantal as an heroic image for which the rebels can die since they will not fight to the death for *reasons*. The Chief of Police and the Court Envoy know this, which is why they are always serenely confident that the revolution will be put down and that it will happen again and again in the future, as it has happened again and again in the past:

> THE ENVOY: . . . Chantal's image is circulating in the streets. A stylized image that resembles her and does not resemble her. She towers above the battles. At first, people were fighting against illustrious and illusory tyrants, then for freedom. Tomorrow they'll be ready to die for Chantal alone.[15]

We are now in a position to see what Genet is driving at in *The Balcony*. The play gives us a panoramic picture of society with its violence, oppression, injustice, vice, and falsity. With the exception of Roger (and he fades later, too) everyone in this microcosmos is unreal. They have all lost their own individuality through trying to be someone else. Some of them, like Mme. Irma, the cynical high priestess of falsity, and the Court Envoy, who manipulates everything like an unctuous Mephisto, seem never to have had any definite individuality of their own. They seem rather to be pieces of the very fabric of falsehood that have become animated.

In order to show us this Weltanschauung, Genet once more sets in motion the whirligig of his mind. The clients of the Balcony, all representative human beings, are stripped of layer after layer of unreality. Every part of them is the fabrication of some socially inspired fantasy. They are all hollow men, but after the various strata that seem to constitute their existence have been peeled off, it is seen that they have no husk as well as no core. The first client, for instance, is unreal to begin with because he needs a fantasy to feel real. So he comes to the

15. *Ibid.*, p. 77.

Balcony to dress up as a bishop, pretend to give absolution, and thus attain a second level of unreality. The third level comes when he pretends the fantasy is real and convinces the populace; the fourth, when he becomes convinced that his imposture has been so successful that he now really *is* a bishop. When he gets to this point, he starts appointing priests and planning a basilica; the "judge" starts appointing magistrates and revising the legal code; and the "general" typically meanders around ineffectually, hoping someone will tell him what to do. In a sense, then, we have here a play within a play within a play within a play: the action is spinning perilously close to the center of the whirligig, where everything will disappear.

The individual characters are not the only things stratified by Genet here. The revolution has been put down, thanks to the impostors, and the Chief of Police is the new head of the state. As he meets with his "cabinet," he gives us Genet's view of the social structure:

> THE CHIEF OF POLICE: Well, gentlemen, above God are you, without whom God would be nothing. And above you shall be I, without whom . . .
>
> THE JUDGE: What about the people? The photographers?
>
> THE CHIEF OF POLICE: On their knees before the people who are on their knees before God.[16]

Here we have an elaborate hierarchy: the photographers are the image-creators who cater to the people's desire to be deluded; the people create God, and God is sanctified by the functionaries of the social order. Above all is the hero symbol, the dictator, the arbiter of the social order, Genet's bête noire —in this case, the Chief of Police.

The Chief of Police is uneasy, however. Despite his success in crushing the revolution, he has still not attained the dignity of having an imitator. None of Mme. Irma's clients has yet had the idea of impersonating a chief of police. Bishops, judges, generals, corpses, kings, saints, crucified missionaries, even

16. *Ibid.*, p. 102.

Christ in person—but no chief of police. The trouble is that
people want to imitate the archetypal figures that are embedded
in the collective unconscious; figures who, as the bishop com-
placently remarks, have the tradition of two thousand years
behind them. A chief of police, the hated and despised power
figure of the modern totalitarian state, is a mere parvenu in
such company. Who would choose to embody a police chief
when he could just as easily be a leper healed by the Virgin
Mary or a policeman deflowering an archduchess? It gets so
bad that the chief is reduced to entertaining the suggestion that
he be personified in the form of an erect phallus as tall as himself. The Chief *is* finally imitated. Ironically, the new client is
the Chief's greatest enemy—Roger, the rebel leader, who had
abducted Chantal from the Balcony in the first place. He fell
in love with her but lost her when she became the revolution's
symbol ("In every revolution," says Mme. Irma, "there's the
glorified whore who sings an anthem and is virginified."). When
Chantal was killed and the rebellion suppressed, Roger, the
only person in the whole mess who had any reality, lost the will
to be himself: "Yes. Everything's washed up . . . and what's
saddest of all is people's saying: 'the rebellion was wonderful!'
. . . outside in what you call life, everything has crashed. No
truth was possible." [17] So now he has come to submerge himself
in the person of his archenemy. At the end of his fantasy he
does something which is at the same time the ultimate gesture
of hate against the abstraction he is personifying, the ultimate
gesture of renunciation, and (because performed in a whorehouse) the ultimate affirmation of falsity—he castrates himself.
After this the Chief retires into his "tomb" in the House of
Illusions. There he will wait two thousand years until he too
will become an archetypal figure.[18] As he disappears, renewed
machine-gun fire bursts out. "Who is it?" asks Mme. Irma,
"Our side? . . . Or rebels? . . . Or? . . ." And the Court Envoy,
enigmatic as ever, answers, "Someone dreaming, Madame . . ."

    17. *Ibid.*, pp. 111–14.
    18. Benjamin Nelson, "*The Balcony* and Parisian Existentialism,"
Tulane Drama Review, VII (Spring, 1963), p. 70, points out that Genet
probably intends a reference to Franco's Valley of the Fallen here.

Then the play ends as Mme. Irma turns out the lights and, stepping out of her role, addresses the audience:

> In a little while, I'll have to start all over again . . . put all the lights on again . . . dress up . . . (*A cock crows.*) Dress up . . . ah, the disguises! Distribute roles again . . . assume my own. . . . (*She stops in the middle of the stage, facing the audience.*) . . . Prepare yours . . . judges, generals, bishops, chamberlains, rebels who allow the revolt to congeal, I'm going to prepare my costumes and studios for tomorrow. . . . You must now go home, where everything—you can be quite sure—will be even falser than here.[19]

The whirligig grinds to a stop, and, as usual, there is nothing on it anymore.

The Blacks (Les Nègres, 1958) deals with the levels of unreality in the relations between whites and Negroes. According to Genet, this lack of reality is inherent in the institution of colonialism. The artificial superiority of the whites leads to the usual subjective-objective dichotomy. The subjective reality of the Negroes can never be understood by the white man; all that exists for him is the objective reality he sees. But this objective reality has been specially prepared by the Negro as a protective smoke screen: he shows the white man what the white man expects to see. And thus we have the ludicrously unreal spectacle of the happy, primitive, inferior native blissfully gamboling about his jungle clearing and asking nothing better than to be "civilized" by missionaries and permitted to work on the plantations for nominal wages. In *The Blacks* Genet tries to make the Negro's real attitude clear to the whites. His play is written for Negro actors and white audiences. This relationship is essential to Genet's scheme. He will not permit white actors to perform the play,[20] and he insists that

19. Genet, *The Balcony*, pp. 117–18.
20. Cf. the letter Genet wrote to Jerzy Lisowski, who had translated *The Blacks* into Polish, refusing him permission to produce the play in Poland on the ground that no Polish-speaking Negroes were available to act in it. (Jean Genet, "To a Would-be Producer," *Tulane Drama Review,* VII [Spring, 1963], pp. 80–81.)

there be at least one white man or one symbol of a white man
(the two are, after all, essentially the same in Genet's system)
in the audience:

> . . . a white person, male or female, should be invited
> every evening. The organizer of the show should welcome
> him formally, dress him in ceremonial costume and lead
> him to his seat, preferably in the front row of the orchestra.
> The actors will play for him. A spotlight should be focused
> upon this symbolic white throughout the performance.
>   But what if no white person accepted? Then let white
> masks be distributed to the black spectators as they enter
> the theater. And if the blacks refuse the masks, then let a
> dummy be used.[21]

The action of *The Blacks* is very simple. A group of Negroes
enacts the ritual murder of a white woman. Another group of
Negroes, wearing white masks and dressed in the trappings
that give the whites their illusory authority, sits in judgment
on them. Instead of being judged, however, the Negroes "kill"
the "Whites." While the Negroes on stage are going through
this mock catharsis, the real action of the play is transpiring off-
stage. A Negro traitor is condemned and shot, and at the end
it becomes clear to the white audience that the whole play was
merely an elaborate, conscious cover-up to disguise an incident
in the war of the Negroes on the whites. When the white
spectators leave, they realize at last that this war has been declared. Susan Taubes points out that *The Blacks* is not an ordinary play within a play, but a play within a situation: the confrontation of the dominating and the dominated in the only
way that is still possible.[22] Direct communication between the
two races is no longer possible: only the completely impersonal
clown show can still bridge the gap. What happens when the
war between the dominating and the dominated comes out into
the open Genet shows us in his next play.

21. Jean Genet, *The Blacks: A Clown Show*, translated by Bernard
Frechtman (New York: Grove Press Inc., 1960), p. [11].
22. Susan Taubes, "The White Mask Falls," *Tulane Drama Review*,
VII (Spring, 1963), p. 87.

In *The Screens* (Les Paravents, published 1961) the Negroes
are the Algerians and the whites are the French colonials. The
main character is Saïd, the poorest and lowest of the Arabs.
Saïd is the paradoxical hero par excellence. He is Genet's hero
because he is unheroic. Saïd's poverty has put him outside
society; and all his efforts are devoted to remaining outside.
He marries the ugliest woman in the area, lives by stealing,
not from his employers but from his fellow Arabs, and finally
informs on his comrades. The contempt and ostracism he earns
by this conduct are accepted cheerfully, even gleefully, by Saïd,
for they testify to his devotion to himself and to his situation.
Joseph McMahon points to some interesting parallels between
the character of Saïd and Genet. The latter had lived for years
outside society, its sworn enemy, accepting its opprobrium as
a sign of his steadfastness to his ideal of individuality. Now, with
the popular success of his plays, he runs the risk of being cor-
roded by the approval of society:

> . . . he wants nothing to do with passing from the *enfant
> terrible* he was at the beginning of his literary career to the
> *enfant gâté* he seems to be becoming as the bourgeoisie,
> against whom he has organized his most acerbic attacks,
> assimilates his ideas, talks about them, and either accepts
> or rejects them. He wants no part of this because the very
> process by which he is spoiled is the process he has been
> attacking in all his later works: the presupposition that it
> is the bourgeoisie, the *decent* people, who rule ultimately
> on this earth and whose assent to any body of ideas is the
> modern world's imprimatur and canonization without which
> no man can be assured he has made his impact.[23]

In apotheosizing Saïd, Genet is in a way writing his own vindication. But there is more to the play than self-justification.
Saïd's act of betrayal is also a vindication of the revolution because in rebelling against the masters' conception of him (as the
Negroes are preparing to do in *The Blacks*), the rebel, if he is
successful, becomes like his masters, for their conception of life

23. Joseph H. McMahon, "Keeping Faith and Holding Firm," *Yale
French Studies*, No. 29 (Spring–Summer, 1962), pp. 27–28.

is inherent in their position.[24] Thus the unwilling impostors in
The Balcony immediately adopt the traditional attitudes of
bishop, general, and judge as soon as they put on their trappings.
Similarly, the planters, Sir Harold and Mr. Blankensee, in *The
Screens* are perfectly aware of the fact that their authority resides in their appearance rather than in themselves. Hence Sir
Harold's panic when he realizes that his huge mechanical pig-
skin glove no longer intimidates the natives as it used to do, and
Mr. Blankensee's when he discovers the loss of the pads he
wears around his midriff to give him an appearance of solid
dignity: "A man of my age who doesn't have a belly and an ass
hasn't much prestige. So one has to fake a little. . . . In the
old days there were wigs." [25] Saïd's treachery is a recognition
of the fact that the success of the revolution would mean the
repetition of the same abominations as before. The rebels would
simply become darker Sir Harolds and Mr. Blankensees. Saïd
realizes that every man has to stand alone and not for a cause,
even if standing alone means burying oneself in degradation and
filth. The vocation of men is "to refuse the fate others impose
on them and to deny the cultural conspiracy which maintains
the illusion of their freedom." [26] The manner in which the
revolution will be betrayed by itself is illustrated in this scene:

> THE SOLDIER (*severely*): You shouldn't talk that
> way any more. And to speak of a traitor the way you do is
> wrong. And what else? A thief, a bastard, a beggar . . .
>
> OMMU: Aha! . . . that was to be expected! Be-
> cause you boys have now reached the stage of uniforms,
> discipline, jaunty marches and bare arms, parade and heroic
> death, while singing "Madelon" and the "Marsellaise" and
> martial beauty. . . .
>
> THE SOLDIER: Why not? There are other things
> than shit and filth. . . .

24. Marc Pierret, "Genet's New Play: *The Screens*," *Tulane Drama
Review*, VII (Spring, 1963), p. 95.
  25. Jean Genet, *The Screens*, translated by Bernard Frechtman. Copyright © 1962 by Bernard Frechtman. (New York: Grove Press Inc., 1962),
p. 73.
  26. Pierret, *op. cit.*, p. 97.

OMMU: You lousy little stinker, you snotnose, go join the other side where there's stately beauty, you little snotnose! But maybe you've done it, you're joining them, and copying them excites you. To be their reflection is already to be one of them.[27]

Ommu, one of Genet's prophetic old beggar women, knows that man is eternally immersed in vileness and she knows "the consequent importance of remaining vile if one is to remain a faithful witness to one's situation." [28]

OMMU: Do sins scare you? We've nothing else to live but sins, we've got to live them. I have nothing against God, but he can see that all he's left us is sins. And what's meant by going into mourning, gentlemen, if not to make oneself ugly? To cover oneself with crape, with ashes, with mud, with flies, with cow dung, to let one's beard grow, to let filth accumulate in the folds of the skin, to pluck out one's eyes, to scrape one's fingers, what's meant by going into mourning, gentlemen? [29]

Beneath the empty trappings of social position all men are filth, and one must remain faithful to one's reality, which is filth. Genet plays an even more cynical variation on Burke's cynical aphorism when he maintains that defecation is a mighty leveler:

THE SERGEANT: . . . when you squeeze, you get glassy-eyed, something clouds over . . . and . . . what is it that clouds over and blots out? The world? . . . The sky? . . . No. Your rank of sergeant, and that of captain! And all that goes with it: the uniform, the stripes, the decorations and the officers' school diploma when you've got one! . . . And what's left? Emptiness.[30]

In being true to his own filth Saïd becomes the lowest kind of criminal and at the same time a saint. For Genet the criminal

27. Genet, *The Screens*, pp. 134–35.
28. McMahon, *op. cit.*, p. 31.
29. Genet, *The Screens*, p. 133.
30. *Ibid.*, p. 170.

and the saint are the same because both rebel against society.[31] Obedience to temporal power and subservience to social conventions are the worst crimes. Every other act, no matter how bestial, pales into moral insignificance by comparison. To say that crime is "immoral" or sexual perversion "bestial" is to make a value judgment based on social values. The pejorative value of such words as "immoral" and "bestial" is thus, in Genet's eyes, nil. Genet sees the act of betrayal as an act which requires courage and will power. It is also the most dishonorable of all acts in the eyes of society. In Genet's system it is therefore the most worthy of acts. To Genet, Judas's act of betrayal makes him more virtuous than Christ.[32] He would agree with the paradoxical conjecture of Nils Runeberg in J. L. Borges's short story, "Three Views of Judas," that Judas Iscariot and not Jesus Christ was God because in deliberately bringing upon himself the vituperation and hate of all Christians through the centuries Judas commits the greatest of all acts of self-abnegation.[33]

Like all members of the current dramatic avant-garde, Genet writes his plays as a protest against society and the restrictions it imposes on the actual or spiritual freedom of the individual. Much of the confusion that surrounds the plays of Genet and of his fellow avant-gardists can be traced to the influence of Artaud's belief that true drama had its roots among primitive, nonrational peoples. The drama as we know it reflects the artificial and hollow society in which we live. Real drama reflects only the basic human emotions as they were before they were covered up with artificial behavior. Artaud felt that drama should not appeal to the mind but to the emotions—and to such an extent that a process of communion takes place between actor and spectator in which both are roused to a high pitch of excitement. Artaud compared this condition to a man losing his reason under the influence of the plague. He also maintained

31. Leonard Pronko, "Jean Genet's *Les Paravents*," *L'Esprit Créateur*, II (Winter, 1962), p. 182.
32. *Ibid.*
33. J. L. Borges, *Ficciones* (New York: Grove Press Inc., 1962), pp. 151–57.

that drama should show "cruelty," by which he meant it should give the impression that man is controlled from birth to death by blind and merciless forces. At the same time drama should be a defiance of these forces, no matter how ineffectual such defiance is doomed to be, and a protest against the encroachment of civilization upon man's naturally free spirit.

Genet conforms fairly closely to Artaud's specifications. The bias against contemporary society may be seen in his choice of scene. *The Maids* takes place in a wealthy household depicted with the utmost viciousness. *Deathwatch* and *The Balcony* take place in the two most antisocial milieus possible: the one in a prison, the other in a whorehouse. *The Blacks* and *The Screens* take place in savage settings where the actual conflict between the social and the antisocial forces is being fought. In all of the plays, moreover, we have the element of cruelty which Artaud claims as an essential ingredient of all true drama. In *The Balcony* this cruelty takes the form of the enacted sadomasochistic fantasies of the bishop, the judge, and the general. In *The Blacks* we see the reenactment of the ritual murder and the shooting of the jury. In *Deathwatch* Maurice is strangled on the stage; and in *The Maids* there is the attempted murder of Madame and the suicide of Claire. And, finally, in *The Screens* we have a constant stream of references to violence and scatology.

In all the plays the *intention* is to arouse the audience to an emotional frenzy in which they will instinctively reject the social structure disintegrating before their eyes on the stage and accept instead the atavistic emotions that Genet sends surging through them. This frenzy is analogous to Artaud's "plague," which sweeps through the audience like an epidemic and frees them from their socially impressed inhibitions, like a disease that leads to death inevitably will do. When Mme. Irma says of the rebellion, "Contagion? The rebellion is an epidemic. It has the same fatal and sacred character," we see that Genet uses the rebellion's ominous threat (emphasized by the intermittent machine-gun fire) as a device to whip up the audience's emotions and make the theater once more a ritual and a ceremony as it was in the theatre of Aeschylus and Sophocles and in the

"theater" of the Orphic and Eleusinian mysteries and as it
still is in the theater of the Orient. All this is straight out of the
atavistic theater of savagery and irrationalism with which
Antonin Artaud wanted to bring back drama to its original
function of hypnotizing the audience into a frenzied communion with the action: to strike not at the brain but at the
core of the human soul.

The German-Speaking Drama

THE CONTEMPORARY German-speaking drama differs from the French avant-garde drama in being more rational and more topical. It is influenced by Shaw and Brecht rather than by Jarry and Artaud. The themes of protest and paradox are still there, but speech is once again the medium of communication, although dramatic form continues to be broken down. The use of violence and cruelty continues, but it is now once more explicable and politically involved instead of cosmic and mysterious, as in the violence and cruelty of the "Savage God."

FRIEDRICH DÜRRENMATT
The Sardonic View

WHEN *The Visit* opened on Broadway on May 5, 1958, it was an instant success, and the name of Friedrich Dürrenmatt, known throughout Europe for some years, was suddenly brought to the attention of the American theater world. So profound an impression did this one play make that Dürrenmatt has shot up in the estimation of American theater people to a place on a level with Jean Anouilh as one of Europe's foremost current dramatic authors.

Dürrenmatt's plays can be characterized as fantasies from which lessons may be learned. The imputation of preaching frightens writers nowadays for some reason. They are convinced that they have no function other than to entertain. The pendulum, always erratic in the theater, has come full swing since the fervor of the turn-of-the-century social-propaganda play. Indeed, it seems to set Galileo's theory at defiance, for, instead of spending all its time in the journey from one end of its swing to the other, it spends all of it standing stock-still at one end and then flashing across to the other end in no time flat. Now we are at the nondidactic end again. Philosophy, Dürrenmatt insists, cannot be transmitted through drama. He feels that the theater exists solely as a medium for the creation of a special world—that the audience, in other words, comes to peep in at a new, wonderful, and strange world, a contrived set of circumstances in which fantastic things can happen quite as matter-of-factly as the spectators wistfully wish they might in real life. Beyond this Dürrenmatt refuses to go. He maintains that he does not care what lesson may be drawn from his plays, if any. Like T. S. Eliot, he is often enlightened as to the inner meaning of his works by reading the critics. His own attitude is simply that each person will choose from these created worlds whatever appears desirable or useful to him.

All of Dürrenmatt's created worlds seem to fasten upon and revolve (in a manner sometimes savage and bitter, sometimes impersonal and amused, sometimes ferociously jocular— but always detached and bitingly sardonic) around death. In Dürrenmatt's works death seems to be almost personified—a vague, grey shape leaning mockingly over the shoulders of his leading characters and edging them slyly on. Unlike Thornton Wilder, to whom death is only the last incident in life and who places the emphasis always on the process of living, Dürrenmatt sees life only as a long futility working up to an ultimate futility. Death is the culmination of life, but it is an anticlimactic and basically insignificant culmination. A process that culminates in an anticlimax can only be treated as a ridiculous joke. Hence the mordantly sardonic, lacerating note in Dürrenmatt's plays—"Man is ridiculous because he must die." Dürrenmatt's world is like a Punch and Judy show in which audience and puppeteer are part of the ridiculous antics.

They laugh at the futile wriggling of the puppets in their vain attempts to squeeze some consolatory meaning out of their tragedies; but the laughter is self-lacerating. Dürrenmatt's other principal theme is the effect of the possession of power on the human soul. His preoccupation with this theme may be summed up in Lord Acton's axiom, "Power tends to corrupt; absolute power corrupts absolutely." In all of his plays there is some figure unbalanced by the possession of power.

Dürrenmatt's best play is undoubtedly *The Visit*, originally titled *Der Besuch der alten Dame* (The Visit of the Old Lady). More than any other of his works it demonstrates his sardonic view of human behavior. *The Visit* takes place in Güllen, a seedy, run-down town somewhere in the German-speaking part of Europe. The inhabitants, most of them unemployed, spend their time sitting around talking wistfully of the former glories of the town. One group of four citizens, which acts as chorus to the action, spends its days lolling around the railroad station watching the trains roar by and reminiscing with vague bitterness about the days when all trains, even the crack trans-European expresses, used to stop regularly at Güllen. Now at last a ray of hope has penetrated the prevailing gloom: Güllen's most illustrious native is coming back for a visit. For Güllen is the home town of the world's richest woman, Claire Zachanassian, who left at an early age with the cloud of an unsavory affair over her and became a prostitute in Hamburg. There Zachanassian, the world's richest man, saw her and married her. Now he is dead and she owns everything—Armenian Oil, Western Railways, the North Broadcasting Co., and the Hong-kong red-light district. The townspeople hope to persuade her to pour some money into the town during her stay, and to this end they have appointed Alfred Ill, her former sweetheart, as her escort and charmer-in-chief with instructions to get at least a million. Alfred, we learn, was once a handsome young fellow who had a secret love affair with Claire. Now he is a run-down old man with a family, the keeper of the general store.

Mme. Zachanassian arrives with her entourage, which includes a butler, two blind eunuchs, a black panther, and an empty coffin. At first things go swimmingly: Ill, set on by the mayor and schoolmaster, who sniff around after the couple like a pair of unpractised but pathetically eager bloodhounds, takes Claire to all the places where they used to make love. He tries to recapture those days, but finds that every time he touches the old lady he touches ivory: she is made up mostly of artificial limbs. Nonetheless, he succeeds in eliciting a promise that she will give the town "millions."

Then, at the ceremonial banquet, comes the bombshell. Claire recounts how Ill refused to acknowledge his child and publicly proclaimed her a whore by means of bribed perjurers. She then offers to give the town a billion—half for the town and half to be equally divided among all the families—if in return they will give her justice:

CLAIRE: I will give you a billion and I want justice in return.

MAYOR: How am I to understand that, dear lady?

CLAIRE: Just as I said it.

MAYOR: But justice cannot be bought!

CLAIRE: Everything can be bought.

MAYOR: I still don't understand.

CLAIRE: Come here, Boby.

The Butler comes forward and takes off his dark glasses.

BUTLER: I don't know if any of you will still be able to recognize me.

SCHOOLMASTER: Chief Judge Hofer.

BUTLER: Correct. Chief Judge Hofer. Forty-five years ago I was chief judge of the Güllen Court. Later I became judge in the Court of Appeals at Kaffigen and remained there until Mme. Zachanassian offered to take me into her service as butler twenty-five years ago. I accepted. A somewhat peculiar career for an academic person, but the salary offered was so fantastic that . . .

CLAIRE: Come to the point, Boby.

BUTLER: As you have heard, Mme. Claire Zachanassian offers you a billion and wants justice in return for it. In other words, Mme. Claire Zachanassian offers you a billion if you undertake to correct the injustice done to Mme. Zachanassian in Güllen. Mr. Ill, if you please.

Ill gets up, pale, startled, amazed.

ILL: What do you want with me?

BUTLER: Come forward, Mr. Ill.

ILL: Certainly.

BUTLER: In 1910 I was Chief Judge in Güllen and sat on a paternity case. Claire Zachanassian, at that time Klara Wäscher, accused you, Mr. Ill, of being the father of her child. You contested the case, Mr. Ill, and produced two witnesses.

ILL: Old stories. I was young and didn't know what I was doing.

The two eunuchs are brought forward.

THE TWO: Here we are, here we are!

BUTLER: Do you recognize them, Mr. Ill?

Ill remains silent.

THE TWO: We're Koby and Loby, we're Koby and Loby.

ILL: I don't know them.

THE TWO: We've changed, we've changed.

BUTLER: Give your names.

THE FIRST: Jakob Hühnlein, Jakob Hühnlein.

THE SECOND: Ludwig Sparr, Ludwig Sparr.

BUTLER: Well, Mr. Ill?

ILL: I don't know anything about them.

BUTLER: Jakob Hühnlein and Ludwig Sparr, do you know Mr. Ill?

THE TWO: We are blind, we are blind.

BUTLER: Do you recognize his voice?

THE TWO: Recognize his voice, recognize his voice.

BUTLER: In 1910 I was the judge and you were the witnesses. What did you swear to the Court at Güllen?

THE TWO: That we slept with Klara, that we slept with Klara.

BUTLER: That is what you swore before the Court and before God. Did you swear the truth?

THE TWO: We swore falsely, we swore falsely.

BUTLER: Why, Jakob Hühnlein and Ludwig Sparr?

THE TWO: Ill bribed us, Ill bribed us.

BUTLER: With what?

THE TWO: With a bottle of gin, with a bottle of gin.

CLAIRE: Now tell what I did to you, Koby and Loby.

BUTLER: Tell.

THE TWO: The lady searched for us, the lady searched for us.

BUTLER: True. Claire Zachanassian had you searched for. Over the whole world. Jakob Hühnlein had gone to Canada and Ludwig Sparr to Australia. But she found you. What did she do with you then?

THE TWO: She gave us to Toby and Roby. She gave us to Toby and Roby.

BUTLER: And what did Toby and Roby do to you?

THE TWO: Blinded and castrated, blinded and castrated.

BUTLER: That is the story: a judge, a defendant, two false witnesses, a miscarriage of justice in 1910. Is it not so, Plaintiff?

CLAIRE: It is so.

ILL: Dead and buried long ago! Just a crazy old story.

BUTLER: What happened to the child, Plaintiff?

CLAIRE: It lived one year.

BUTLER: What happened to you?

CLAIRE: I became a whore.

BUTLER: Why?

CLAIRE: The decree of the Court made me one.

BUTLER: And now, Claire Zachanassian, you want justice?

CLAIRE: I can afford it. A billion for Güllen—if someone kills Alfred Ill.[1]

1. Friedrich Dürrenmatt, *Komödien I*. With permission of and copyright © 1958 by Peter Schifferli Verlags AG "Die Arche" (Zürich: Verlag der Arche, 1958), pp. 292–95.

This is a typical Dürrenmatt scene. Its structure may be compared to the piling on of straws until the camel's back breaks. Casually the evidence starts building up, dropping negligently, apologetically almost, on the imperceptibly, yet very really, increasing pile, until suddenly the whole innocent-and-insignificant-seeming mass is brought into focus by Claire's self-assured, deeply venomous remark, "One billion for Güllen—if someone kills Alfred Ill." It is like pulling a string that brings the whole structure tumbling down, jerking everyone, actors and audience, back to a startled and shocked attention. Dürrenmatt uses this enormously effective technique again and again. He uses it in the proposal scene of *Die Ehe des Herrn Mississippi* (The Marriage of Mr. Mississippi); in the scene of Archilochos' promotion in *Griechе sucht Griechin* (Greek Seeks Greek, a novel); in Odoacer's submission scene in *Romulus der Grosse* (Romulus the Great); and in the trial scene in *Die Panne* (The Breakdown, a novel adapted for the stage as The Deadly Game).

Things begin to move rapidly after the offer. The mayor at first indignantly turns it down in the name of humanity. Gradually, however, Ill's fellow citizens, starved of all luxury for so long, get deeper and deeper into debt as they buy things on credit in neighboring towns. Slowly their attitude toward Ill changes. They become more and more hostile as they "discover" the heinousness of his crime. Eventually Ill realizes that even his family wants him to die (his son has a new car and his wife a new fur coat—on credit); and, in a superbly ironic scene, a veritable tour de force of cynicism, he is sentenced to death while reporters from all over the world and TV and newsreel cameras look unsuspectingly on. The murder takes place immediately afterwards. Claire accepts the body for removal to the elaborate mausoleum she has constructed for it on the Isle of Capri. As she goes out, she calls the mayor, and, with a gesture of regal contemptuousness, drops the check at his feet. As the mayor stoops to retrieve the fluttering piece of paper— worth a billion, or a man's life, or the newly burdened conscience of the town—the curtain falls.

That is the story of a typical Dürrenmatt play. The two principal themes of death and the corruptive influence of power are already fully developed in *Es steht geschrieben* (It Is Writ-

ten), performed in Zürich in 1947. In this, his first play, Dürrenmatt chose as his subject the Anabaptist blood bath in Münster
under John of Leyden. The play deals with John's fanatical
vanity, his gradual moral disintegration under the pressure of
power, and the final "joke" of his horrible death as his broken
body is thrown into the same dung cart in which he first arrived
in Münster.

In *Romulus der Grosse* (Romulus the Great, 1949) the demonstration of futility assumes a more sophisticated character.
The play is about the last days of the West Roman Empire.
As in the play about John of Leyden, Dürrenmatt has taken a
historical character and a historical series of events and altered
them to suit his own purposes. Nothing could be more remote
from the historical last Roman emperor than Dürrenmatt's
Romulus. Dürrenmatt turns the end of the Roman Empire,
under the child emperor Romulus Augustuius in 476, from an
almost imperceptible death rattle, the inevitable last stifled sigh
that follows centuries of inefficiency and corruption, to a sardonic commentary on idealism and self-sacrifice. The real
Romulus reigned for less than a year (475–476) and was only
about fourteen years old, but Dürrenmatt's emperor is an old
man who has ruled for twenty years. Twenty years was a fantastically long time for a late Roman emperor to reign. Dürrenmatt's emperor manages it by not ruling. After becoming emperor by marrying the illegitimate daughter of the Emperor
Valentinianus, he has spent the entire twenty years raising
chickens in his country villa. Under his do-nothing policy the
strength of the Roman Empire has been undermined and now
German hordes led by Odoacer threaten to take Rome and
exterminate the Imperium.

Dürrenmatt's Romulus poses as an urbane cynic with the
mind of an eighteenth-century rationalist; but hidden beneath
the worldly exterior is the moral fervor of a Puritan divine. Some
idea of the type of person and ruler he is may be had from this
conversation with his two chamberlains:

ROMULUS: . . . Fetch the Finance Minister.
ACHILLES: The Finance Minister has absconded,
Your Majesty.

ROMULUS: Absconded???

PYRAMUS: With the State Treasury, O Emperor.

ROMULUS: But why? There wasn't anything in it.

ACHILLES: He hopes that his action will hide the fact that the country is bankrupt.

ROMULUS: An intelligent man. The best way to hide a big scandal is to start a small one. Let him be invested with the title, "Savior of his Country." [2]

As the play progresses, Romulus becomes more and more of a Shavian character (the whole play, in fact, might be straight out of the Shaw canon). He reveals to his wife that the sole reason he married her was to become emperor and thus fulfill the sentence he had passed on his country. For twenty years he has deliberately mismanaged and bankrupted the country. He has waited for twenty years to see the moment that is about to come: the fall of the Roman Empire to the Germans. With the implacability and steadfast purpose of a Catonian Roman he has pronounced his verdict and unflinchingly carried it out. Rome has failed; therefore Rome must die. He discloses all this in a conversation with his amazed wife, who for twenty years had thought him feeble-minded:

ROMULUS: . . . My political policy is to do nothing.

JULIA: You didn't have to become emperor to do that.

ROMULUS: Naturally enough my do-nothingness only made sense as long as I was emperor. To laze around as a private citizen is totally pointless.

JULIA: And to laze around as emperor endangers the state.

ROMULUS: Well, there you are!

JULIA: What do you mean by that?

ROMULUS: You have discovered the reason for my laziness.

JULIA: You can't possibly doubt the necessity of the state.

2. *Ibid.,* pp. 13–14.

ROMULUS: I don't doubt the necessity of the state: I merely doubt the necessity of *our* state. It has become an international empire and an institution which killed, plundered, suppressed, and ravaged other peoples—until I came.

JULIA: I don't see why you had to become emperor if that's the way you feel about the Roman Empire.

ROMULUS: The Roman Empire has existed for the last few centuries only because it had an emperor. Consequently there was no other alternative for me than to become emperor myself in order to be able to liquidate the Imperium.

JULIA: Either you are crazy or the world is.

ROMULUS: I have resigned myself to the latter alternative.

JULIA: Then you only married me to destroy the Roman Imperium.

ROMULUS: For no other reason.

JULIA: You have thought about nothing else besides Rome's downfall right from the beginning.

ROMULUS: About nothing else.

JULIA: You consciously sabotaged the safety of the Imperium.

ROMULUS: Consciously.

JULIA: You've played the cynic and clown all the time only so you could stab us in the back.

ROMULUS: You can put it that way too, if you like. . . .

JULIA: You are Rome's betrayer!

ROMULUS: No, I am Rome's judge.[3]

This view of the last Roman Emperor as a man who judges Rome for its sins and deliberately destroys it is in itself a sufficiently novel and interesting reinterpretation of history to justify a whole drama. But Dürrenmatt adds two more twists to his plot. He is not interested in the decline and fall of the Roman Empire; he *is* interested in the dissection of the rationalist-moralist, Romulus.

3. *Ibid.*, pp. 57–58.

F

Romulus is not a power-crazy judge, dispassionately consigning Rome to the devil. He has only been able to justify his objective to himself all these years by promising himself that he will give his own life in expiation for his betrayal. The pure rationalist would have seen Rome's destruction was "necessary" and would have watched the consummation of his plans with considerable self-satisfaction; but the moralist has the martyr complex: he must find "justification" for the "necessity" in the sacrifice of his own life. Both types, Dürrenmatt is trying to tell us, are equally dangerous. They are guilty, among other things, of *hubris*. Like Hector in *Tiger at the Gates*, Romulus tries to halt the invincible phalanx of fate. Inevitably he fails.

The night before the Germans are due to arrive, Romulus' household leaves him after a farcical scene in which he discovers no less than nine potential assassins hidden in his bedroom. Only the sudden outcry announcing the imminent arrival of the Germans saves him. The next morning Romulus quietly awaits the German chieftain, Odoacer. Urbane as ever, faithful to his lifelong creed of "Face the world fearlessly, fearlessly do the right," he fully expects to be beheaded on the spot by the barbarians. Then, as in the banquet scene of *The Visit*, comes the surprise. Odoacer turns out to be a rationalist-moralist too. As urbane and cultivated as Romulus, instead of cutting his head off, he throws himself on his knees before the emperor. It turns out that Odoacer has conquered Italy for the specific purpose of abasing himself before the head of the Roman Empire and handing the German people over to him. He has realized that his nephew, Theodoric, is a true barbarian, a war-loving, savage machine (Dürrenmatt's intentional parallel to modern Prussianism is obvious) who will turn the Germans into a conquest-mad horde if he succeeds to the leadership. Theodoric has all the most dangerous symptoms: he doesn't like girls, drinks only water, sleeps on the hard floor, practices fighting daily, and does calisthenics in every spare moment; and the people love him. Odoacer sees only one solution: to conquer Rome and throw himself and his people under its humanizing influence. Like Romulus he has judged his people, and like Romulus he has misjudged them. Romulus becomes "Great" only at the end when, defeated in all his plans, he accepts the fate that is his. Instead of being the implacable judge, his role is to be a retired and superannuated emperor living out his life on a pension in a country villa while Odoacer governs. Both of them now know that they are only marking time during an interim, for as soon as he feels himself strong enough Theodoric will kill them both and the progress of history, which they have tried to impede, will resume.

In *Romulus the Great* we can clearly see the two themes that run through Dürrenmatt's work: the themes of death and power. Romulus is the type of the benevolent despot, and he is just as bad, Dürrenmatt tells us, as the more conventional type of despot. As soon as he gains absolute power, Romulus becomes, strictly speaking, insane. From the best and most reasonable motives he calmly proposes to destroy a nation. Despite his kindliness in his personal relations, with his family and the members of his household, despite his strong sense of personal justice, despite his genuinely felt humanitarian impulses, Romulus suffers from the disease of all morally fervid idealist reformers: he loses the human element when applying his theories. People in the mass are not individualized for Romulus, and so he consigns the people under his care to destruction. His proposed sacrifice of his own life becomes suddenly ridiculous when he comes face to face with the German chieftain. Nor, we then realize, would the sacrifice have been of any significance at all—certainly not as an expiation. The laughter of the gods seems to tinkle faintly through the conversation as the two old idealists, Romulus and Odoacer, sit discussing their situation amid the ruins of their grandiose plans.

In *Die Ehe des Herrn Mississippi* Dürrenmatt takes his two principal themes of death and power one step further. Again he is absorbed by the hideous results of absolute power in the hands of a single-minded idealist, only this time he extends the range of his subject by using symbolic characters in a symbolic setting. The death theme is also carried one step further—instead of being treated sardonically, it is treated with off-hand jocularity. Three of the four main characters are murdered in the last scene, but one of them has already been murdered in the first scene, so that we see the same murder twice—somewhat like seeing a movie trailer and then the movie itself. Furthermore, each of the corpses comes to life again immediately in order to explain the significance of his death to the audience.

The play, as Dürrenmatt tells us in his opening stage direction, is about the room in which it takes place. This room "stinks to high heaven" and represents the ordinary, everyday world in which the majority of people live. It is a room that has been depersonalized: a little of everything is to be seen in it. There are pieces of cheap bric-a-brac, Louis XVI mirrors, fin-de-siècle mirrors, Louis XIV chairs, a Louis XV buffet, Empire sofas, Spanish walls, Japanese vases, Meissner porcelain, and a Gothic grandfather clock. Russian elements, Dürrenmatt tells us, can be left out if the political situation makes such an omission desirable. In short, the room is an utter hodgepodge of styles— what the Germans call a Biedermeier room, which is the type of room most people would have if they had the money to buy the stuff. There are two windows in the rear wall, one giving a view of a Gothic cathedral and an apple tree, the other of a cypress and the ruins of an antique temple. The chief characters are similarly generalized through their names: Anastasia, Florestan Mississippi, Frederic Réné Saint-Claude, and Graf Bodo von Übelohe-Zabernsee.

Basically, the complicated plot concerns the reactions to each other of two fanatical ideal-pursuers, Saint-Claude and Mississippi, and one humanitarian, Count Bodo, as they revolve around their catalyst, Anastasia, the eternal femme fatale, the Whore of Babylon, as she is called at one point, the scabrous underside of *das ewig Weibliche*. The plot itself is pure melodrama. Dürrenmatt has created as banal a plot as possible in order to fix the audience's attention while he exposes the characters and philosophies of his protagonists. Anastasia poisons her husband and is blackmailed into marriage by Mississippi. At various times she takes Bodo, Saint-Claude, and Diego, the Minister of State, as lovers. In the end she tries to poison Saint-Claude, poisons her husband instead and is herself poisoned by him. Purely as a plot nothing could be more satisfactory. What lies behind this erotic blood bath is quite serious, however.

Like Romulus, Mississippi and Saint-Claude have single-mind-edly fought to attain an abstract ideal and like him they have ceased to be human beings and have become fanatical blinkered automatons instead. Mississippi and Saint-Claude (names they adopted when they began their careers) have grown up together in the gutters of some great city. With the money they earned as male prostitutes they opened a brothel. Both young men made money and set out on the path determined for them by the first books they read. In Mississippi's case the book was the Bible, and he goes to Oxford to study law, obsessed with the idea of restoring absolute justice to the world in the form of the Mosaic law. In pursuit of this ideal he has already succeeded in forcing through over 200 death sentences in his capacity as state's attorney at the time the play opens. He is slowly chang-ing the laws to return more and more of the offences listed in the Mosaic law as punishable by death to the status of capital crimes. By the end of the play he has over 350 death sentences in 30 years as state's attorney to his credit. Saint-Claude, on the other hand, read Marx: he has become a professional revolu-tionary, citizen of the Soviet Union, colonel in the Red Army, honorary citizen of Rumania, member of the Polish parliament, and member of the Cominform Politburo. None of these things mean anything to him, however, since he cares no more for Com-munism than for capitalism. His hand, like Mississippi's, like Romulus', like that of all determined ideal-pursuers, is against everyone. Saint-Claude, at least, has the clear-sightedness to recognize what has happened to him and Mississippi, although he is now powerless to change himself: "We are the two last great moralists of our times, and we have both gone under. You behind a hangman's mask and I behind a Russian spy's." [4]

Mississippi and Saint-Claude meet again in the symbolic room in Anastasia's house twenty years after they parted in the brothel. The room is now Mississippi's as well as Anastasia's, for he has been married to her for five years at this point. Five years

4. It is amusing to note parenthetically that Dürrenmatt told me he deliberately gave Saint-Claude the kind of youth that most European Com-munists (many of whom were intellectuals of good family) wished they might have had.

before, Anastasia had poisoned her husband when she discovered that he was having an affair with Mississippi's wife. Similarly, Mississippi had poisoned his wife—executed her in accordance with the Mosaic law, he calls it—when he discovered she was having an affair with Anastasia's husband. Then he forced Anastasia to marry him for purposes of mutual punishment and expiation. Their marriage was to be a hell for both so that their sins might be refined and purified. This Mississippi fondly believes to have happened: he himself has become inspired to the point of having succeeded in ramming through 150 death sentences in five years, and she has become known as the Angel of the Dungeons because of her solicitude for the men her husband has had condemned. Meanwhile Saint-Claude has entered the country illegally for the purpose of starting a revolution. He has decided to use his old friend as a target because the people hate him. Anastasia becomes Saint-Claude's mistress when she sees which way the wind is blowing. And when she sees that the government will not back Mississippi, thus knocking the heart out of Saint-Claude's little revolution, she becomes the chief minister's mistress. In the end Mississippi begins to suspect that she has been unfaithful and poisons her. At the same time he carelessly drinks another poisoned cup of coffee that Anastasia had prepared for Saint-Claude. All of this does Saint-Claude no good, for he is shot by the Communists for failing to put the revolution over. During the whole play the figure of Count Bodo von Überlohe-Zabernsee is present either in spirit or in person. Bodo is a direct contrast to Mississippi and Saint-Claude. A nobleman who has given away all his fortune in order to become a physician and open a clinic for the poor, he is the type of the good and useful idealist—the idealist who is interested in helping the individual and looks upon each individual as a separate human problem.

Mississippi, Saint-Claude, and Romulus deal in generalities: Mississippi feels that everyone must be bent to fit an arbitrary, abstract concept of justice; Saint-Claude feels that hunger and oppression must be eradicated by force; Romulus feels that Rome must die and lets the present citizens suffer for the sins of their ancestors. Bodo, on the other hand, deals in particulars:

he feels that sickness must be stamped out by giving each
sufferer complete medical care. Bodo's good work is ruined by
Mississippi's legal fanaticism. He is driven out of the country
because he has technically broken a law by giving Anastasia,
whom he loves, the poison to kill her husband under the impression that it was for her sick dog. He flees to Borneo, where he
opens a hospital but loses all his money and ruins his health.
The hospital is a dud too, since it cannot compete in effectiveness and popularity with the local witch doctors.

At the end of the play Dürrenmatt points his moral. Anastasia, Saint-Claude, and Mississippi have been killed and now
rise again and speak to the audience:

> ANASTASIA: A whore who meets her death without
> remorse.
> SAINT-CLAUDE: Yet whether we lie here in this ruin
> MISSISSIPPI: Or whether we die backed up against
> a white-washed wall, or on a pile of blazing faggots or bound
> upon a wheel, between Heaven and Earth
> SAINT-CLAUDE: Ever again we return, as always we
> have returned again
> MISSISSIPPI: Always in new disguises, always long-
> ing for ever-receding paradises
> SAINT-CLAUDE: Rejected by you now and again
> MISSISSIPPI: Nourished by your indifference
> SAINT-CLAUDE: Thirsting for your brotherhood
> MISSISSIPPI: We sweep over your cities . . . driv-
> ing the mill which grinds you down.[5]

This is followed by a vision of Bodo dressed as Don Quixote
tilting at a windmill: "the eternal comedy goes on . . . fed by
our helplessness."

In *Ein Engel kommt nach Babylon* (An Angel Comes to
Babylon, 1953) Dürrenmatt puts less emphasis on the two
themes that I have suggested underlie the plays discussed thus
far. The acidulously jocular view of death is still there in the
farcical key figure of the hangman, but the theme of the corrup-

5. Dürrenmatt, *op. cit.*, p. 167.

tive influence of power in the hands of a single-minded person is definitely relegated to a subordinate role. *Ein Engel kommt nach Babylon* is a rather unsuccessful attempt at a symbolic portrayal of human history in terms of individual character types. The play itself is fascinating because more than any other of Dürrenmatt's plays it takes place purely in a stage world. The trouble with it lies in the symbolism, which is suggestive but unclear and often even muddled, somewhat like the symbolism in a Bergman movie. All the chief characters are eternal types. Nebuchadnezzar and Nimrod and their ministers, as well as Akki the beggar, have lived since before the Flood. The other important characters are the angel and Kurrubi, a young girl recently personally produced by God out of the void.

The play is about the angel's mission to bring Kurrubi, who represents the quality of selfless love, to the lowest of men. The lowest of men, according to the angel's road map (a wonderful document that appears to combine the functions of a cosmic atlas, the *Encyclopaedia Britannica*, and the *Farmer's Almanac*), is Akki of Babylon, the last living beggar on earth. Unfortunately, King Nebuchadnezzar chooses this moment to disguise himself as a beggar in order to persuade Akki to give up begging and join the Babylonian civil service. Nebuchadnezzar has just become king again after serving for 900 years as King Nimrod's footstool and has decreed that begging must be abolished. All who disobey are to be hanged, but Akki has nonetheless remained obdurate; and so, in the best Haroun al-Raschid or "benevolent tyrant" tradition, Nebuchadnezzar has disguised himself as a beggar in order to bring Akki round. Akki and Nebuchadnezzar decide to hold a contest to see who is the better beggar, and of course Akki, the old pro, wins going away. This solves the angel's difficulty: obviously the loser in the contest is the lowest of men. Nebuchadnezzar's helplessness has meanwhile won Kurrubi's love. But in his rage at the fact that he has been given this gift of God as the lowest of mortals instead of as the highest, Nebuchadnezzar mistreats Kurrubi and gives her to Akki in exchange for Nimrod, whom Akki has won in the begging contest.

That is the basic situation out of which the rest of the play grows. Kurrubi becomes Akki's begging companion for ten days, and the whole town falls in love with her. The people insist that she marry the king, and she learns that the lowest of mortals and the highest are one—King Nebuchadnezzar is the beggar whom she loves. She refuses to marry Nebuchadnezzar unless he becomes a beggar again, but of course he cannot do this. Nor is anyone else willing to do it, despite the "love" they all profess for Kurrubi. In fact, when they see what Kurrubi's conditions are, the populace's "love" turns to hate and they demand her death. She is handed over to the hangman, but— Happy End!—the hangman is really Akki in disguise and they escape together into the desert.

Dürrenmatt is dealing with two parallel symbolic themes here: the impossibility of selfless love on earth and the ultimate triumph of the type of human being represented by Akki, the independent man. When she first appears, Kurrubi is only fifteen minutes away from having been formed by God—she is innocence and purity personified. Her first introduction to human ways, i.e., to evil, is when she sees the brutality of the soldiers who are in charge of Nimrod. The angel's explanation, "Be calm, my child. A simple accident only, which has no effect on the harmony of things," represents the viewpoint of the celestial powers, the viewpoint *sub specie aeternitatis*. Dürrenmatt's depiction of the angel is not specifically religious. The angel simply stands for the viewpoint of whatever superhuman powers the spectator may believe in; for those who do not believe, he can simply stand for the lack of understanding in a mindless cosmos. The angel's character throughout is that of a bumbling and absent-minded professor. An amusing example of this is the following passage, in which the angel tries to explain why Heaven is not concerned with kings:

> ANGEL: I am an Angel of God.
> NEBUCHADNEZZAR: What is your wish, Exalted One?
> ANGEL: I have come to you from Heaven.
> NEBUCHADNEZZAR: Why have you come? What do you want with a beggar of Nineveh? Go, Messenger of God,

to Nebuchadnezzar the King. He alone is worthy to receive thee.

ANGEL: Kings, O Beggar Anaschamaschtaklaku, do not interest Heaven. The greater a man's lowliness, the greater his acceptability to Heaven.

NEBUCHADNEZZAR: (*amazed*) Why?

ANGEL: (*thinks*) No idea. (*thinks harder*) Actually it *is* rather peculiar. (*apologetically*) I'm not really an anthropologist. I'm more interested in the physical sciences. My specialty is suns. Principally red giant ones. My mission is to go to the lowest of men, but I have no means of knowing Heaven's reasons.[6]

Throughout the play the angel completely fails to grasp what is going on around him. It is all too insignificant, and besides he is busy collecting botanical specimens. His attitude is summed up in a remark he makes to Kurrubi near the beginning of the play. Kurrubi has been created to go among men and already has some of the human susceptibilities. When the angel tells her she is to go to the lowest of men, she answers that the lowest of men must surely be unhappy. The angel's answer is, "Whatever is created is good, and whatever is good is happy. In my extended travels throughout creation I have never seen the smallest atom of unhappiness." The evil that the angel is unable to see is the evil of human institutions, the means by which the power-possessors coerce the helpless majority. The accident of Kurrubi's falling in love with the disguised Nebuchadnezzar brings her directly into contact with the very apex of this pyramid of evil. Nebuchadnezzar and Nimrod, who alternately share the supreme power over their fellow human beings, represent the incessant historical see-sawing of political power from one tyranny to another. However new the tyranny seems, Dürrenmatt is saying, it is really always the same: it is either Nimrod or Nebuchadnezzar. And the end result of this loveless tyranny (it cannot accept Kurrubi) will be the chaos embodied in the product of this system—the grinning idiot hopping back and forth in front of the throne whom both

6. *Ibid.*, p. 197.

Nebuchadnezzar and Nimrod acknowledge as their son and heir. As the opposing force to that of the two interchangeable kings and their political and theological ministers, Dürrenmatt has created the figure of Akki the Beggar. Dürrenmatt appears to be saying that only by disassociating completely from society and its laws—and thus becoming the lowest of the low from a worldly viewpoint—can one preserve independence and, consequently, dignity. Akki is far and away the most dignified character in the play. And he preserves his dignity by refusing to have anything to do with the things that might tend to associate him with those whom he despises: all the money and jewels that he accumulates each day by begging he throws into the Euphrates in the evening. The only thing he keeps is food—"The culinary art, properly cultivated, is the only facet of human endeavor about which nothing bad can be said." Dürrenmatt looks upon Akki and his kind as a sort of dike holding back the impatient floods of ignorance:

> AKKI: We are secret teachers, educators of the people. We go in rags for the sake of man's wretchedness; we obey no laws in order to celebrate freedom. We eat as greedily as wolves, and drink like sots in order to expose the terrible hunger and the burning thirst which is poverty. And the arches of the bridges under which we sleep we fill with the belongings of the vanished rich in order to show that all things come to the beggars in the fullness of time.[7]

Frank V—Oper einer Privatbank (Frank V—Opera of a Private Bank, 1959)—a rather ambitious title, for the work is really a satirical comedy with music (by Paul Burkhard)—was first produced at the Zürich Schauspielhaus in 1959. Frank V is the president of a private bank founded by his great-great-grandfather, Frank I. Even since its founding this bank has operated on two inflexible business principles: "Never make an honest deal" and "Never pay back any money." The play relates how, by sticking faithfully to these two maxims, which in years gone by had made the firm one of the richest and most power-

7. *Ibid.*, p. 196.

ful banking houses in Europe, Frank & Co. goes bankrupt. As
the play opens, the firm is already in such a desperate position
that Frank has to fake his death so that he can stick his life
insurance into the business. The company is bombarded with
one disaster after another. One of the biggest depositors with-
draws his account, but, faithful to its second motto, the company
sends out its most attractive teller to get the money back in a
hotel room. Unfortunately she is thwarted by the vice squad.
In another scene a new recruit is given an orientation lecture by
Frank's wife, who, in the classical tradition of the female of the
species being more deadly than the male, is the real brains behind the business. "You're murderers!" the horrified recruit ex-
claims when the full extent of the bank's operations is revealed
to him. "No, no, not at all, my dear boy," Mrs. Frank says re-
provingly, "Only business people in difficulties." The difficulties
become more and more severe, and at the end *Frank* V fully
measures up to Mrs. Frank's demands for a classic play. When
the maid asks permission to watch *Richard III* Mrs. Frank
grants it with the words, "a classical play. Doubtless there will
be plenty of bodies." If the body count is any criterion, *Frank*
V is at least as classical as *Richard III*. At the end the survivors
sit around the safe, warily pointing submachine guns at each
other. Dürrenmatt solves the mess by having Frank's children
drive the crooks out and take over. Under Frank VI the firm
of Frank & Co. becomes honest for the first time in its long
history. The days of the robber barons are over—but not because the capitalistic private enterprise system has been cleaned
up. Frank V and his tribe are outdated because their free-wheel-
ing business anarchy is no longer exclusively their method of
operation: everyone is doing it. Frank fails because he is behind
the times. He has not learned to substitute the gloss of legality
for the old-time strong-arm methods.

Dürrenmatt has also written several radio plays, of which
only *Das Unternehmen der Wega* (Operation Wega, 1954) is
significant for our discussion. In this play Dürrenmatt drama-
tizes the East-West conflict, which he believes is due mainly to
willful bullheadedness on both sides. Fear and lack of under-

standing lead the "free" nations (in this play) into the most
grotesque imaginable moral perversions. The *Wega* is a space
ship on which the chief ministers of state of the Free United
States of Europe and America travel to Venus in the year 2256
A.D. The use-honored and mischievous old saw that "war with
Russia is inevitable" has at last come true, and the ministers are
now on a mission to persuade the inhabitants of Venus to join
their side. Venus has been used for years both by Russia and
the West as a human garbage dump—it is a penal colony for
habitual criminals and people whose politics happen to be in-
compatible with those of the place in which they lived on Earth.
In the coming war the strategic position of Venus and its in-
visibility behind a permanent cloud bank will make its possession a decisive factor. The mission from the Free and United
States is therefore under instructions to destroy Venus with
cobalt bombs should the inhabitants prove intractable. If they
prove tractable they are to be permitted to return to Earth once
the war is won. However, the mission, under Sir Horace Wood,
finds it rather difficult to negotiate. There is no government on
Venus. The people live on small ships and are too busy fighting
to survive to bother about government. Whoever is free at the
moment designates himself as representative of the planet and
speaks to the mission. Sir Horace finally locates Bonstetten, a
former classmate of his at Oxford and Heidelberg, who was
sent to Venus as commissar and deserted. Bonstetten tells Sir
Horace that the people of Venus refuse to take sides in any war
and that none of them wants to return to Earth. On Venus
the weather consists of constant thunderstorms and constant
hot rain; the ground is everlastingly being shifted by earth-
quakes; the sea is radioactive, and all sorts of strange monsters
roam the planet; but no one wants to leave it. Bonstetten explains. On Venus men are at last free: they are too busy trying
to stay alive to make laws. On Venus men have at last realized
their ideals in practice: it is the only way to survive.

       WOOD: What have you exchanged for the mildness
of the earth? Steaming oceans. Burning continents, glowing

red deserts. A raging sky. What knowledge has it given you?

BONSTETTEN: That Man is worth something and that his life is a boon.

WOOD: Ridiculous. We have known that on earth for a long time.

BONSTETTEN: Well? Do you live in accordance with this knowledge?

WOOD: And you?

BONSTETTEN: Venus forces us to. That is the difference. If we don't help each other here, we perish.[8]

Sir Horace tells Bonstetten that the *Wega* carries bombs, but that he will of course not order their use. He is amazed to hear that the Venusians had anticipated this. "After all, we too lived on Earth once" (Bonstetten explains). Nor does Bonstetten put any trust in Sir Horace's promise not to use the bombs. In a thoroughly cynical speech that is pure Dürrenmatt he tells his former friend just what will happen:

You will break your promise. Your mission is a failure. Now you still have pity for me, but once you get back to your ship your pity will fade and your mistrust will replace it. The Russians could come and make an agreement with us, you will think. You will of course know how impossible that is, that we will treat the Russians as we have treated you, but a little grain of fear that we could after all perhaps make a treaty with your enemies will remain in your mind. And because of this little grain of fear, because of the slight uncertainty in your heart, you will release the bombs. Even if it is senseless, even if they will hit innocent people—and so we will die.

And that is just what does happen. At first Sir Horace is horrified by what Bonstetten says:

WOOD: You are my friend, Bonstetten. I couldn't kill a friend.

8. Friedrich Dürrenmatt, *Das Unternehmen der Wega* in *Hörspielbuch 1955*. With permission of and copyright © 1955 by Peter Schifferli Verlags AG "Die Arche" (Frankfurt a. M.: Europäische Verlagsanstalt, 1955), p. 74.

BONSTETTEN: It is easy to kill when you don't see the victim and you won't see me die.

WOOD: You speak as if it were an easy thing to die!

BONSTETTEN: Everything that is necessary is easy. One only has to accept it. And the most necessary and most natural thing on this planet is death. It is with us always and everywhere. There is too much heat and too much radiation. The sea itself is radioactive. There are worms which burrow under our skin and into our entrails, bacteria which poison our blood, viruses which destroy our cells. The land is full of impassable swamps, seas of boiling oil and volcanoes, and ghastly monsters are everywhere. We do not fear your bombs because we live with death and have had to learn not to fear it.[9]

The play ends as Wood, who was, after all, quite sincere in his promise to Bonstetten, weakly gives the order for the bombing. And then in Sir Horace's last speech, Dürrenmatt adds his characteristic bitterly sardonic twist:

I'm fed up with everything. That Venus is horrible. They're all criminals there, after all. I'm sure Bonstetten wanted to make an alliance with the Russians. They were just putting on an act for us . . . Now the bombs have dropped and soon they'll drop on the earth. Thank goodness, I have a bomb-proof shelter as a public official. And what's more I'll have a vacation—Foreign Ministers always go on vacation during wartime. But I'll have to forget about fishing. I'll read the classics. T. S. Eliot preferably. He's the most soothing of them all. There's nothing unhealthier than exciting reading.[10]

The East-West conflict continues to obsess Dürrenmatt in his latest play, *Die Physiker* (The Physicists, 1961). If Dürrenmatt were as conscientiously didactic a playwright as Shaw, he would have called this play *The Physicist's Dilemma*. Dürrenmatt is mordant and sardonic where Shaw is genial and

9. *Ibid.*, p. 77.
10. *Ibid.*, p. 80.

optimistic, but the ethical problem of *The Doctor's Dilemma* and *Die Physiker* is essentially the same. Shaw examines the problem of the healer who has to step out of his accustomed purely medical realm of knowledge and make a moral decision about his profession. For the healer the problem is simply whom to heal when there is a shortage of medicine. His dilemma is that he cannot give enough. The physicist's dilemma, as Dürrenmatt sees it, is that he can give too much, and his problem is whether he should withhold his knowledge. Given the enormous inroads the physicists have made into areas of knowledge previously thought impenetrable, it is not inconceivable that at some time in the near future a key may be found that will enable men to understand all natural phenomena. Dürrenmatt postulates precisely this eventuality. A young physicist works out a formula for all possible discoveries. Horrified at the thought of what the politicians would do with his formula were he to publish it, he pretends to be mad and has himself shut up in a lunatic asylum. Only thus can he continue the mental exercises which are his life without at the same time endangering the future of humanity. Rather than be hailed as the greatest thinker of all times, he prefers to spend his life imprisoned and to die unknown. He has realized that absolute freedom of thought could be undesirable in a situation where all knowledge is possible and where all thinkers are at the mercy of political planners. He announces that King Solomon appears to him and, in an act of self-abnegation comparable to Romulus's, prepares to spend the rest of his life in a mental institution. When the play begins, Möbius has been in the sanatorium for twenty years. He has recently been joined by two other apparently insane physicists, one under the impression that he is Sir Isaac Newton, the other that he is Albert Einstein. They soon reveal themselves to be perfectly sane secret agents, Sir Isaac for the West, Professor Einstein for the East, bent on persuading Möbius to join their side. They are each famous physicists in their own right and have been able to gauge the tremendous potential broached in Möbius's doctoral dissertation. They have therefore been sent by their respective secret services to take him away. This turns out to be impossible, first of all because

they have suddenly become ringed around by armed guards,
secondly because Möbius has burned his papers and does not
want to leave. The two secret agents realize that they are imprisoned forever, but they also realize, at last, that Möbius is
right: their knowledge is too dangerous to be published. The
Western physicist, who thought that the scientist's duty was to
seek knowledge without caring what use might be made of it,
and the Eastern physicist, who thought that the scientist's duty
was to subject his knowledge to a political party, both realize
the truth of the paradox that for thinkers freedom exists only in
a lunatic asylum: "Only in the mental hospital can we still be
free. Only in the mental hospital can we still think. Out there
our thoughts are dynamite. . . . Either we remain in this lunatic asylum or the world becomes one. Either we extinguish ourselves in the memory of men or mankind itself is extin-
guished." [11] "Einstein" protests for a moment that they are
caged like wild beasts, and Möbius calmly replies that they *are*
wild beasts—"they must never unleash us on mankind again."
Then, heroically, the three physicists resign themselves to their
fate:

> NEWTON: Lunatic, yet wiser than before.
> EINSTEIN: Caged, yet freer than before.
> MÖBIUS: Physicists, yet guiltless.[12]

With the statement of the paradox that mankind can be saved
only through the suppression of knowledge, the lesson of the
play is complete. Dürrenmatt, however, has to insert his sardonic touch. Unconsciously carrying the method of paradox
over into his technique, he turns the play into a meaningless
melodrama with the addition of a superbly dramatic scene.
Their heroic resolve to save humanity by suppressing their
knowledge has made the three physicists technically guilty of
hubris, for, as Möbius says, what has once been thought can
never more be taken back again. They discover that the chief
doctor and owner of the sanatorium, a grotesquely humpbacked

11. Friedrich Dürrenmatt, *Die Physiker* (Zürich: Verlag der Arche,
1962), pp. 61–62.
12. *Ibid.,* p. 63.

old maid, is *really* mad and, acting on instructions from her own private vision of King Solomon, has stolen Möbius's formulas. She tells the three physicists that their sacrifice has been in vain and that they will be imprisoned forever while she takes over the whole universe with Möbius's formula for attaining the key to all knowledge.

Throughout his works Dürrenmatt has a viewpoint that can best be described as sardonic. Dürrenmatt is a disillusioned analyst of the human character. Even the plays with political themes are ultimately about the human beings rather than the issues. Like Ionesco, like Beckett, like all the writers of the dramatic avant-garde in fact, Dürrenmatt feels deep down in himself that the problems of humanity are insoluble. And so he takes refuge from this knowledge in a mordantly sardonic portrayal of life. He himself remains detached. Romulus and Mississippi, Saint-Claude and Nebuchadnezzar, Frank V and Sir Horace Wood are viewed and dissected, laid out on slides and meticulously picked apart with scalpel and tweezers. Perhaps the only character in all of Dürrenmatt's works who is looked at with any kindness and compassion at all is Archilochos, the inoffensive little assistant bookkeeper who becomes head of the factory as a result of marrying the country's leading courtesan in the novel *Grieche sucht Griechin.*

Although Dürrenmatt derives his technique more from Thornton Wilder than from Antonin Artaud and the surrealists, he does resemble the authors of the current dramatic avant-garde in that his plays are dominated by the two qualities of protest and paradox. Dürrenmatt's two main themes are based on (i) the paradox that the power to do good corrupts the doer so that the goodness is negated and the power becomes purely evil; and (ii) the paradox that the omnipresence of death renders human acts trivial. What distinguishes Dürrenmatt from Beckett, who also feels that the events of life are basically meaningless, is that Beckett feels this to the point where he asserts that all events are flattened out and equally insignificant, whereas Dürrenmatt does recognize that events may have an immediate significance to those affected. It is here that the element of protest comes in: Dürrenmatt always implies that events must be resisted. Nothing is inevitable and determined in Dürrenmatt. The fact that things are insignificant from a cosmic viewpoint does not alter the fact that they are significant in the immediate present: it merely argues that they are finally insoluble and will always repeat themselves. The monomania of Mississippi and Saint-Claude, of Romulus and Nebuchadnezzar, and of the political leaders who lurk behind the action of several of the radio plays *must be resisted*. Dürrenmatt's protest, unlike that of the other current avant-garde writers, is not against the cosmos: it is against the world as it is and against the people who rule it.

MAX FRISCH
The Drama of Despair

MAX FRISCH was born in Zürich in 1911. Trained as an architect, he abandoned that profession for a writing career only after a long and painful struggle during which he actually forced himself to stop writing for a number of years. During the war, however, he was called to active service on the Swiss-German frontier when it was thought the Germans would invade. The Germans very wisely thought better of it, but the Swiss Army remained on guard anyway, and Frisch whiled away the long hours by keeping a diary, later published as *Blätter von dem Brotsack* (Leaves from the Knapsack). With that, Frisch's writing career was begun again and after his first successes (his plays are as popular in the German-speaking theater as Dürrenmatt's) he abandoned the practice of architecture altogether.

Frisch's plays, unlike those of Dürrenmatt, are not expressive of a particular Weltanschauung. This may result in somewhat naïve plays, such as *Santa Cruz* and *Als der Krieg zu Ende War* (When the War Was Over), but when Frisch is at his best, as he is in *Die Chinesische Mauer* (The Chinese Wall) [1] and

1. Max Frisch, *The Chinese Wall*, translated by James L. Rosenberg (New York: Hill & Wang, Inc., 1961).

Biedermann und die Brandstifter (Mr. Biedermann and the Arsonists),[2] there is no better dramatic author alive today.

The unevenness of Frisch's work can be attributed to the lack of any one guiding theme and to his own involvement in it. In this respect he differs from Dürrenmatt, who carefully detaches himself from the world he describes. Dürrenmatt's attitude is sardonic as he stands aside and shows us a world he considers absurd. He is like the manipulator of a puppet show who occasionally draws apart the curtain above the stage to reveal himself quizzically smiling and jiggling the strings playfully with his fingers. At such moments (e.g., the opening and closing scenes of *Die Ehe des Herrn Mississippi*, the forest scenes in *The Visit*, the little monk's scenes in *Es steht geschrieben*) Dürrenmatt mocks his characters, the audience, and —necessarily—himself as well. The interest of Dürrenmatt's plays arises out of the *strength* of the dramatic conflicts in the various situations he creates—but the sardonic viewpoint is always primary and always the same. Frisch, on the other hand, writes plays about whatever happens to interest him at the moment, and as he is always passionately involved in the situations and characters he creates, the quality of his plays tends to fluctuate sharply. With Dürrenmatt we are always on the outside looking in: his theater is a peep show in which humanity is caricatured in order to prove a point. With Frisch we are on the inside, we are involved, we identify. Dürrenmatt leaves us with an acidulous, bitter, astringent taste; Frisch at his best rouses in us at least the terror part of the Aristotelian formula.

Although lacking a common, basic theme, Frisch's plays do have an idea that shows up in all of them: that men learn nothing from experience.

Frisch's plays can be divided into two categories: plays of the mass and plays of the individual. In other words, political polemics and analyses of individual but typical psychological attitudes. The only one of Frisch's plays that does not fall into either category is *Als der Krieg zu Ende War* (1949), in which a Russian colonel and the wife of a Nazi officer conduct a sema-

2. Max Frisch, *The Firebugs*, translated by Mordecai Gorelik (New York: Hill & Wang, Inc., 1963).

phor love affair (he cannot speak German, she cannot speak Russian) in the rubble of occupied Berlin. This is the only one of Frisch's plays that is a complete failure. He has written seven other plays, divided between the two categories.

PLAYS OF THE INDIVIDUAL

The psychological problem that fascinates Frisch is the inability of man to stand by himself, wholly independent of all other human beings. Man always strives to *be himself*. But, like Peer Gynt, he can do this only in his dreams. Man in search of himself is constantly either dreaming of running away to some idyllic paradise where he can live his own life away from all encumbrances and responsibilities, or he actually is running away. In either case he is invariably disillusioned, whether by awakening from the futile dream or by coming to the harsh reality of the wished-for paradise. "No man is an island . . .," Donne tells us, but most men spray their energies away trying to be one. Not surprisingly, Frisch connects this drive to be free with the everlasting battle of the sexes: the freedom for which men strive is equated with freedom from the bonds of marriage. In marriage the longing to be free, to do what one pleases, the longing for distant, delusive paradises, the longing, in short, to realize oneself, has to be curtailed. Money has to be earned through stultifying work, responsibilities have to be worried about, and children add fetters to tighten the mesh. Frisch caps his treatment of this theme with another play about that universal farcical-tragic hero, that Peer Gynt of the bedroom, Don Juan.

Santa Cruz (written 1944, published 1947), Frisch's first play, sets the freedom-and-marriage conflict in a fairy-tale milieu. A cavalry captain and his wife have lived together in his castle for seventeen years. During that time the regular, day-to-day, repetitive routine of married life has petrified their emotions so that they go through their days like mediocre actors condemned to play the same scenes for eternity to an ever-empty house. Seventeen years ago, just before their marriage, the couple were visited by a certain Pelegrin, who, although concrete

enough (he is the real father of the wife's child), is a symbol
for the longing to be free. Pelegrin had persuaded both the
young man and the woman to come away with him to Hawaii,
which here represents the elusive paradise where one can be free,
independent, and true only to oneself. On the way to Hawaii,
however,—at Santa Cruz—the two get married. The instinct to
marry and multiply, to be safe, secure, and certain of the future
triumphs. And now, after seventeen years, Pelegrin returns. His
presence activates the old longings that have been lying dormant
in the husband and wife during their whole marriage. The husband succumbs, leaves a farewell note, and goes off to make
his own way at last. But in the wife the instinct for domesticity
is stronger. She vanquishes Pelegrin in argument, whereupon
Pelegrin dies and the husband returns. The symbolic circle is
completed when we are made to realize that the spirit expressed
by Pelegrin lives on in the daughter, who must go through the
conflict between hearth and horizon in her turn.

  Graf Öderland (Count Öderland, 1951) is technically and
philosophically an advance from *Santa Cruz*. Here the problem
is not so much freedom from the bonds of marital domesticity,
but freedom from the monotonous routine imposed upon our
lives by social position and profession. Technically the play is a
precariously balanced tour de force, the whole action being an
exposition of a megalomaniac dream that flits in a few seconds
through a frustrated man's mind. The action takes place late at
night in the study of a public prosecutor who is preparing a
case against an obscure bank clerk. After fourteen years of
unimpeachable probity and invariable punctuality, this clerk
has suddenly grabbed a hatchet one evening and chopped up
the first person he could find. To his consternation, the prosecutor realizes that the bank clerk has killed out of boredom and
that he himself understands this state of mind very well. He
understands that the man has reverted to an instinctual form of
action in his attempt to break through the fetters imposed upon
him by social convention, just as the Malayan natives do when
they run amok. The prosecutor, too, has been becoming in-
creasingly desperate under the pressures of his social and personal life (his wife is the defense attorney's mistress, but that

can be forgiven Frisch as a permissible dramatic convenience).
The more he thinks about the bank clerk's problem, the more
absurd does his position of prosecutor seem to him; and as he
broods about the crime, a similar explosion is triggered off in
him. Since he is a more intellectual and a less elemental type
than the bank clerk, however, the explosion is purely cerebral,
though all the more violent in intensity.

In his dream the prosecutor runs away to a forest where
he meets a young girl. He crosses the border with her, killing
three frontier guards with a hatchet on the way. The hatchet
becomes a sort of reassuring amulet for him, and he always
carries it with him in a briefcase so that he can touch it and
feel free whenever he wants to. His goal is the Isle of Santorin
in the Aegean Sea, a place where one is completely free to be
oneself. Santorin fulfills the same function in this play that
Hawaii does in *Santa Cruz*; but just as the husband and wife in
Santa Cruz never get to Hawaii, so the prosecutor, who has by
now adopted the title of Count Öderland, never gets to Santorin. Instead he somehow gets sidetracked (like Pierre of
Sartre's *Les Jeux sont faits*) and we next see him as the leader
of a nihilistic underground movement operating in the sewers
of the city in which the Count was formerly public prosecutor.
The emblem of this movement is the hatchet, the symbol of
freedom and independence and self-realization, but the movement has become a strictly militaristic organization composed
of social outcasts (escaped convicts, misfits and malcontents,
etc.) trying to overthrow the established order. In other words,
there is no escape. The invisible walls that hem us in are not
solely composed of social pressure: they are inherent in the
psyche of the human animal. Madness is the only way out.
Count Öderland finds himself the head of a complete miniature
society even more rigid than the one from which he fled. Monotony led him to seek freedom, but the search for freedom only
leads to another form of organization based on authority and
submission and thus back to monotony. Frisch brings his round
dance of irony and paradox full circle when he has Count
Öderland overthrow the government and then installs him in
the house he once occupied as public prosecutor. He has

achieved his wildest dreams. He is the head of the state and
has supreme power. He can order anyone to do anything: he is
free—theoretically. But he is actually as enmeshed as ever. The
triumphant dream turns into a frenzied horror of frustration—
as it must. The Count finds his wife and her lover in the house.
He shoots them, but the pistol shots have no effect. In a final
gesture of defeat and ultimate frustration, he throws himself
out of the window. The dream has ended.

Throughout his dream Count Öderland is accompanied by
a young girl who changes identity several times, but always
remains exactly like the prosecutor's maid. Similarly, the various
enemies that the Count meets all have the face of Dr. Hahn,
his wife's lover. These various roles are all played by the same
person. Over and over, no matter how far he seems to get away
from his old self, he encounters the same people:

> How do we know each other? Every now and again it seems
> to me—how shall I put it?—that there are only three or four
> faces one meets in one's lifetime in the final analysis. Even
> if one goes from one end of the earth to the other there is
> always a girl . . . and there is always a policeman who has
> to know one's name and where one wants to go, and every-
> where there are fences to prevent one's going where one
> wants to go . . .[3]

At the end he realizes that everything is useless:

> Life is an illusion—I'm slowly beginning to realize that.
> Repetition, that's all it is. Repetition—that's the curse, that's
> the barrier, and no hatchet is any use against it even if one
> succeeds in bursting through the walls. Repetition! till one
> wakes up at the point of death and it's as if nothing had
> been at all, absolutely nothing, nothing but desires which
> flared up and glowed and were snuffed out. Desire for joy
> and for happiness. And error, anxiety, darkness; . . .[4]

3. Max Frisch, *Graf Öderland* (Frankfurt a. M.: Suhrkamp Verlag,
1951), pp. 35–36.
4. *Ibid.*, p. 125.

It is useless to protest, useless to run amok, useless to do any-thing except to think as little as possible and get along as best one can.

With *Graf Öderland* Frisch produced a play which crystal-lizes the two most important themes of the contemporary drama, isolation and protest. One of the chief themes of the older drama was the achievement of perfect communion through romantic love. The contemporary drama deals mainly with the impossibility of communion, with the eternal mutual isolation of human beings. Frisch forces us to consider the problem of resigning ourselves to bear a world where we realize no communion is possible—ever. Unlike the playwrights who stick strictly to Antonin Artaud's dictum of protest in drama, Frisch does not confine himself merely to protest per se. He shows us that protest, too, is useless. The condition of freedom turns out to be just as stifling as the condition of social bondage. Artaud's protest is more in the nature of a communal release mechanism: actors and audiences are emotionally purged by their cry of defiance so that they can go back to build up their tensions once more. Frisch carries the process a step further to true tragedy, for he shows us that the protest is futile.

In his last play dealing with the individual, Frisch takes up that perennial dramatic hero Don Juan. Again Frisch's theme is the urge to be free. He uses the Don Juan theme be-cause Don Juan is the perfect embodiment of a man striving to be independent and resisting domesticity. Don Juan (up to now) has never had to run amok to release his tensions because he has always been free. As the seducer par excellence he has always been a social outsider since the cardinal sin against society is flagrant violation of sexual mores. Don Juan has re-mained totally himself by seducing 1003 women instead of only one.

Frisch's theory, already expressed in *Santa Cruz* and *Graf Öderland*, is that man cannot be free. He is always either bound to domestic responsibility, like the husband in *Santa Cruz*, or he finds that freedom is no better than bondage, like Count Öderland. Don Juan, according to Frisch, is the personification

of the youthful conceit that a man can realize himself completely alone. Frisch wants to show that such an attitude is at
variance with reality. Don Juan never grows up. He retains the
immature delusions of youth.

In Frisch's play Don Juan is not so much a ladies' man as
a mathematician (the full title of the play is *Don Juan, or The
Love of Geometry*, 1953). His seductions are purely accidental.
He hopes to become free by immersing himself in the pure
knowledge of mathematics. When we first see him, Don Juan
is about to get married. He says "No" when he should say "Yes"
at the altar and flees. On the way he seduces his best friend's
fiancée and his intended mother-in-law, kills his intended father-
in-law (the future stone statue) and callously helps his own
father to a fatal heart attack. His own fiancée, whom he had
seduced in the park on the night before the wedding without
knowing who she was, drowns herself; and Don Juan's reputation is made. His whole purpose in all this has been to get rid
of everything that might stop his complete absorption in the
study of geometry. But Don Juan is never to achieve the freedom he believes resides in the exclusive exercise of pure reason.
Women succumb to his reputation as a seducer. It is not that
Don Juan is particularly attractive to women or that he makes
any special effort to captivate them; it is simply that his initial
escapade (committed in order to rid himself of women once
and for all) has had the effect of making it de rigueur for every
woman to succumb to him. To meet Don Juan and not to go
to bed with him would have been a disgrace too deep for any
woman's reputation to bear. And thus Don Juan, who is so in-
different to sex as to play chess when he is dragged along to a
whorehouse, becomes history's foremost sexual hero.

Frisch's punishment for Don Juan's *hubris* is pure ironic
farce. Since a Don Juan play without the Stone Guest is un-
thinkable, Frisch includes it; but since he is also writing for a
hypermodern audience, he treats it as a deliberate hoax of Don
Juan's. Twelve years and 1003 women after the beginning of
his career Don Juan is bankrupt and fed up. He gets the idea
of inviting several women and the Bishop of Cordoba to a last
dinner, dressing up the madam of the local whorehouse as the

Commandant's ghost, and then jumping through a trap door to "hell." To the bishop he proposes that in return for thus giving the Church a legend, he be permitted to spend the rest of his life studying geometry in a monastery. The latter part of the plan backfires when the "bishop" turns out to be one of the many husbands Don Juan has cuckolded. Despite the false bishop's denunciations, however, everyone else is taken in by the transparent hoax, and the Don Juan legend is completed. Don Juan still has no money, and he cannot get any more since he officially no longer exists. He winds up as the husband of a former prostitute who is now the widow of a nobleman, and the play ends as she informs the Don that he is about to become a father. It is the final indignity. The man who wished to stand alone is given poetic justice for his presumption in challenging the gods, as he does at the end of the first part of the play when the drowned body of his fiancée is laid at his feet: "Do not expect me to cross myself and do not hope to see me weep. Bury the poor thing. And stay out of my way. I no longer have any fear. We'll see now which of us, Heaven or I, makes a fool of the other!" [5] It is Don Juan who turns out the fool, for—and this is man's tragedy, Don Juan's and Count Öderland's, the cavalry captain's and everyone's—no man can stand alone. Protest is futile. We see the light but our psychology binds us: that is Frisch's paradox in his plays of the individual.

PLAYS OF THE MASS

If the paradox of the plays of the individual leads us to resignation, the paradox of the plays of the mass forces us to despair. It is the paradox (by no means put forward for the first time here) that man does not learn by experience. No matter what happens to him, man is still the same blind fool at the end as at the beginning. The presence of this idea makes Frisch's dramas despairing pleas, somewhat like the sermons of a dressed and basted missionary to the cannibals. The four plays in this group are Nun singen sie wieder (And Now They Sing

5. Max Frisch, Don Juan oder Die Liebe zur Geometrie (Frankfurt a. M.: Suhrkamp Verlag, 1957), p. 79.

Once More), *Die Chinesische Mauer, Biedermann und die Brandstifter,* and *Andorra.*

Nun singen sie wieder (published 1946) is Frisch's play about the war. It deals with a group of hostages shot by the Germans. The spirits of these hostages meet in a sort of limbo where they exist in communal brotherhood and sing. The only really interesting aspect of the play is Frisch's analysis of the two German officers in charge of the shooting. The two are old schoolmates and one of them is the son of their teacher. The latter cannot stand the consciousness of his guilt, deserts, goes back home, and hangs himself. His father, on seeing this, makes some treasonable remark and is sentenced to be shot. The other officer, his son's former colleague and the best student he ever had, is put in charge of the old schoolmaster's execution.

Frisch deals with what was perhaps the most horrifying aspect of the Nazi regime in this play: the schizophrenia of the German intellectual. How was it possible for persons like Herbert, the former star pupil, persons who were familiar with the culture of their own and other countries, to become moral monstrosities? Herbert gives his old schoolmaster an answer just before he orders him shot. It is an inadequate answer, as all such answers must be, and certainly not a true one, but Frisch is not trying to give an answer here but to fix a portion of the guilt. That portion falls—and quite rightly—on the harmless and well-meaning old schoolmaster whom Herbert accuses of prevaricating when his students asked him for the truth. When his students saw that the schoolmaster was too cowardly to stand up for the truth, they lost faith in it and decided to dedicate themselves to destroying it as a false god—to destroy it in the name of a better and purer god whom they could respect. Thus the worship of Race and Nation replaced the worship of Truth and Ethics.

Neither the warped and self-indulgent philosophy of the officer nor the cowardly one of the schoolmaster will survive, Frisch implies. What will survive is the spirit represented in the tranquilly singing dead, the direct and indirect victims, respectively, of the two doomed philosophies.

Die Chinesische Mauer (1946; revised 1955) is one of the

most brilliant plays of the modern theater. Frisch was stimulated to write it by the explosion of the atomic bomb over
Hiroshima and Nagasaki. Frisch makes no use of the usual grotesque sensationalism. What he is horrified by is the fact that
with atomic power one man can destroy the human race for a
personal whim. He disposes of the argument that the release of
atomic power is a blessing since no one is going to start a war
knowing that it will inevitably destroy his own side as well as
the enemy. Man is controlled by impulse and does not pause to
ponder the results of actions triggered by his rancid gastric
juices or the water on his brain or his irritation at his parlor-
maid's frigidity. Above all, man does not learn by experience,
he does not improve—and we have many figures in our history
who were restrained in the extravagance of their megalomania
only by the limitations of the instruments and methods at their
disposal. *Die Chinesische Mauer* is a brilliant play, but also a
cosmically despairing one.

In order to give the play a universal quality, Frisch has
chosen to create a *Welttheater* encompassing all areas of the
world and all ages of humanity. The scene is medieval China
just before the building of the Great Wall. The Emperor of
China, Hwang Ti, serves as Frisch's universal symbol of political tyranny. He is the ever-successful conqueror who is never
quite sure of the loyalty of his people. He has just subjugated
the last of the "barbarians" (i.e., enemies, in the semantics of
tyranny) and now proposes to keep his people busy by building
a great wall which will make his empire safe forever. Only one
thing worries him: there is a certain Min Ko among his subjects
who makes up defamatory jingles about him. These jingles are
sung along the banks of the Yangtze-Kiang and in the yellow
mud and slimy manure of the Hangkow rice paddies no matter
how industriously the Imperial Secret Service lays about it with
thumbscrew, bastinado, and Mongolian bamboo wheel. The
action of the play takes place at a party Hwang Ti gives to celebrate his victory. Among the guests—besides the expected Oriental contingent—we find such figures of history and human imagination as Romeo and Juliet, Philip of Spain, Pontius Pilate,
Napoleon, Brutus, Don Juan, Cleopatra, Christopher Colum-

bus, and L'Inconnue de la Seine. Binding all these together is the narrator, an anonymous Man of Today. Dressed in an ordinary business suit, he is the focal point for the audience, bringing the colorful and diverse crowd within the range of their own experiences.

There are two parts to the plot. One is the Man of Today's relationship—*our* relationship—to the historic figures; the other is the Emperor's search for Min Ko the dissenter and its effect on the Man of Today. The historic figures are divided into two groups. There are the actual historic figures—Brutus, Columbus, Philip of Spain, Cleopatra, Napoleon, Pontius Pilate—who represent the mistakes from which Man will not learn, for they keep coming again and again; and then there are those figures which are the products of the human mind—Romeo and Juliet, Don Juan, etc. These, as well as L'Inconnue de la Seine, who represents the great anonymous mass of past humanity, are in danger of being destroyed by the Philips and Napoleons and Hwang Tis and their present-day counterparts, whom we know well enough. The Man of Today circulates among them, vainly sounding his warning:

> I am worried, yes. We can no longer stand the adventure of absolute monarchy, Excellency, nowhere ever again on this earth; the risk is too great. Whoever sits on a throne today holds the human race in his hand, their whole history, starting with Moses or Buddha, including the Acropolis, the Temple of Maia, Gothic cathedrals, including all of Western philosophy, Spanish and French painting, German music, Shakespeare and his youthful pair: Romeo and Juliet. And included in it all, our children and our children's children. A slight whim on the part of the man on the throne, a nervous breakdown, a touch of neurosis, a flame struck by his madness, a moment of impatience on account of indigestion—and the jig is up! Everything! A cloud of yellow or brown ashes boiling up toward the heavens in the shape of a mushroom, a dirty cauliflower—and the rest is silence—radioactive silence.[6]

6. Max Frisch, *The Chinese Wall*, translated by James L. Rosenberg. Copyright © by James L. Rosenberg (New York: Hill & Wang, Inc., 1961), p. 28.

None of the characters listens to him. All they want to do is come back and do the same things all over again. Napoleon wants to go on conquering, Philip of Spain wants to continue the Inquisition, Brutus wants to go on fighting for ideals, Columbus still wants to discover new lands, and Cleopatra still wants to "inspire great men." The figures these characters represent are still with us, and they have learned nothing. The same abominations are blandly committed again and again. Frisch's Man of Today makes one last frantic appeal:

> . . . All of you, my lords, all of you, you must not return. It is too dangerous. Your victories, your kingdoms, your thrones by divine right, your crusades hither and thither, they just don't make sense any more. We want to live. Your way of making history—we can't put up with it any longer. It would be the end, a chain reaction of madness—[7]

The appeal is choked in the omnipresent trivialities of social behavior, the demands of which muffle so much that is vitally important, as waiters come on and drown out the appeal with cocktails.

The second part of the plot deals with resistance to political tyranny, represented in Hwang Ti. The Emperor takes as his jester the Man of Today, whom Frisch uses as a representative of the intellectual class, and orders him to defend a dumb peasant who is accused of being the subversive Voice of the People. The Man of Today knows perfectly well that the peasant boy cannot possibly be Min Ko, the Voice of the People, because he cannot speak at all. But the Man of Today suffers from the universal disease of intellectuals: he is powerless against brute force. He suppresses his instincts and even works actively for what he knows to be wrong (except in those very rare cases where the intellectual is also a man of exceptional physical courage). In those cases he is crushed for his principles —and what good does that do? Frisch's typical intellectual is too rational and too cynical about himself to make even the semblance of a protest: "How could I doubt, Your Majesty:

7. *Ibid.*, p. 37.

have I not seen your naked dagger? . . . I want to live." And so he stands aside, making no protest as the mute peasant boy is handed over to the Imperial torturer. Mee Lan, the daughter of Hwang Ti, who represents love and idealism in Frisch's symbolic system, has fallen in love with the intellectual, but she shies away in horror at his passiveness, for like all idealists she is irrational and not cynical. The intellectual explains his moral impasse to her:

> MEE LAN: You knew he was mute.
> THE MAN OF TODAY: Yes.
> MEE LAN: And you are going to permit this mute boy to be tortured—you, who know everything?
> THE MAN OF TODAY: Permit?
> MEE LAN: You shrug your shoulders. And that's all! Shrug the shoulders, light another cigarette—while they torture a mute to force him to scream; and you, who can speak, stand there and keep silent—and that's all!
> THE MAN OF TODAY: What can I do?
> MEE LAN: You with your learning! Time and space are one; how comforting! Destruction of the world by heat, how exciting! And the speed of light is unsurpassable; how interesting! Energy equals mass times the speed of light.
> . . . .
> THE MAN OF TODAY: What can I do? He will be tortured. I know. As thousands before him have been. First the thumbscrew, then the nailed whip, then the business with the block and pulleys (which tear the tendons so that he will never again be able to lift his arms), then the white-hot wire, then the bone-breakers, repeated as often as necessary —all that, I know, has been going on right up to today. And whether we cry or laugh, whether we dance, sleep, read— there is probably not a single hour that goes by today in which some man somewhere is not being tortured, flayed, martyred, disgraced, murdered. But has any intellectual ever been able to forestall destiny simply because he foresaw it? We can write books and make speeches, even angry speeches: "Why this can no longer go on!" And yet it goes

on. Precisely so. Great and learned persons arise and call to
mankind: "The cobalt bomb, which you are now producing, will be the end of you!"—and people go on making the
cobalt bomb.[8]

The explanation is, of course, true; and Frisch's irony reaches
a crescendo of derisive barking. The play ends as the intellectual and the idealist, the powerless and the despised, look at
each other helplessly, as surely bound fast by their natures in
this world as if they were locked in iron fetters.

Frisch tells us right at the beginning that this is a play without a solution. No one learns anything, and everything goes on
as before. Only this time there is a possibility that the repetition of the same old imbecilities will result in the self-extinction
of the human race. The play is therefore in the strictest sense
a *farce*; and Frisch has thus described it. It is a warning, a warning that has to be made even though it is foredoomed to be
ignored. Great Walls can no longer be thrown up to hold off
the inevitable. The play takes place now, "in an era when the
building of Chinese Walls has become . . . a farce." [9] Man's
mind has become lopsided: its scientific development has completely outstripped its humanistic development. It no longer
has the power to give a moral synthesis to its newly uncovered
facets. Consequently it has lapsed into a narcotic complacency,
fatalistically accepting everything that happens or lazily jug-
gling things around a bit until they seem less menacing. It is
this modern mental habit born, probably, of a multishock-
induced numbness that Frisch is crying out against when he has
Hwang Ti step out of his part and address the audience in the
most important speech of the play:

> HWANG TI: I know well enough what you're think-
> ing, you out there. But I laugh at your hopes. You're thinking,
> this very evening you will see me hurled from this throne,
> for the play must have an ending and a moral, and when I
> am dethroned then you can complacently return home and
> drink your beer and nibble on a cracker. That's what you

8. *Ibid.*, pp. 96–97.
9. *Ibid.*, p. 23.

G

would like. You with your dramaturgy! I laugh. Go out and buy your evening newspaper, you out there, and on the first page you will find my name. For I do not intend to be dethroned. I don't believe in dramaturgy. I just sit on my throne with my hydrogen bomb ready to hand and smile as I watch you peacefully going home . . .[10]

Frisch's best play is *Biedermann und die Brandstifter* (Mr. Biedermann and the Arsonists, 1958). This is a carefully worked out political allegory about the rise of totalitarian governments. Frisch's thesis is that the final coup d'etat by which totalitarian governments come to power is purely incidental: by the time that final act happens, the disaster is ineluctable. The coup is the culminating point of a long series of small incidents, each of which seems unimportant, yet any one of which could have been prevented. Had it been prevented, the whole structure would have toppled. Frisch's play is a warning—again. But, like *Die Chinesische Mauer*, it is a despairing warning: Frisch knows that what has happened many times before will inevitably happen again. Human nature, he believes, is static: Man is no more developed now than when he was scratching his pithecanthropic armpits. His only advances have been in technical knowledge, which his nature has led him to use for deleterious purposes. It is the belief that men cannot learn (at the end Biedermann, in hell, wonders whether he is damned) that differentiates Frisch's play from Bertholt Brecht's *Der Aufhaltsame Aufstieg des Arturo Ui*. Brecht's play is a point-to-point allegory of the rise of Hitler told in terms of a Chicago gangster. His thesis is that at any one of a number of points Arturo Ui could and should have been stopped. Frisch's play is a point-to-point allegory of the rise to power of any totalitarian system, but his thesis is that although the gangsters could and should have been stopped at any one of a number of points, the nature of Biedermann (*homo ordinarius-Jedermann*) incapacitates him. Biedermann is cowardly and guilt-ridden and

10. *Ibid.*, p. 65. The last sentence of this quotation does not appear in the Rosenberg version. It is my own translation from the German edition (Max Frisch, *Die Chinesische Mauer* [Frankfurt a. M.: Suhrkamp Verlag, 1955], p. 75).

incapable of learning that the exposure of his own failings would be a lesser evil than the wholesale disaster his reticence helps to promote.

Structurally the most interesting aspect of the play is Frisch's use of a chorus of fire fighters who hang about the peripheries of the scenery and occasionally come forward to sound Cassandra-like warnings in verse. They represent the unused power that can destroy the arsonists. Their constant refrain is that they are always ready to come but cannot do so until they are called. The tiers of watchful firemen all round the action provide a timeless setting for the contemporary story of the Biedermanns and their foolishness.

On its primary level the story is simple. Biedermann is a typical businessman, owner of a very successful hair-lotion manufacturing concern. Like all very successful businessmen (Biedermann is a millionaire), he has accumulated his money by ruthless methods, keeping just this side of the border of legality, though not of morality. His hair lotion is a fake—his customers might just as well bathe their bald heads in their own urine, he tells his wife. In addition he has just fired his oldest and most faithful employee, the inventor of the process by which the hair lotion is made. The employee kills himself. These two facts leave our businessman without a moral leg to stand on when he tries to face down the frankly immoral arsonists. "Every citizen above a certain income," says one of the arsonists, "is, strictly speaking, legally punishable."

Biedermann knows exactly what to expect from the arsonists. Their method of operation is always the same. One of them pretends to be homeless and asks for a night's lodging, and the next day the house is a heap of ashes. Just as Biedermann is meditating on the newspaper reports of the latest fire, an enormous man practically forces his way into his house, and, always behaving with an excessive cordiality that occasionally switches to an Uriah Heep-like obsequiousness, installs himself in the attic. Gradually Biedermann sees the arrangements for his own destruction being completed. First another arsonist is smuggled into the attic. Then barrels of gasoline are dragged up. Biedermann makes a feeble attempt to assert himself and

threatens to call the police; but just then the police do arrive—
with the news of the unjustly discharged employee's suicide.
Ensnared in his own guilt, Biedermann feels himself helpless.
The arsonists are completely established now, and Biedermann
knows it. He decides to make friends with them, to ingratiate
himself with them in the hope that they will relent. Surely they
will not burn his house if they see he is on their side, if they see
what a fine fellow he really is! The arsonists have dropped all
pretense now. They tell Biedermann they are going to burn
his house. Biedermann affects to take this as a joke and invites
them to dinner. At the end of the dinner, fire sirens are heard.
"A good thing it isn't us," Biedermann piously murmurs as the
engines rush by. The arsonists tell him it's only a ruse of theirs,
though: they always have a false alarm sounded in a remote
part of town when they are about to do a job. They plan to fire
several other houses in the vicinity, they tell Biedermann. With
luck and a favorable wind the fire should carry to the tanks of
the municipal gasworks. As they leave, they ask Biedermann
for a box of matches. Completely defeated, he hands them
the instruments of his own destruction.

The allegory and lesson of the main part of the play are
quite plain. Frisch is giving his audience both a historically
correct parable and a warning. The arsonists represent the
insidious forces of totalitarianism, first worming their way into
bourgeois society, then, once they have gained the foothold of
tentative or apprehensive acceptance, asserting themselves, and
finally engulfing and destroying their victims. It is an example
of two classic clichés—of giving an inch and having an ell taken
and of having the hand that fed, bitten. The lesson is don't
give an inch and don't feed. The manner in which the two
arsonists gain a foothold in the Biedermann household is precisely the manner in which the Nazis gained a foothold in
Weimar Germany. It is the usual pattern for internal revolu-
tionaries in the initial stages of their campaign. Their task is
made all the easier by the moral helplessness and cowardice of
the bourgeoisie, which should be a solid, resilient, antagonistic
mass against which the arsonists should be as helpless as fire in
an asbestos-lined vacuum, but which instead is as soft as mildew

and as porous as a termite-infested log. This is no farfetched analogy. Frisch makes his allegorical intention clear with the name he chooses for his representative bourgeois. Biedermann in German has the same connotation as Babbitt in English. Gottlieb Biedermann: Godlove Babbitt. The Babbitts and the Biedermanns are helpless against the forces of arson and destruction because they are themselves guilty. When Willi says to his fellow arsonist that everyone above a certain income is, strictly speaking, punishable, he may be exaggerating a little. What is true, Frisch tells us, is that everyone above a certain income has a guilty conscience and is thus ready to compromise. "If I report them to the police," reasons Biedermann, "I'll make enemies of them. What's the good of that? One match and our house goes up in flames. What's the good of that?" In this state of mind it is no wonder that Biedermann actually *helps* the arsonists to destroy him. Like a condemned man trying to ingratiate himself with the hangman by greasing the rope, he holds the fuse so Willi can measure off the requisite length. Then he goes and salves his conscience by contributing money to the fire department. Of course, after contributing the money he has to go and compromise with his enemies in order, as he thinks, to be able to make more money: "I don't know if Gottlieb is always right," sighs his wife, "He's gone through this before—Of course they're hoodlums, he tells me, but if I antagonize them, then I may as well pour our hair lotion down the drain. And no sooner had he joined the Party—" What happens when he joins the Party we can see for ourselves.

In the epilogue, which was unfortunately omitted from the New York production, but which is as essential to the play as is Shaw's epilogue to *St. Joan*, Frisch shows us Biedermann and his wife after the disaster. They have been burned to a crisp and are in hell, of course—although they can't bring themselves to believe it. "Why shouldn't we be in Heaven?" Biedermann says, "Everyone we know is in Heaven, even my lawyer. For the last time—this must be Heaven. What else? We have to be in Heaven. People like us haven't *done* anything!" [11] They

11. Max Frisch, *Biedermann und die Brandstifter* (Frankfurt a. M.: Suhrkamp Verlag, 1958), p. 134.

are finally informed by a long-tailed monkey who bears a
peculiar resemblance to a friend of the arsonists that they really
are in hell. They are going to escape the fires, however, because
hell is about to go on strike. Satan and Beelzebub are fed up
with getting only puny, insignificant sinners like "Babbitts and
intellectuals, pickpockets, adulterers, ladies' maids who stole
their mistresses' nylons, and draft dodgers." All the really big
sinners have been pardoned: "Whoever goes around in uniform, or wore one when he killed, or promises to wear one
whenever he kills or orders killings, is saved." This is the news
that the Devil (who, by the way, is none other than Willi the
arsonist) has just brought back from heaven. Disguised as a
bishop, Willi has tried to find God in order to arbitrate the
dispute, but he has been unsuccessful. Heaven, he says, is not
what it was the last time he was up there:

> I very much doubt what I saw was really Heaven. They said
> it was, but I doubt it. . . . They wear medals there and all
> the loudspeakers have got clouds of incense coming out of
> them. I saw a whole Milky Way of medals—enough to make
> the Devil feel sick. All my clients were there, all my mass
> murderers with the angels cruising around their bald spots.
> Everyone greets everyone else and rolls around drinking
> hallelujah and whispering of remission of sins. The saints
> are noticeably quiet, since they're made out of wood or
> stone, and the princes of the Church (I circulated among
> the princes of the Church in order to find out where God
> is) are quiet too, even though they're not made of wood or
> stone. . . . I disguised myself, and those in power up there
> were so busy forgiving themselves they didn't recognize me
> —they let me bless them.[12]

Things being as they are, the Devil decides to bank the fires
of hell and go back to earth to try and drum up some more
business. Once again he and Beelzebub change back to the
costumes in which we first saw them at the beginning of the
play, and off they go to earth to burn down once more the

12. *Ibid.*, pp. 156–57.

cities which the Biedermanns have built up again. At the end,
Biedermann and his wife are left alone on the stage. Organ
music swells up, they fall on their knees, and "Do you think
we're saved?" the wife asks. And Biedermann, having, as always, learned nothing, still self-righteously convinced of his
innocence, answers, "—I think so . . ."

Frisch's latest play, *Andorra* (1961), is an examination of
anti-Semitism. Andorra is a tiny republic with no native Jews.[13]
It borders on a violently anti-Semitic, militaristic state that has
systematically wiped out all its Jews and is now threatening
to invade Andorra. Twenty years previously Andorra's schoolmaster had fathered an illegitimate child in the neighboring
country of the Blacks. Too cowardly to admit that the baby
was his (since this would have hurt his social position in
Andorra), the schoolmaster gave out that the child was Jewish and that he had rescued it from a Black pogrom. Andri, as
he is called, has therefore grown up as the schoolmaster's foster
son. The Andorrans, although they have never known any Jews,
know all the anti-Semitic clichés and attribute them to Andri.
They are not overtly prejudiced against him at first—not until
the militantly anti-Jewish Blacks threaten to invade. Their attitude is that they are trying to be friendly to Andri but that he
is forever rebuffing their good intentions with his "Jewish" over-
sensitiveness. The irony of it all, of course, is that Andri is not
a Jew at all. But by the time he discovers this, his hate against
those who have made him suffer because of his supposed Jew-
ishness is so great that he refuses to cease being one.

Frisch's main purpose is an analysis of the anti-Semite's
hypocrisy. Interspersed between the scenes are little speeches
given by the various characters, in which they explain their actions as if on a witness stand years later. They have, of course,
learned nothing. They are totally unrepentant, and their one
purpose is to emphasize that it wasn't *their* fault. Through each
of their speeches runs the refrain, "We didn't know he wasn't

13. Frisch states in a prefatory note to the play that the name "Andorra" has nothing to do with the real country of that name, nor with any
other specific country. (Max Frisch, *Andorra* [Frankfurt a. M.: Suhrkamp
Verlag, 1961], p. [4].)

a Jew," so that they unconsciously assert their guilt as they imply that their actions would have been excusable if Andri really had been a Jew. Lest this may sound strangely specious to English or American ears, let it be said here that Frisch is not inventing or even exaggerating anything for his polemic purposes. A speech such as the following by the Andorran physician can be heard in private conversation today in any German-speaking city:

> I should like to express myself briefly, though much that is being said today needs correction. It's always easy to say afterwards how one should have acted—quite apart from the fact that, as far as I'm concerned, I really don't see why I should have acted otherwise than I did. What, after all, did we do? Absolutely nothing. I was the town physician, and I still am today. I don't remember any more what I was supposed to have said in those days. That's the way I am—I say what I think, in the good old Andorran fashion. . . . I admit that we were all mistaken, which is something which can only be regretted. How often do I have to say it? I'm not in favor of such horrible things—I never was. . . . All I can say is that it wasn't my fault, quite apart from the fact that his bearing (unfortunately it cannot be denied) became more and more (let us be frank) somehow Jewish, although, to be sure, the young man may well have been an Andorran like the rest of us. . . . Let us not forget that those were troubled times. As far as I'm concerned, I never took part in any of those unpleasant acts, nor did I ever encourage anyone else to. . . . To be sure, it was a tragic affair. It's not my fault that it happened. I think I speak for everyone when I say once again that we can only regret the course of events—back then.[14]

Despite Frisch's refusal to link his play with specific events, one cannot help noticing the strong parallel between Germany's Anschluss with Austria and the Blacks' bloodless conquest of Andorra. Many of the speeches put into the Andorran

14. Frisch, *Andorra*, pp. 101–102.

townspeople's mouths read like parodies of Viennese talk. If the leading citizens can speak like this after the event—and they do—then there is ample reason to look upon *Andorra* as Frisch's most complete expression of despair in the potential of human nature.[15]

In the plays here discussed, particularly the last three, Frisch reveals himself as a traditionalist. The trend in the contemporary drama—and this includes also Frisch's countryman and rival, Friedrich Dürrenmatt—is to treat characters impersonally. With the principal "experimental dramatists" (Beckett, Ionesco, Adamov, etc.) this impersonal treatment is motivated by the conviction that in modern society individuality has been castrated. These writers see modern man as a sort of blind, groping creature playing a perpetual game of blindman's buff. Dürrenmatt treats modern man in the same way, but he assumes the Olympian position. He is an aged and very wise lecturer indulgently explaining the foibles of mankind. Frisch is none of these things. He is a human being like everyone else. It is a status that he never forgets and never rejects. He is *involved.* His characters are human beings, and we understand them through recognition, through a sort of intuitive Bergsonian identification. They are not the bloodless specimens split open on the dissecting table that Dürrenmatt and the experimentalists provide for us. Frisch's characters are fully rounded psychological beings. His themes—the psychological impossibility of human self-sufficiency and the inability of men to learn by experience—are presented in a personal manner, sometimes to the extent of becoming personal pleas. Frisch's two best plays, *Die Chinesische Mauer* and *Biedermann und die Brandstifter,* are consciously foredoomed pleas for a better world. The irony implicit in them no longer sounds like the scornful laughter of the gods we hear in Dürrenmatt; it sounds like the self-reproaching wailing of the damned.

15. Frisch's specific instructions in the text that all overt reference to past events (through the design of the uniforms, for example) should be avoided implies that he is writing about a possible future.

FRITZ HOCHWÄLDER
The Drama within the Self

Fritz Hochwälder was born in Vienna in 1911. Like so many other prominent theater people in Germany and Austria, he fled to Switzerland when the Nazis came to power. It was in Switzerland that Hochwälder wrote his first important play. *Das Heilige Experiment* (The Holy Experiment, 1943) was written while Hochwälder was on leave of absence from the labor camp in which he and many other political refugees had been interned by the Swiss. The play was first performed in Biel, Switzerland, in 1943, and was subsequently played at the Burgtheater in Hochwälder's native Vienna, as well as in Germany, France, Holland, Sweden, Finland, Norway, Argentina, Brazil, and Greece. After the phenomenal run of over 400 performances at the Theatre de l'Athénée in Paris, the play opened on Broadway in September, 1953, and closed after seven performances. The American failure was probably caused by two principal factors: Hochwälder's plays are distinctly more suitable for an off-Broadway audience than for a Broadway one, and the version used was an adaptation by Eva Le Gallienne of the French adaptation and was thus twice removed from Hochwälder's original text.[1] At any rate, a Broadway failure is no reason for discounting a serious playwright.

Fritz Hochwälder's dramas deal with conflict within the human mind. All drama is conflict of one sort or another, but the drama of conflict within one human mind is the oldest and purest form of drama. With the introduction of the second actor by Aeschylus it became possible to present the drama of conflict between *two* human minds. In the modern theater (which means roughly since the first World War) we have seen further refinements of this in the drama of conflict between a human mind and an idea and even in the conflict of two or more ideas.

1. The Le Gallienne version was performed under the title, *The Strong Are Lonely*. The authorized American translation is by the present writer under the title, *Faith Is Not Enough*.

Of the trio of writers who have made the most significant contribution to the contemporary German-speaking theater, Fritz Hochwälder is the only one who has concentrated on the most basic form of drama. The other two, Frisch and Dürrenmatt, have branched out for the most part into the drama of personified ideas.

A dramatist ideally raises a conflict in the mind of the protagonist and lets us see him grow to an awareness of it. The purest drama is condensed into that moment in which the character, for the first time, sees himself as he is, when he becomes conscious of the difference between the illusion he has lived and the reality he should have lived. It is the moment of self-realization for the character and for the audience watching him. It is the horror of looking into a kaleidoscope and suddenly seeing the randomly scattered crystals fall into a rigidly ordered array of graduated prisms. This horrifying destruction of illusion and rearrangement of personal values is the basis of Fritz Hochwälder's drama.

Hochwälder's most representative play, *Das Heilige Experiment,* deals with the expulsion of the Jesuits from Paraguay in 1767. The Jesuits had established what amounted in effect to a sovereign state within the Spanish-held territory of Paraguay. This state acknowledged the sovereignty of the king of Spain, but maintained its own army in order to keep out the Spanish colonists, who simply wished to enslave the Indians. The Jesuit state in Paraguay was, in fact, a true communist state, with all sharing equally in the benefits and profits of the community as a whole.

The creation of a Utopian state in the midst of a non-Utopian one inevitably creates an intolerable economic situation. The inhabitants of the Utopian communal state obviously produce goods better and more economically than the inhabitants of the non-Utopian competitive society. The latter become jealous and start intriguing to have the Utopians declared immoral, dishonest, illegal—whatever you please. In Hochwälder's play the Spanish settlers have secretly transmitted slanders about the Jesuit state to the Spanish crown. The king of Spain perceives that these slanders, if accepted at face value, will enable him to confiscate the rich territory of the Jesuits. He therefore accepts them, draws up the edict dissolving the Jesuit state, and *then* sends out a commission to "investigate" the accusations. The commission is to hear both sides, but it already has the king's signed sentence in its possession. In other words, the investigation, like all investigations in which the investigator is one of the interested parties, is to be a deliberate farce. It is at this point—with the arrival of the commission—that Hochwälder's play begins.

The head of the commission, Don Pedro de Miura, is an old friend of Alfonso Fernandez, the Jesuit Father Provincial. He is determined to conduct a completely fair and impartial investigation for the show of the thing and also in order to satisfy himself personally of the truth or falsity of the accusations. He knows, of course, that the sentence is already passed, but he wishes to satisfy himself of its justice. The investigation quickly brings out the obvious fact that the accusations are *untrue*; that, in fact, they are slanders invented by the Spanish colonists who envy the Jesuits their rich harvests and devoted laborers. Nevertheless, though he privately acknowledges to the Father Provincial that the charges are untrue, Don Pedro has to carry out the sentence. He pronounces the Jesuit state dissolved. Father Alfonso's answer is to arrest him: he and his fellow Jesuits have decided to fight to maintain their Kingdom of God on earth. All this time an elderly, dapper little Italian traveler has been watching the proceedings with a genteel air of disinterest. This Signor Querini, as he calls himself, now tells Father Alfonso that he is the emissary of the general of the Jesuit Order. He orders Father Alfonso to release the king's commissioner and obey his demands. The reason that he gives is that the Jesuits of Paraguay have committed a sin in founding a state based literally on the teachings of Christ. The miseries and injustices of this world are no concern of theirs, he asserts, since the task of the Jesuits is to prepare people for the world to come. The Jesuits should side with the cruel, the unjust, and the powerful in the hope of converting them to virtue and charity. What is behind all this, of course, is the same thing that is behind the Spanish colonists' hatred of the Jesuit state: economics. Querini says that hundreds of thousands of Indian souls and lives must be sacrificed because otherwise the hatred of political forces in Europe might injure the order. Despite the obvious cynicism of this attitude, Father Alfonso is forced to obey the rules of the order. He hands his written surrender to Don Pedro and commands the reluctant fathers under his charge to obey. With the exception of Father Oros, the military commander of the Jesuit state, they, like their Father Provincial, are too numbed at this point to do anything but mechanically obey in accordance with the vow of obedience they have taken. Father Oros alone renounces his vow. He is the only one to perceive that a vow of obedience, however fearsome the threats of damnation with which it is enjoined, is invalidated the moment it exacts an immorality. Despite the Father Provincial's orders, fighting breaks out—whose fault this is is not made clear—and he is himself wounded while trying to stop it. In his fury he tears the map of Jesuit Paraguay from the wall and curses his work.

And now comes Hochwälder's psychological turning point. As Father Alfonso lies dying of his wound and as he watches Don Pedro sign the death warrants of Father Oros and a number of Indian hostages, he realizes he was wrong—wrong to obey his vow, wrong not to do what he felt to be right. At the same time he realizes that to meet violence with violence, to defend the right with blood, is also wrong. Nothing is solved:

FATHER ALFONSO: . . . Should we place ourselves on the side of force?—Never! Should we serve the mighty of the world?—Never! Should we surrender everything without resisting?—Never! Should we renounce the Kingdom of God on Earth? Never . . . Oh—I hear the rebellious voice in my breast saying, Never! Never! Never! I listened to it —but my mouth spoke otherwise. I told my voice it was right—but to my men I said . . . "I command you! Listen to me! I am the Provincial! I command—obey me!"—and I myself obeyed! Obeyed—obeyed—the rebellious voice in my heart . . . First I cursed, in anger and in the blindness of my pain, this state—as the wound bit into my flesh, I

> destroyed it with my own hands—I destroyed this work
> . . . and thus I leave this world still ruled everywhere by
> oppression—slavery—and everything was in vain . . .
> whispers . . . the voice . . .[2]

At the time of critical decision life becomes an impasse, Hochwälder is saying. Father Alfonso realizes at the moment of
death that everything he had ever believed in and lived by was
wrong. He has wavered between two courses of action, both
wrong; and there were no other alternatives. Devoutly religious
all his life, he is faced at the moment of death with the knowledge that religion has no solution to the problem of life. Hochwälder's play is the tragedy of moral frustration.

In *Der Flüchtling* (The Fugitive), written in 1945, Hochwälder treats a psychological problem that has always puzzled
and horrified thinking men all over the world. It is the problem
of the apparent schizophrenic nature of the world's monsters.
We all know the stories, which the tabloids gleefully serve up
to us whenever they have the opportunity, about insanely
vicious murderers or child-rapists or animal-torturers who are
found upon investigation to have a happy family, admiring
neighbors, doting parents, and an unctuously approving superior
at the office. Jack the Ripper was very probably a staid and
highly respected member of Lincoln's Inn Fields. This Dr.
Jekyll and Mr. Hyde duality in human nature is the subject of
Hochwälder's play.

Der Flüchtling takes place in what seems to be the south-
west corner of Germany, near the French and Swiss borders.
There are only three characters: the fugitive, the border guard,
and the guard's wife. The fugitive is trying to get across the
border to a neutral country, and the wife feels herself obligated
to help him when he stumbles exhausted into her house. The
border guard is the real protagonist, however. It is his duty to
catch the fugitive and hand him over to the secret police. He
knows quite well they will torture him and kill him, but that,
of course, is none of his business. In the border guard, Hoch-

2. Fritz Hochwälder, *Das Heilige Experiment* (Basel, Switzerland:
Kurt Reiss Theaterverlag, 1946), p. 88.

wälder gives us a picture of the people who formed the back-
bone of the Nazi regime. These are the petty officials who are
able to compartmentalize their lives and live as upright burghers
in one part and as inhuman monsters in the other. We have
always had this type festering among us: the public executioner
used to wipe the honest sweat off his brow, roll down his sleeves,
and go home to play with his children after a hard day with
the thumbscrews and the rack. Such people do not lack moral
sense; they merely have the faculty of transferring their guilt.
They are not responsible, *they* have not given the order. Hochwälder's border guard is a perfect example of this type. At
home he is a model husband, deeply and sincerely in love with
his wife; on duty he is an automaton, ready to do anything that
he is ordered to do. His moral sense is not dead: he realizes
what he is doing, but he rationalizes everything by convincing
himself that he is doing it for his wife's sake. To preserve his
wife's peace of mind he would do anything—and besides, he
does it because he is ordered to do it, and therefore he is not
morally responsible. The old argument.

When the guard learns that his wife is hiding the fugitive,
he is horrified. Their whole happiness is jeopardized. What
should he do? Pretend to help the fugitive to escape and then
shoot him in the back as soon as he is outside the house—
obviously! Death will be instantaneous, the fugitive need never
know anything, and the happy home life will be preserved: the
perfect plan. There is just one hitch: the wife, who has been
sheltered from reality up to now, refuses to yield to expediency
when she is at last faced with a real moral problem of her own.
Leaving her husband contemptuously, she barricades herself
in the bedroom with the fugitive. Later she falls asleep and the
fugitive comes down and offers to try and cross the border alone
before she wakes up. The guard, appreciating the decency of
the proposal, offers the fugitive his hand. It is scornfully rejected:

> GUARD: What have I done that you won't . . .
> FUGITIVE: You've got a clear conscience, haven't
> you? Innocent as a newborn babe! Wouldn't hurt a fly!

Waters the flowers in his garden every evening, feeds his
rabbits, and thanks God he lives in peace. The whole country's shot to pieces and dried up, but that doesn't bother
him—oh no, he just sits at home and thinks the hell with
those outside!—And watch out, anyone who dares disturb
his sacred peace! Then he becomes a beast and doesn't ask
whose fault it is. At one stroke the good-humored fellow
becomes a devil and quickly draws up a list of his fellow
citizens to denounce and murder—murder! at the first opportunity.

> GUARD: No! That's not true! I just thought . . .
> FUGITIVE: Innocence in person! He just thought!
Doesn't care what happens all around him, doesn't care
that bloody gangsters are setting the world on fire. None of
his business if they round up free men and send them into
slavery! He just obeys orders! But whose orders he obeys—
that he doesn't care to know and whoever tells him the
truth is his enemy, for if he listened maybe he'd find out
he was a gangster himself and not even as much as a hair's-
breadth better than his masters. . . . And still he just
wants to live in peace. At any price! [3]

As he realizes why no decent man can shake his hand, the
events of his life suddenly rearrange themselves in the guard's
mind and drop into their proper places. He looks down the
long corridor of his past, as it were, and it is like looking into
the abyss itself. He helps the fugitive to escape with his wife,
and then calls out the news of his treachery to the approaching
militia. They answer with a shot, and he falls dead across the
threshold that he had ruined his life to protect.

As might be expected from a writer whose political disagree-
ments with the Nazis had forced him to flee his native country,
the rise of the German despotism continued to fascinate Hochwälder. A conscientious artist feels the compulsion to explain
to himself what is wrong with the world; and it is in responding to his explanation or in denying it that his audience either

3. Fritz Hochwälder, *Der Flüchtling* (Elgg, Switzerland: Volksverlag
Elgg, 1954), p. 56.

learns more about the world or becomes convinced that it is
impossible to learn anything—which is a solution of sorts too,
as the writers of the theatre of the absurd have demonstrated.
In *Der Flüchtling* Hochwälder explored the effect of a totalitarian state on an average individual mind; in *Esther* he wrote
a complete allegory of the rise of the Nazi mentality in terms
of the Biblical story of Esther, Mordecai, and Haman.

The story of Esther is, of course, tailor-made for the project.
The plans of Haman and Hitler are so similar that Hochwälder hardly has to stretch any facts to create his allegory:
he merely has, for the most part, to transpose names and transfer situations from one milieu to another. Hochwälder does,
however, make certain significant changes in the character and
career of Haman to make him correspond more closely to
Hitler. Instead of being a nobleman elevated by the king, Hochwälder has Haman start out as a servant in Mordecai's household. Later he is thrown into the king's prison and, while confined there, hears of and joins a secret organization which seeks
to improve the state (which is in the midst of a profound economic depression) by violent means. Haman contrives to make
himself leader of the organization, which up to now has been
little more than a society of discontented talkers, by impressing
upon it the need for action. It is his idea that the Jews would
make ideal scapegoats and he soon makes himself a powerful
demagogue among the discontented lower classes of the city.
He comes to power when the nobles persuade the king to call
him in, although they thoroughly disapprove of him. Both the
nobles and the king look upon the elevation of Haman to
supreme power as a measure of temporary expediency, but of
course it is Haman-Hitler who is master of the expediency
device. Pleading expediency, he obtains the king's consent to
the extermination of the Jews and is only foiled when Esther
finally intervenes. The parallels are so obvious that they hardly
need to be pointed out: the only thing wrong with Hochwälder's allegory, in fact, is that in 1940, when he wrote it, the
execution of Haman was unfortunately only a piece of self-
indulgent wishful thinking on his part.

The characteristic Hochwälder touch of inner revelation

comes at the very end in *Esther*. Unlike the Biblical heroine, Hochwälder's has not been particularly anxious to save her people. Mordecai's lesson of concealment has been so well driven into her that she no longer considers herself a Jewess and feels disinclined to concern herself in any political affair. In the Biblical story Esther obtains the king's favor and the privilege of having any wish granted. She simply accuses Haman of treachery, and that is that. Haman is taken out and hanged; Mordecai is made the chief minister; and the Jews are granted the privilege of using the time set aside for their own extermination to slaughter their enemies. Hochwälder's Esther does not have so simple a task, nor could Hochwälder, writing in 1940, present so sanguine an ending. Esther traps Haman with an elaborate plot that reveals he had been planning to overthrow the king. But even so the Jews' troubles are not over. The king recognizes that the country does need a scapegoat and that the Jews are the obvious choices for the position. He will not, of course, exterminate them, he assures Esther, but merely persecute them a little whenever the people need to have their attention diverted from official corruption and inefficiency. To show that he is not really prejudiced against Jews, he will marry Esther (she has been his concubine up to now) provided she keeps her origin a secret, and he will ennoble Mordecai. The latter tears up his charter of nobility and tells the king he will not be singled out but will share the fate of his people. As Esther quietly watches the scene, she experiences the typical Hochwälderian inner revulsion and announces that she gives up her chance for the throne to go with Mordecai. Until such time as justice reigns in the world and her people are judged on an equal basis with other peoples, she can do nothing—nor has she any right to save herself alone.

In *Der Flüchtling* and in *Esther*, more than in any other of his plays, we can see Hochwälder's use of the flash of moral enlightenment as a dramatic and didactic device. One decisive key event occurs that changes a man's whole life by rearranging the perspective of his memories. What could be more dramatic than this moment of inner realization? The same "moment of truth" appears in most of Hochwälder's other plays.

In *Donadieu* (published 1953), for example, the problem is the
rejection of revenge. Again a complete reversal of a man's purpose in life is involved. The action takes place during the
Catholic-Huguenot conflicts in France. Donadieu is the leader
of a self-contained Huguenot community in southern France
where fugitives from all over the country are welcomed. Donadieu's one passion in life is revenge. During his absence from
the garrison several years previously, his wife was brutally murdered and the rest of the villagers burnt alive in the church by
a group of Catholic banditti. Since then, Donadieu has lived in
suspended animation, so to speak, until the moment when he
will have the murderer in his power. But when one of two
travelers wearing the king's uniform is recognized as the leader
of the murderers, Donadieu is unable to do anything, for the
murderer is entrusted with the king's declaration of indulgence
for the Huguenots. If he takes his revenge, Donadieu prevents
the Huguenots from obtaining their rights. He refrains. Again
the psychological enlightenment that Hochwälder shows us is
complete. Donadieu does not refrain merely because the circumstances make it expedient: he refrains because he has realized the futility of his desire for revenge. Like the border guard
and like the Father Provincial, he has been granted a moment
in which the whole course of his life has become visible to him;
and his life, like theirs, has been—as it must be—totally changed
by it. Even when the man who has killed his wife deliberately
taunts him, hoping to provoke a fight and thus invalidate the
declaration of indulgence, Donadieu remains firm. Even though
those who had previously urged him to forego the luxury of his
revenge now urge him to silence the vicious taunts, Donadieu
maintains his claim. And so the general cause is saved—through
Donadieu's moment of self-revelation.

Similarly, in *Meier Helmbrecht* (published 1956), Hochwälder tells the story of a medieval landowner whose son becomes a bloodthirsty robber who pillages the countryside until
he is finally caught himself. The point of the play comes in the
third act, when Helmbrecht is tried by a jury of his peers on the
smoking ruins of his farmhouse. Slowly he is made to realize that
his protestations of innocence are willful self-delusion and that

he too is responsible for his son's crimes. What his son has become Helmbrecht's neglect and indulgence made him: the sins of the children must be visited upon the fathers. Hochwälder unfortunately gives his play a rather weak ending by reconciling Helmbrecht with his now crippled and blinded son as he starts to rebuild his house.

Since most of Hochwälder's plays were written during or immediately after the war, it is only natural that he should be so taken up by this question of the placing of guilt. In *Meier Helmbrecht* he argues that the fathers are responsible for the children. In *Der Flüchtling* he argues that a man is responsible for his own integrity—that the plea that he is only a cog in the machine is valueless. The plea that "orders are orders" and one has no choice but to follow them was, of course, one that became almost an automatic, rhythmic refrain after the war, when every German chanted it like a daily prayer. Hochwälder deals with the justice of this plea on the part of the older generation in *Meier Helmbrecht,* on the part of the man in the street in *Der Flüchtling,* and in *Der Öffentliche Anklager* (The Public Prosecutor, published 1954), a melodrama about the French Revolution, he deals with the leaders of the people—the politicians, officials, and generals. Like these people, Fouquier-Tinville, the cold-blooded public prosecutor who engineered the Reign of Terror, pleads that he is a servant of the state and that it is his duty to obey orders:

> Here we only obey our orders. No blame attached to us, we can serve all parties with a clear conscience. We follow whoever is in power. Keep that in mind, . . .
>
> . . . .
>
> Reactions? I am not concerned with politics. I obey the law and carry out such orders as may come to me. I don't question whether they are good or bad.
>
> . . . .
>
> I was merely employing the means I was given—carrying out my orders. That is why I feel I can reject any personal responsibility.[4]

4. Fritz Hochwälder, *The Public Prosecutor,* translated by Kitty Black in J. C. Trewin, ed., *Plays of the Year* (London: Elek Books, 1958), pp. 334, 337, 361.

Nobody is enlightened in this play. Fouquier-Tinville satisfac-torily falls into the trap he has been tricked into setting for him-self and that is that. He fully deserves his end, for Hochwälder makes it clear that his explanations are consciously specious and that his actions are dictated by cynical opportunism and an insane thirst for power.

Hochwälder has written three other plays that are outside the main philosophical stream of his work. They are *Hotel du Commerce* (published 1954), an adaptation of Guy de Maupas-sant's "Boule de Suif," *Der Unschuldige* (The Innocent Man, published 1958), a melodrama about the deceptiveness of cir-cumstantial evidence, which he wrote as a bravura piece for At-tila Hörbiger of the Vienna Burgtheater, and *Donnerstag* (Thursday), an extremely confused and clumsily constructed modern morality play written for the Salzburg Festival.

Some may quarrel with Hochwälder's theory of psychology. Man, they will say, is not transformed, except in the rarest of rare cases, into a completely different psychological being by one occurrence. Few men are that sensitive. In fact, it is probably nearer to the actual human truth to say that man never learns by experience, that he is irredeemably set in child-hood upon a labyrinthine and enclosed psychological path. But Hochwälder's view of human nature is nonetheless the most dramatic possible. The luxury of precise psychology must be left to the novelist, who has the space and the structural flexi-bility to indulge in whatever he will. The dramatist is bound by the exigencies of the stage. He must depict the events of the world at their highest intensity, regardless of whether or not they would happen precisely thus in real life.

The New English Dramatists

The Experimentalists

THE DRAMATIC avant-garde movement has flourished in England like aspidistra in the Gobi desert. The old cliché about the hidebound Englishman is nowhere so true as in art. This is not to say that the Englishman is incapable of holding revolutionary ideas. Slow as the English nation as a whole has always been to change and adapt, individual Englishmen have traditionally burst forth with visionary religious ideas or radical political ones that have made the most independent thinkers of other nations blench. These revolutionary ideas, however, have always appeared sub rosa, so to speak. As Shaw pointed out, the English seem to associate art with "immorality," i.e., socially rebellious conduct, and too often regard the practicing artist in somewhat the same light as a paroled felon: they await with bated breath the appearance of any overt aberration from the norm. Then they pounce—or, rather, they blandly disregard. The effect is the same: the artist is crushed. It is not surprising, therefore, that the English artist shies away from experimentation with the techniques of his craft. There are always plenty of new *ideas* floating around the back streets of Hampstead and Chelsea, but there are hardly ever any new *forms*. The play of traditional construction with realistic dialogue is still the form British authors seem instinctively to turn to. For the most part the young British dramatists appear to be unaware of the avant-garde movement of Beckett, Ionesco, Genet, and Adamov in France; Martin Esslin quite correctly includes only Harold

196

Pinter and N. F. Simpson in his survey of the theatre of the absurd. Failure to adhere to the principles of the avant-garde drama is, of course, not in itself a crime. The drama of protest—the only kind of worthwhile and serious drama—can be incorporated just as well (*vide* Shaw) within the framework of the conventional play form.

The rapturous ecstasy with which the English critics have received the "new British drama" represented by Harold Pinter, John Osborne, Bernard Kops, Arnold Wesker, John Mortimer, Shelagh Delaney, N. F. Simpson, Doris Lessing, Nigel Dennis, Brendan Behan, and John Arden would seem to indicate that the English theater has undergone its greatest renaissance since the days of Elizabeth I. Unhappily, this is not the case. The English critics have apparently been overcome by the sudden flood of competently written dramas produced in the latter part of the nineteen-fifties. Their critical faculties dulled by this unexpected eruption, they have been pontificating about the regeneration of the English theater and the rebirth of intellectual responsibility in the English drama. To critics fed for so long on the post-Pinerotic pap of the West End drama, the plays of the new English dramatists necessarily seem masterpieces. Unfortunately, one is forced to suspect that much of this enthusiasm is attributable to thankfulness for boredom relieved and for national sensitivities assuaged.

HAROLD PINTER
The Comedy of Allusiveness

NOTHING demonstrates more clearly that the avant-garde movement in the theater is essentially a French movement than the work of Harold Pinter. Pinter is England's only major exponent of the avant-garde technique in playwriting, yet his plays irresistibly remind one of particular works by French avant-garde authors. The impression that Pinter's plays give is that of eclectic scholarship rather than of creation. He seems to have read all of the secondary sources—Beckett, Ionesco, and

Genet, particularly—but not the all-important primary source, Antonin Artaud.

Pinter has an extremely acute sense of stage situations—a perception of what will "go" on stage. In all of his plays, static and incomprehensible though they may often seem, Pinter demonstrates a truly extraordinary ear for the speech patterns of ordinary people, as well as a highly developed ability to create interest and suspense by means of a series of momentarily sustained conflicts. The dialogue in Pinter's plays fascinates by its very monotony and repetitiousness because the audience *recognizes* it—they have heard this sort of talk before. Ionesco does the same thing with ordinary speech patterns in *The Bald Soprano,* but whereas he deliberately extends the monotony and repetitiousness until they become caricature, Pinter knows where to stop: precisely where real-life speech patterns stop. Pinter uses human dialogue as a verbal sparring match in which the participants feint and parry with words to avoid involvement with each other. His characters are not strapped tight within separate cocoons, as Adamov's and Ionesco's are: they remain convinced, just as ordinary people do in reality, that they *can* touch each other with the verbal jabs they flick out, but they live in terror of the moment when they will hit their mark.[1]

Pinter himself has indicated that his purpose is to observe what happens to people.[2] In order to do this, he usually chooses as his central image a room—any ordinary room where people live—to serve as a microcosm of the world. In the room people feel safe. Outside are only alien forces; inside there is warmth and light. It is a womb in which people can feel secure. The conflict in Pinter's plays occurs when one of the outside forces penetrates into the room and disrupts the security of its occupants. Pinter's role is that of dispassionate observer, and much of the apparent difficulty of his plays stems from the fact that he writes them as if he were eavesdropping on his characters

1. Bernard Dukore, "The Theatre of Harold Pinter," *Tulane Drama Review,* VI (March, 1962), p. 48.
2. Martin Esslin, *The Theatre of the Absurd* (Garden City, N. Y.: Doubleday & Company, Inc., 1961), p. 199.

and recording their often pointless stream of consciousness. He
has described the genesis of three of his most important plays
as coming from a simple curiosity as to what could happen to
two people in a room: "*The Room* came after going into a
room with one person standing and one sitting. *The Birthday
Party* after going into a room with two persons sitting. *The
Caretaker* after looking into a room with two persons standing." [3]

The Room (1957), Pinter's first play, is a simple story about
two people living in a tiny globe of light set in an immense and
menacing void of darkness. People venture out into the dark
occasionally, but only fearfully and unwillingly. People come in
from the dark occasionally, but only to bring danger to the people in the light. The room is inhabited by an elderly couple. The
man has to go out and the woman is left alone. We learn that
she never goes out and that she does not even know how the
house she lives in is laid out. Furthermore, the landlord, who has
lived there for years and years, does not know either. When the
woman goes to put out the garbage, she finds a young couple
standing at the door. Coming as they do from the mysterious,
nebulous outer regions, their sudden appearance has a distinctly
eerie effect, which is intensified when they inform the woman
that they have been wandering all over the house for a long
time without finding any light except that in the room. They
are looking for living quarters, they tell the woman, and while
groping around the pitch-black basement they heard a disembodied voice politely telling them that No. 7 was to let. The
woman tells them that they are in No. 7 but that she intends
to stay. She ushers them out, but her sense of security has been
shattered: the outer forces are beginning to encroach on her.
Then the landlord comes in and tells her that a mysterious
stranger has been waiting for days to see her. He has been
patiently lying in the damp basement waiting for her husband
to go out. The woman is unwilling to see anyone, but the landlord insists and brings in an old blind Negro. The Negro seems
to know her, although she frantically denies knowing him. Her

3. Harold Pinter, "Writing for Myself," *Twentieth Century*, CLXIX
(February, 1961), p. 174.

name is Rose but he calls her Sal, apparently a childhood name, for she seems to recognize it, and tells her he has a message from her father asking her to come home. The husband returns and speaks for the first time. When he has finished boasting about how fearlessly he drove his van along the dark, icy roads, he sees the Negro, kicks him out of his chair, and beats him unconscious (possibly he kills him). Rose suddenly screams that she is blind, and the curtain falls.

The Room shows all the defects of a first play by a young author, but it also shows the germs of Pinter's very considerable technical skill. As a mood piece—the mood being horror —the play is excellent—almost a subdued Grand Guignol piece. Unfortunately, Pinter has spoiled the play by succumbing to the temptation to put in some juvenile symbolism. With the entry of the blind Negro, whatever he represents, the play disintegrates. The Negro may symbolize death, the woman's past, or some hidden guilt complex—probably the latter, since she is struck blind when her husband beats the Negro. But there is no hint as to what his function really is nor as to why the husband beats him so savagely. He is simply an emissary from the outside who has succeeded in breaking into the circle of light. As a result, the womb is broken, and the dwellers are cast out from the light into the darkness.

The Dumb Waiter (1957–1960), another one-act play about a room, is far more successful. Here we have a pure Grand Guignol play. Two men are staying in a miserably furnished room that does not even (horrors!) have proper facilities for making tea. The men chat about football teams and various items in the newspaper. As they talk, Pinter very skillfully makes us gradually aware that the two men are hired killers under the orders of a mysterious, hierarchical organization, which sends them around the country murdering people. All their time is spent in various rooms to which they are sent awaiting their next assignment. Like Rose in The Room, they feel secure in their haven, although, knowing they will have to go out soon, they are made extremely jumpy by any signs of intrusion from the outside. Pinter creates a really remarkable effect of suspense by simply having footsteps approach the door. An

envelope is then shoved under the door and the footsteps fade
away. The gunmen put their revolvers away and breathe easily
again. Some more casual talk ensues, and then suddenly a
dumbwaiter, hitherto unnoticed by the two men, starts operating at the rear of the room. The two "torpedoes," Ben and
Gus, find a waiter's order slip on it. They decide that there
must be a restaurant above and that they are in what used to
be the kitchen. (In England the kitchens of restaurants are
usually below the dining room and communication between
the two is maintained by means of a dumbwaiter.) Frantically
Ben and Gus search their pockets for food and send whatever
scraps they have. The dumbwaiter comes down again and again
bearing orders for progressively more and more exotic food.
Pinter plays with this excursion into pure absurdity for all it is
worth, since he uses it to lead into the contrast with his "shock-
of-horror" climax. Gus goes into the next room (out of the
safe world in Pinter's system) and Ben receives some instructions through the dumbwaiter's speaking tube. When Gus
comes back he is stripped down to his shirt and his gun is gone.
As the curtain falls we realize that Ben has been ordered to kill
his partner.

In Pinter's full-length play, *The Birthday Party* (1958),
we catch more than ever the quality of allusiveness that seems
to pervade all of his works. I am not, obviously, implying that
Pinter is a plagiarist. His works simply tend to remind one of
other works in an allusive manner—in a manner, that is to say,
as if Pinter had been unconsciously influenced by something
he had read. There would be nothing wrong with this, of course,
even if the influence were markedly direct: a writer should be
judged not by the originality of his plots but by his treatment
of them. And Pinter's treatment of his plots is for the most
part masterly. What I mean by Pinter's allusiveness is that
reading *The Room* reminds one of Beckett—specifically, of the
atmosphere of a Beckett play. Similarly, reading *The Dumb
Waiter* makes one think that Pinter has remembered a distant
Grand Guignol play. *The Birthday Party* irresistibly reminds
one of Hemingway's "The Killers."

The Birthday Party is about the death of Stanley Weber,

a small-time piano player who had apparently once offended
some extremely powerful forces. He has been hiding out in a
seedy rooming house in a seaside resort town, thinking himself
safe from pursuit. He does not seem to know in what way precisely he has offended his pursuers. All he knows is that his
promising career as a piano player was ruined when his second
concert was called off without warning. His description of this
incident in his life reads like a paranoid's nightmare:

> STANLEY: Played the piano? I've played the piano
> all over the world. All over the country. (*Pause.*) I once
> gave a concert . . . Yes. It was a good one, too. They were
> all there that night. Every single one of them. It was a
> great success. Yes. A concert. At Lower Edmonton. . . .
> I had a unique touch. Absolutely unique. They came up
> to me. They came up to me and said they were grateful.
> Champagne we had that night, the lot. . . . My father
> nearly came down to hear me. Well, I dropped him a card
> anyway. But I don't think he could make it. No, I—I lost
> the address, that was it. . . . Yes. Lower Edmonton. Then
> after that, you know what they did? They carved me up.
> Carved me up. It was all arranged, it was all worked out.
> My next concert. Somewhere else it was. In winter. I went
> down there to play. Then, when I got there, the hall was
> closed, the place was shuttered up, not even a caretaker.
> They'd locked it up. . . . A fast one. They pulled a fast
> one. I'd like to know who was responsible for that. . . . All
> right, Jack, I can take a tip. They want me to crawl down
> on my bended knees. Well I can take a tip . . . any day
> of the week.[4]

Soon after, two ordinary-looking men, an Irishman and a Jew,
rent rooms in the house. It soon becomes apparent that their
job is the same as Gus and Ben's in *The Dumb Waiter*—they
have been sent by some mysterious, high-up power to kill
Stanley.

Pinter's handling of the scenes in which McCann and

4. Harold Pinter, *The Birthday Party and The Room* (New York:
Grove Press, 1961), pp. 23–24.

Goldberg appear is masterful. The two killers become more and more sinister, and the horror of the situation accumulates as the audience contrasts its knowledge of the two men's real function with their behavior. Goldberg, the leader of the two killers, is portrayed alternately as a stock East End Jew, replete with nostalgic memories of his Mamma's gefilte fish and sententious maxims about familial togetherness, and as a cold-blooded hoodlum who has killed dozens of people. He talks about his eminence as a murderer with the same complacent pride that a bright young executive might talk of his rise from an office-boy's job; and he steadies the less-experienced McCann's nerves in the manner of a football coach reassuring a third-string halfback before his first big game. They organize a birthday party for Stanley although the latter keeps insisting that it is not his birthday. However, it makes no difference what Stanley says. As soon as he learns that one of the visitors is named Goldberg, he seems to know he is doomed, and from that point on he acts like an ox being led to slaughter. During the party, in which he is an unwilling participant, Stanley breaks down and goes berserk. On the next day he comes down from his room dressed in formal funeral clothes. He seems to have no will of his own anymore; and he is in fact nothing but a walking corpse by this time. Goldberg and McCann take him away in a big, black, hearselike car with a large ("There's just room . . . for the right amount.") trunk.

The Birthday Party is Pinter's best play, and in it he has made his closest approach to the French avant-garde school. Both the first-act–curtain scene where Stanley marches round the room frenziedly beating on a toy drum and the second-act–curtain scene in which Stanley goes berserk during a game of blindman's buff and tries to strangle one woman and rape another would have been highly approved of by Antonin Artaud.[5]

5. This approximation of Artaud's ideas appears to be fortuitous. Pinter has specifically rejected the suggestion that he has a preconceived plan or idea before writing a play. His dramas grow out of an imaginative development of characters in a situation (Esslin, *op. cit.*, p. 205). Pinter, in other words, claims, like Shaw, that his plays are not planned in advance, but grow naturally as he writes them, as if he were recording the conversation and actions of characters performing in his mind.

Pinter again uses his "room" theme here, but this time he uses it far more effectively than in the two previous plays. In *The Room* and *The Dumb Waiter* the enclosed space was a safe place in a vaguely defined void. Characters ventured out of the room occasionally—when they had to—but never seemed really to know what the outside was like. It was as if only the room *really* existed—a snug refuge in a sea of impersonal hostility, like an igloo on an ice floe. In *The Birthday Party* there is nothing sinister or undefined about the outside world, and the room is a refuge only for Stanley. Stanley, we learn, never leaves the house. He is conscious of guilt, and the area outside the house seems sinister only to him because it is from there that retribution will come. It does not matter that the retribution is unjust or that he has convinced himself it is unjust. Justice does not enter into the matter. The victim's viewpoint is not important. Stanley might be anyone, and he might not have done anything in particular. He has simply perceived his own helplessness, has recognized the illusory solidity of the bulwarks every person builds around himself. The anesthetic of existence as a social being has worn off for Stanley and he is thus exposed to the vengeful and implacable "forces" that govern human existence. On one level Goldberg and McCann are certainly emissaries of the hostile, unknowable power that takes the place of God in the avant-garde drama's philosophical view of the human condition.[6] But they are also at the same time ordinary, common-or-garden killers on the temporal level of the play's action. It is the contrast made by their macabre casualness and their victim's conscious helplessness that gives the play its ironic force. Stanley's "birthday party" is really his death, and when he comes down the next day in striped trousers, black jacket, white collar, and bowler hat, it is as if he had already been laid out in his coffin. Like two particularly unctuous funeral directors, Goldberg and McCann lead Stanley, who

6. Dukore, *op. cit.*, p. 52. Dukore sees Goldberg and McCann as being the agents of society come to pour Stanley into the collective mold. I do not myself feel that Pinter's meaning in this play can be narrowed down so specifically, though Dukore makes out a plausible case for his view by citing Goldberg's constant use of clichés.

is now moving with the robotlike gestures of a ·somnambulist, out to the big black car; and he disappears forever from the sight of his friends, who notice nothing wrong. They will simply go on living and forget. Like Stanley they have amounted to nothing in life, but unlike him they do not know it. Stanley knew and therefore had to pay the penalty: he is dissolved and washed away, like the victims of Peer Gynt's button-molder.

In his other full-length play and first big success, *The Caretaker* (1960), Pinter leaves the macabre and savage humor that characterized his previous plays and takes us to a Beckett-like static drama about three men who are waiting for something that will never come. Again the characters are encased in a room that represents safety. This time the room is a huge, cluttered one on the top floor of a large house, the rest of which is shut up. The house belongs to Mick and is being taken care of by his older brother Aston, who lives in the room. Aston brings Davies, an old tramp whom he has rescued from being beaten up, into the room. Davies turns out to be one of those belligerently self-assertive personalities who feel that everything is theirs by right. As soon as Aston offers to put him up in the room until he can get himself straightened out, Davies starts acting as if the room were his. Gradually he seems to get the idea that he is doing Aston a favor and that Aston's insistence on keeping the room as it has always been is a personal affront to him. Despite Davies's constant nagging dissatisfaction, Aston continues to be kind to him and offers him the job of caretaker while he redecorates the house. He even reveals that he once received electric-shock treatments in a mental institution. Davies cannot resist playing the two brothers off against each other, first trying to persuade Mick (who also offers him the job of caretaker) that his brother is still insane and ought to be put back in the institution; and then, when Mick finds him out, trying to wheedle himself back into Aston's good graces. All that Davies succeeds in doing with his troublemaking is, paradoxically, to bring the brothers closer to each other. At the end Davies is left pleading tearfully and vainly with Aston for another opportunity to "belong."

Like all plays of the avant-garde, *The Caretaker* is open to several interpretations. On the surface it is about two brothers who have drifted away from each other and are now brought closer together again by their contact with a tramp that one of them has taken in. But it is also, like all the plays discussed up to this point, the story of the room in which it takes place. The room is cluttered, dirty, and draughty. The roof leaks, the gas is disconnected, and the sanitary facilities are of the most primitive; but to the three people in the play it represents a haven in which they can hide from the world. To Davies, the homeless old tramp, it comes to be a place where he can settle down at last; and, insofar as the play is a tragedy, it is the tragedy of his failure to qualify for a place in this contracted, modern-world paradise because of his inability to curb his natural maliciousness. To Aston it is a refuge from the world with which he was unable to cope. As long as he remains in the room and keeps his mind strictly on the needs of the house which he is supposed to be decorating, he is safe from the lunatic asylum and the electric-shock treatments. His existence is a careful and deliberate attempt to keep his mind off the things with which he cannot cope by absorbing himself in the precise, step-by-step performance of routine actions. Throughout the play he calms himself by fiddling with an electric plug he is trying to repair, somewhat in the manner of Hemingway's Nick in "Big Two-Hearted River" going through the routine of fishing to keep his mind off less pleasant things. To Mick, the younger brother, the room is a haven in reserve. He does not live in it, but keeps it as a place to fall back on. The bed Davies sleeps on is his, and his antagonism to Davies when he first meets him and later when he chases him round the dark room with the vacuum cleaner is based on his fear of being dispossessed. All three men—Aston, Mick, and Davies —are waiting for something that the audience realizes will never happen. Like the two tramps in *Waiting for Godot*, they are marking time through life, buoying themselves up with the hope of an unattainable ideal. Davies's one thought in life is to get down to Sidcup and recover the papers that will prove his identity. Aston's one thought in life is to build the shed in the garden, the symbol of his recovered sanity. And Mick dreams of someday turning the run-down old house into a nightmarishly tasteless parody of a millionaire's penthouse apartment with teal-blue, copper, and parchment linoleum squares, oatmeal tweed armchairs, and mahogany and rosewood bedroom furniture. None of these things will ever happen, but they will go on thinking about them; and in thinking about them they will obtain the illusion of having a purpose in life.[7]

Harold Pinter has also written a number of minor plays for radio and television. These include *A Slight Ache, A Night Out, The Dwarfs, The Collection,* and *The Lover.*

A Night Out (1960), is a slight, though well-written, reversion to the conventional play form. The allusiveness here is to Sidney Howard's *The Silver Cord* as Pinter tells the story of a young man helplessly shackled to a self-pitying, domineering mother. He has one outburst of defiance as he threatens to hit his mother with an alarm clock and rushes out of the house. He allows himself to be picked up by a prostitute and at last it looks as if the cord is to be snapped. But all he is capable of doing is a repeat of the scene with his mother. His rage is merely transferred to the prostitute and he threatens her with the alarm clock and says to her all the things he has never dared to say to his mother. Then he goes home and resumes his "little boy" role. In its way this play is a small masterpiece. The only trouble is that ever since Freud popularized it, the mother-fixation theme has become commonplace in literature and consequently no longer carries the shock value it still ought to have.

In *A Slight Ache* (1959) and *The Dwarfs* (1906), both radio

7. *The Caretaker* has been interpreted in a number of different ways, all of which suffer from being too specific. Bernard Dukore (*op. cit.*, p. 50) sees Aston as the one-time social rebel rendered impotent by society through the symbolic brain operation. Ruby Cohn (*Tulane Drama Review*, VI [March, 1962], pp. 55–68) suggests that Mick and Aston represent the System, which crushes Davies. They tantalize him with faint hope in order to crush him all the more completely at the end. J. R. Taylor sees the whole play as an elaborate plot by Mick to get rid of Davies with Aston's unconscious consent so that he can continue rehabilitating his brother (Taylor, *Anger and After* [London: Methuen & Co., Ltd., 1962], pp. 246–47). To Esslin (*op. cit.*, p. 211) Davies's expulsion takes on "the cosmic proportion of Adam's expulsion from Paradise."

H

plays, Pinter has gone to the extreme limits of possible experimentation with breakdown of form. These plays are formless even for radio, where, of course, a much looser form is possible in the first place. Both plays are concerned with the elusiveness of identity, a favorite theme of the modern avant-garde drama. In *A Slight Ache* a self-satisfied writer of philosophical essays talks to a mysterious old matchseller who has been standing outside his cottage for weeks without selling anything. The matchseller makes no response to the writer, and gradually the latter's self-confidence breaks down as he goes on talking. At the end he has been so reduced by the long monologue in which he has inadvertently demonstrated his own emptiness that his wife hands him the tray of matches and goes off with the silent old man.

The Dwarfs is more complicated. Here there are three characters, Len, Pete, and Mark, who fade in and out and seem at some points to merge with each other. Pinter is talking here mainly in some personal nightmarish symbols about the sinister army of dwarfs which has invaded the world and is insidiously ruining it. There are also vague suggestions that Len is a Christ figure ("They make no hole in my side. They make a hole in my side.") and equally vague suggestions that Mark is a papal symbol. Mark has a particular key, he is of Latin origin, he has a ring, he bets on the "treble chance," and so forth. Pinter keeps everything deliberately vague and allusive, and it is impossible to get anything definite out of the play at all.

In his latest plays, *The Collection* (1961) and *The Lover* (1963), both originally written for television, Pinter has turned to a rather enigmatic drawing-room comedy style. His television plays give the impression of perfect familiarity and straightforwardness, but they leave the spectators asking themselves, "What on earth was he really talking about?" There is little possibility that *The Collection* and *The Lover* will be successful television plays in the United States, where the audiences demand not only a schoolmasterish clarity but also an ostentatiously gleaming sexual purity culminating in a "moral" ending unexceptionable to even the most rabidly sensitive of the indigenous Puritan groups. In Britain, however, the home audi-

ence seems to be made of sterner stuff, for they were able to
accept even *The Birthday Party:* "While viewers were clearly
exasperated by the lack of the cheap and obvious motivation
to which they were used in their daily fare, they were also
visibly intrigued. For days one could hear people in buses and
canteens eagerly discussing the play as a maddening but deeply
disturbing experience." [8] In the United States, unhappily, there
would only be exasperation at the lack of obvious motivation.

Although *The Collection* would be impractical for American television, it has been produced successfully on the off-
Broadway stage. Both this play and *The Lover* are concerned
in a milder and much less agonized way, with the same problem that obsesses Genet: "What is a person's reality?" To
Genet human beings are composed of layer upon layer of illusion draped around a nonexistent core; to Pinter human beings
are simply inscrutable, to themselves as well as to others. They
may be emptiness surrounded by illusion, but they may also,
without knowing it, possess a solid center of reality. The point
is that they do not know and are too frightened to find out.
It is in *The Collection* and *The Lover* that the image of
Pinter's dialogue being like a verbal sparring match in which
the participants are always just barely keeping out of each
other's reach becomes really pertinent. Even more so is the
comment which Pinter wrote for the program of *The Room*
and *The Dumb Waiter* when they were performed at the Royal
Court Theatre:

> The desire for verification is understandable but cannot
> always be satisfied. There are no hard distinctions between
> what is true and what is false. The thing is not necessarily
> either true or false; it can be both true and false. The as-
> sumption that to verify what has happened and what is
> happening presents few problems I take to be inaccurate.
> A character on the stage who can present no convincing
> argument or information as to his past experience, his pres-
> ent behaviour or his aspirations, nor give a comprehensive
> analysis of his motives, is as legitimate and as worthy of

8. Esslin, *op. cit.*, p. 207.

attention as one who, alarmingly, can do all these things. The more acute the experience the less articulate its expression.[9]

This is precisely the case in *The Collection*, which is about four people, each emotionally affecting all the others, yet none ever succeeding in actually touching one of them and making sense to him. The plot revolves around the question whether or not two of the characters slept together while attending a dress designers' convention in the north of England. The wife comes home and for no discernible reason (is she trying to reach him?) gives her husband a circumstantial and highly spiced account of how she spent a night in bed with someone else. The husband (his name is Horne, interestingly enough) visits his rival and taxes him with his wife's story. The rival denies everything at first, but then, when Horne's urbanely casual manner changes to a thinly veiled menace, corroborates the wife's story, even going so far as to add a juicy detail or two of his own. Horne goes home to brood and be urbanely casual with his wife, and the audience sits back with a sigh of contentment as it recognizes the unfolding of another familiar "eternal triangle" drama. But with Pinter the sides of the triangle obstinately refuse to fit together. It appears that Bill, the rival, is being kept by Harry Kane, an older man, who naturally does not care to have his domestic arrangements spoiled by his protégé's philanderings, hypothetical or otherwise. Harry goes to see the wife and gets her to admit she made the whole thing up. Confronted with this evidence, Bill switches his story again and agrees that nothing happened. Horne goes home and appeals to his wife for confirmation of the new story. The curtain falls as she looks at him enigmatically.

The Lover is specifically written with television-production techniques in mind and would require considerable rewriting for transfer to the stage. This has now been done. As it stands, in its original form, it is one of the most brilliant plays to appear in the English language since the end of the war. The

9. Quoted in Esslin, *op. cit.*, p. 206.

opening scene shows a stuffy businessman leaving his suburban home to go to the city and politely inquiring whether his wife plans to entertain her lover that day. The wife replies that she does and asks him to come home late. Then she transforms herself into a seductive siren and awaits her lover. The bell rings and she goes to answer the door. It is her husband. In the second act we see that these two are in the habit of playing out a series of interlocking semisadistic fantasy scenes which all culminate in an aggressive entrapment of one partner by the other. The allusiveness here is to Genet's *The Balcony*, but although the sexual fantasies remind one of the three opening scenes of that play, Pinter's purpose is not the same as Genet's. Genet's characters indulged in their sadistic fantasies to give themselves the illusion of being someone, whereas Pinter's indulge in them in order to achieve sexual potency. They can achieve physical communication only through an elaborate bypassing of emotional communication. The sterility, both physical and emotional of this typical modern couple is so great that they can come close to each other only in a fantasy world. During the play the husband tries to break out of this vicious circle where illusion equals sexual potency equals mutual understanding equals illusion, but the wife is too far gone and frantically appeals to him to continue the game. In the end he yields, and they drift off into their fantasy life again. *The Lover* is Pinter's bitterest, most cogent, and most expertly written statement of his belief that the tragedy of people today is their "deliberate evasion of communication." [10]

Harold Pinter has established himself as the most promising of England's young playwrights. Without a doubt he has far and away the most original mind (with the possible exception of N. F. Simpson) of any of the new English dramatists, and (again with the exception of Simpson) he is the only one of them who is unafraid to experiment with new dramatic forms and techniques.

10. Statement of Pinter in an interview with Kenneth Tynan, quoted in Esslin, *op. cit.*, p. 207.

N. F. SIMPSON
Parallel to Logic

AMONG THE MORE remarkable results of the current so-called "renaissance" in the English drama has been the work of N. F. Simpson, a London schoolteacher. His three important plays are *A Resounding Tinkle, The Hole,* and *One Way Pendulum;* [1] and, like Mr. Groomkirby in the last-named play, they reside in a world of their own. Like Alfred Jarry and his descendants, the 'Pataphysicians, Simpson has created a parallel reality that runs alongside our reality and clowns at it. Simpson's way of showing up what he considers the ridiculousness of the world is to create a special world in which reality is satirized by being placed in a new context. His plays, like 'Pataphysics, are a perversion of logic—the impossible carried out in accordance with the laws by which the possible exists.

Someone once said that comedy was the most serious art form. The avant-garde drama is rapidly demonstrating that farce is the most serious of all art forms. The appreciation of farce requires a highly developed sense of the ridiculous and an ability to cut the mind loose from prosaic literalness. These are, unfortunately, rare qualities, so that instead of receiving the wholehearted laughter he deserves, Simpson has all too frequently been the victim of humorlessly obtuse analyses such as John Russell Taylor's. Taylor sees Simpson only as a repetitive prankster whose absurdity "rapidly loses its charms in a life-and-death struggle with the law of diminishing returns." [2] As a contrast to this view, Martin Esslin finds that Simpson *is* a serious artist—"a more powerful social critic than any of the social realists"—whose work culminates in *One Way Pendulum* with its picture of "a society that has become absurd because

1. Simpson has also recently written a one-act play called *The Form.* This is a Pinter-type play on shifting identities and not characteristic of Simpson's work.
2. John Russell Taylor, *Anger and After* (London: Methuen & Co., Ltd., 1962), p. 64.

routine and tradition have turned human beings into Pavlovian automata." [8]

Simpson's first play, A Resounding Tinkle (1957), seems to be an exercise in formlessness and free association which he uses as a vehicle for taking jabs at various aspects of social behavior. Like Ionesco, Simpson favors the average middle-class home as a setting. He gets his humorous and satiric effects by turning the natural events of this setting topsy-turvy. In A Resounding Tinkle, for example, we are in the living room of the Paradock home. Two comedians come in and entertain the Paradocks with a vaudeville skit that has nothing to do with the rest of the play. Then they sit down and get drunk on a purple-colored liquid which is supposed to be nectar and discuss ways of making the audience laugh. There is a great deal of this sort of self-conscious intrusion into the play on Simpson's part—a great deal too much, in fact. A character designated as the author's mouthpiece comes on and discusses the play in a long lecture to the audience, and later a "technician" delivers an oration on the "laughter index" of the audience. Finally Simpson puts a crowd of critics on the stage to deliver their judgments on the play. All of this self-conscious fiddling only tends to detract from the real humor of the play, which lies in such inspired idiocies as the Paradock family's dilemma over an elephant they have purchased, which turns out to be too big for their house. They exchange it for an equally dissatisfied neighbor's python, which is so small it fits into a pencil box.

The only point in the play at which Simpson can be said to be really serious is in his satire on the ritual of religious services. Like Beckett, Simpson takes as the cardinal point of his Weltanschauung the paradox that human thought is useless. Man can know nothing, and his attempts to understand the universe and create a coherent place for himself in it, which have resulted in the elaborately and finely spun opacity of the mental network we call religious ritual, are consequently

3. Esslin, *op. cit.*, p. 224.

nothing but convoluted cerebrations continually twisting round on themselves. This is the central theme which both Beckett and Simpson demonstrate in their plays. The difference between the two, apart from the obvious stylistic one, is in their attitude toward it. Beckett's despair is hidden under a sardonic objectivity and a deliberate choice of laconic and allusive speech patterns. Simpson's attitude, on the other hand, is one of hair-clutching hilarity. To him the world is not so much depressing as ridiculous—and therefore to be laughed at. The paradox renders the world so ridiculous to Simpson that he can express his feelings only in the "beyond realm" of nonsense. He becomes serious only infrequently, whereas Beckett does precisely the opposite: he lights the prevailing gloom with occasional flashes of ribald vaudeville humor.

When Simpson does get serious it is some time before the audience realizes it. The seriousness emerges slowly from the torrent of nonsense, most of which is extremely funny but hardly germane either to the philosophy or to the plot of the play. In *A Resounding Tinkle*, for example, Mr. and Mrs. Paradock and the two comedians sit down and "have a read" with their afternoon coffee (in the Paradock household it is customary to take a book with one's coffee) when the radio suddenly starts blaring out a divine service. Nobody listens except the First Comedian, who chants the responses under his breath:

> PRAYER: Let us sing because round things roll:
> RESPONSE: And rejoice that it might have been otherwise.
> PRAYER: Let us praise God for woodlice, and for buildings sixty-nine feet three inches high:
> RESPONSE: For Adam Smith's *Wealth of Nations* published in 1776:
> PRAYER: For the fifth key from the left on the lower manual of the organ of the Church of the Ascension in the Piazza Vittorio Emmanuele II in the town of Castelfidardo in Italy:
> RESPONSE: And for gnats.

PRAYER: How flat are our trays:

RESPONSE: Our sewers how underground and how rat-infested altogether.

. . . .

PRAYER: Let us give thanks for air hostesses and such as sit examinations, for the Bessemer process and for canticles, that all who live in France may be called Frenchmen and that nothing may be called useful that has no purpose.

RESPONSE: Amen.

. . . .

PRAYER: Let us throw back our heads and laugh at reality:

RESPONSE: Which is an illusion caused by mescalin deficiency.

PRAYER: At sanity:

RESPONSE: Which is an illusion caused by alcohol deficiency.

PRAYER: At knowledge which is an illusion caused by certain biochemical changes in the human brain structure during the course of human evolution, which had it followed another course would have produced other biochemical changes in the human brain structure, by reason of which knowledge as we now experience it would have been beyond the reach of our wildest imaginings; and by reason of which, what is now beyond the reach of our wildest imaginings would have been familiar and commonplace. Let us laugh at these things. Let us laugh at thought:

RESPONSE: Which is a phenomenon like any other.

PRAYER: At illusion:

RESPONSE: Which is an illusion, which is a phenomenon like any other.[4]

The same sort of thing occurs in *The Hole* (1957). This one-act play takes place around an open hole in the street.

4. Thomas Maschler, ed., *New English Dramatists 2*. With permission of and copyright © by N. F. Simpson. (Middlesex, England: Penguin Books, 1960), pp. 99–100.

Various people come in and look down into the hole. Each sees there some different aspect of life or each sees some different aspect of the same thing. At the side of the hole sits a queer huddled-up figure, the Visionary, who claims he is forming a one-man queue to see the unveiling of a stained-glass window in the cathedral which he sees in the hole. The other men—Endo, Cerebro, and Soma—represent a more active side of life: they keep seeing games being played in the hole. Dominoes, boxing, badminton, and darts follow each other in rapid succession and are in turn chased away by cards, chess, tennis, high jumping, pool, dice, wrestling, tug of war, and golf. This scene is merely another extension of the "inability to think" theme. Endo, Cerebro, and Soma are always looking for evidence of which game is being played but are never able to make up their minds for long since as soon as they have decided on something, some other bit of evidence floats into view and they are up in the air again. The point is that the human mind is not even capable of grasping *empiric* evidence reliably.

There are three main satiric points in the play. The first of these comes when the watchers catch sight of a tennis game in the hole and start calling the score in unison, standing as though for the National Anthem. Later on Simpson brings in an even more effective jab at religious ritual than the one in *A Resounding Tinkle* when the watchers see a lot of fish in the hole and decide that there must be three different tanks down there—three tanks in one or one tank in three, they can't decide which. Then they stand at attention and recite in unison:

> I believe in one aquarium which was and is and shall be; in which shall be comprehended the sprat and the Black Widow; in it the sole and the carp shall swim together, the swordtail and the water-flea; with the gudgeon shall float the mackerel, with the roach the guppy; duckweed shall be there, and foaming moss; neither shall the water at seventy-five degrees Fahrenheit be at variance with the water at forty degrees Fahrenheit, or eschew it. And the

freshwater shall be salt and the saltwater fresh, and no distinction shall be made between them, for all are of one aquarium and there is no other aquarium, but this.[5]

Finally they spot a prisoner pacing his cell in the hole, and here Simpson satirizes the tendency of people to rationalize everything in accordance with convention. To the mass of people, represented here by Endo, Soma, and Cerebro, ethics are relative and depend on the currently accepted prescription:

> SOMA: He has done wrong, and he has chosen to do it illegally.
>
> CEREBRO: It is the duty of every one of us to avoid those crimes we know to have been blacklisted.
>
> SOMA: To act otherwise is evil. More than that, it is a breach of the law.[6]

The scene in the prison cell gradually changes to another one in which a particularly brutal ritual murder appears to be taking place. The watchers are horrified, but, being ordinary people, their reaction to horrors is to run around shouting slogans and appeals for someone else to do something, thus salving their own consciences. The play ends with another satiric jab at religion as Soma delivers a mock sermon about an electric junction box with three cables, and possibly a fourth, running out of it. The junction box, which has appeared in the hole, takes the place of the mysteries of religious faith:

> For each time we draw near to the cavity and together peer down into the depths, we are not only giving expression by that act to the unquenchable curiosity that is in us, but we are at the same time reaffirming the truth of the eternal and inscrutable paradox—that it is upon this cavity that we build our faith.[7]

The Hole is undoubtedly Simpson's most trenchantly satiric play. Always maintaining his lofty objective attitude, he ridi-

5. N. F. Simpson, *The Hole* (London: Samuel French, 1958), p. 20.
6. *Ibid.*, p. 23.
7. *Ibid.*, p. 40.

cules the accepted forms of belief and behavior in the manner
of a man who feels he ought to cry but cannot stop laughing.
Simpson's feeling about the world is somewhat like the one
about America expressed by H. L. Mencken when he said that
a man would have to have a petrified diaphragm not to laugh
himself to sleep every night. This attitude comes out even more
strongly in Simpson's most successful play, *One Way Pendulum* (1959). If we are to look for any influence in this play
it must be in the work of Alfred Jarry and his cult of 'Pataphysics. As in 'Pataphysics, we have here a deliberate transfer-
ence of events to a track that runs parallel to conventional
logic. 'Pataphysics is the "science of imaginary solutions," a
way of protesting against the evils of the world by making fun
of the thought processes which created them. This is done by
making use of those thought processes to attain utterly ridiculous results. In other words, a new and fantastic world is built
up by a strict adherence to a rigid logical system. This method
is best described in nontechnical terms by Simpson himself in
his dust-jacket note to *One Way Pendulum*. It is, he says, "a
gravely serious attempt to make nonsense out of everything,
including nonsense. It hopes thereby to arrive from time to
time at a kind of sense, but the journey is what really matters.
There is a serious side to the play, for those who nevertheless
want it but it is right underneath, just above the sump and
difficult to get at. . . . It is best left alone . . . it has . . .
appeal for those who want . . . a play in which to find whatever it is they are looking for. They will be able to come back
to it again and again to see whether what they are looking
for has turned up yet or not."

In *One Way Pendulum*, as in all the works of the 'Pataphysicians, a vague aura of discomfort seeps through the curtain of hilarity: when the spectators' laughter is at its peak,
it suddenly turns hollow. As in *A Resounding Tinkle*, the setting in *One Way Pendulum* is a banal, middle-class home in
which everything seems to be just slightly slanted away from
the ordinarily used main track of life. Mr. Groomkirby, the
head of the house, "earns his living" by setting up a row of
parking meters behind the house and then standing next to

each one for an hour a day so that the sixpence he has put into
it will not be wasted. At the end of the week he empties the
meters and collects the money. The reason he always stands
a full hour next to each meter is that he is afraid he might
lose his own patronage if he feels overcharged. Despite this
rather bizarre method of making money, the Groomkirby
household seems to live fairly comfortably—so much so, indeed, that Mrs. Groomkirby frequently has to hire an enormously fat woman, a professional eater, to come in and eat up
the leftovers. Sylvia, the Groomkirbys' daughter, is fairly normal (comparatively speaking), her only real peculiarity being
a feeling that her arms are too short and a consequent desire to
be turned into an ape. Far and away the most offbeat member
of the family is young Kirby Groomkirby. Kirby lives by logic
alone. Having read Pavlov, he can now do nothing unless he
hears a bell rung first. His one obsession in life is to wear
black, but, being a very logical fellow, he feels he can only wear
black as a sign of mourning for someone he knows. He has
therefore so far approached no less than forty-three strangers,
told them a joke in order to establish acquaintanceship, and
then hit them on the head with a crowbar. He has grown
tired of this, however, because his sense of honor requires him
to think up a new joke for each victim, which can get to be a
bit of a strain, and has now embarked upon his grand project
to keep him legitimately i.e., logically, in mourning for the rest
of his life. He has collected five-hundred "speak-your-weight"
machines—weighing machines, common in England, which
not only show the person's weight but also announce it by
means of an internal recording device—and is teaching them
to sing the Hallelujah Chorus from Handel's *Messiah*. His
intention is to take them all to the North Pole, where he
hopes that the enormous crowds of people who will collect to
hear the machines will be so overcome with amazement that
they will jump up and down to relieve their feelings and thus
cause the earth's axis to shift. This should bring the British
Isles into the polar zone and cause a sufficient number of
people to freeze to death to keep Kirby in mourning for the
rest of his natural life. The details of this diabolical plot come

out at Kirby's trial, which takes place in the Groomkirby living room. Mr. Groomkirby, an amateur of the law, has bought a scale model of the Old Bailey Criminal Court and set it up. As soon as he plugs it in, a judge and other officers of the court appear and proceed to trial. Kirby is found guilty but is let off by the judge for the rather bizarre reason that putting him away would deprive the state of the opportunity of punishing him for any future crimes that he might commit if let go free.

N. F. Simpson's plays are perfect examples of the drama of protest and paradox that sprang directly out of Jarry's *Ubu roi*. Although clearly influenced also by Ionesco, he is of all the current avant-garde dramatists—French or English—perhaps the closest in spirit to Jarry himself.

The New English Dramatists

The Traditionalists

WITH PINTER and Simpson we come to the end of the experimentalists in the current English drama. The other writers in the English dramatic regeneration are entirely traditional in their technique. The form of any of Wesker's or Kops's or Osborne's plays in no way differs from the form employed by any of the prewar playwrights: it is a direct descendant of the nineteenth century well-made play. This may not seem to be a drawback at first. Form in the drama is, after all, not of primary importance. In drama, content is all-important. If the content of the drama is interesting, then the form of the drama, as long as it is not so disorganized as to interfere with comprehension of the plot, is comparatively unimportant. The form of the drama can, however, increase the scope of the content. A well-made play is confined to the drama of individual relationships and conflicts, whereas the drama of indefinite form (the avant-garde drama, for example) can take the whole cosmos as its field of action. Within their necessarily limited field of endeavor, however, the new dramatists of the traditionalist group do present fresh viewpoints. The new English drama, whether traditional in form and subject or whether imitative of the avant-garde, is a drama of rebellion. Like the French avant-gardists, the English writers are uniformly iconoclastic. Their purpose is protest against things as they are, and their method usually hinges on a central sardonic paradox. They are dramatists without illusions (with the exception of Kops and Wesker): they have looked conditions full in the face and have not flinched from what they have seen. This honesty and courage distinguishes the new English dramatists and differentiates them from their predecessors.

JOHN OSBORNE
"Angry Young Man"?

THE "NEW MOVEMENT" in the British drama actually began officially on the night of May 8, 1956, when John Osborne's *Look Back in Anger* opened at the Royal Court Theatre in London. The reviews in the daily newspapers the next day were in general cautiously favorable.[1] But it was not until Kenneth Tynan's review came out the following Sunday that the "movement" was properly launched. Tynan climaxed his panegyric by saying, "I agree that *Look Back in Anger* is likely to remain a minority taste. What matters, however, is the size of the minority. I estimate it at roughly 6,733,000, which is the number of people in this country between the ages of twenty and thirty. And this figure will doubtless be swelled by refugees from other age-groups who are curious to know precisely what the contemporary young pup is thinking and feeling. I doubt I could love anyone who did not wish to see *Look Back in Anger*. It is the best young play of its decade." [2] This will strike most people as pretentious, self-publicizing gush rather than criticism, but it had its effect. Overnight, Osborne, previously an obscure provincial actor, became famous; and sundry despairing young playwrights who had been furtively scribbling away in seedy rooming houses on the Earl's Court Road, in Hampstead, Hackney, Poplar, Whitechapel, and Newington Butts suddenly took heart and set to with renewed industry. They were fortunate. John Osborne's timing was

1. The full story of the reviews, with excerpts, is very well told in Taylor, *op. cit.*, pp. 31–32.
2. *The Observer*, May 13, 1956, p. 11.

precisely right. A few years earlier or a few years later *Look Back in Anger* might well have been passed off by the critics as callow breast-beating, but in 1956 the critics and the public were ready for something new. The sincerity of the Osborne play must have come as a tremendous relief after the seemingly endless stream of elephantiasis-afflicted plots trying to be fey that characterized the efforts of the fashionable West End dramatists. There was also the factor of the international success of Arthur Miller and Tennessee Williams. At last someone had appeared who could challenge the Americans' position as representatives of the English-speaking drama. Chauvinism stirred in the critics as they watched *Look Back in Anger*; and the angry-young-man movement was born. Now, one play doth not a movement make; hence the renewed scraping of pens in Earl's Court and Hackney. The new English playwrights got their chance because English national pride was aroused by the success of Osborne's first play.

Look Back in Anger was a rallying point. It came to represent the dissatisfaction with society reflected in the novels of such young writers as John Wain, Kingsley Amis, and John Braine. Jimmy Porter, its rancorous protagonist, was thought to symbolize the fury of the young postwar generation that felt itself betrayed, sold out, and irrevocably ruined by its elders.[3] The older generation had made a thorough mess of things, and there was nothing the new generation could do except withdraw (Jimmy Porter, an educated and cultured university graduate, supports himself by peddling candy in the streets) and indulge in the perverse and vicarious pleasure of nursing its resentment. Society is so rotten that there is no longer any point in attempting to be useful. It is not that Jimmy is *content* to stagnate. He just feels that he has no chance. His withdrawal is not one of choice. He does not even permit himself the consolation of gloating over conditions with the cynical hindsight of superiority. He simply feels

3. Taylor (*op. cit.*, pp. 40–45) recognizes that *Look Back in Anger* is basically a well-made, domestic-psychological drama, but he spoils his analysis by desperately trying to twist it into an angry-young-man play with the aid of isolated passages taken out of context.

himself to be unjustly crushed down with no visible hope of ever getting up again. He reminds one of a fighter who has been knocked down, and, instead of getting up again, just lies there spitting insults at his opponent and grinning with sardonic masochism whenever the latter kicks him in the ribs.

But is this what Osborne really intended when he wrote the play? Or has it been read into it by eager critics who have been searching for a symbol of a new postwar "lost generation" to rival Hemingway's creation of Jake Barnes as a personification of post-World War I disillusionment? Is Jimmy's defeatism a symbol of the numb quiescence of post-World War II youth, as Jake's castration was of the sterile euphoria of post-World War I youth?

John Osborne must have been the most surprised man in England when he suddenly found himself placed at the head of the angry-young-man movement.[4] He had written a carefully and intelligently worked out dramatic study of a psychotic marriage relationship and was hailed instead as the creator of a revolutionary literary movement. Certainly Jimmy Porter makes a good many cutting remarks about contemporary society, but he only makes them as a result of his own peculiar personality problems. There is absolutely no indication in the play that Osborne ever intended Jimmy's remarks to be taken as a general condemnation of society. Jimmy is an extremely unusual young man and anything but representative of the young men of our time. Osborne has not put his diatribes against society in his mouth in order to orate in the manner of a Hyde Park soap-box messiah. Instead, Jimmy's rantings are always the natural outgrowth of his psychotic state: they are a defense mechanism he uses to hurt his wife, whom he suspects of being imperfectly devoted to him, and to avoid facing up to the problem of his own helpless character. Granted that a representative of the generation which reached adulthood in the early fifties would execrate his elders (what generation

4. Osborne himself characterized *Look Back in Anger* as "a formal, rather old-fashioned play," and said that he did not dare "pick up a copy of *Look Back* nowadays. It embarrasses me." (John Osborne, "That Awful Museum," *Twentieth Century*, CLXIX [February, 1961], p. 216).

this side of early Victorianism has not?), his anger could hardly be embodied in Jimmy's rantings if any justice is to be done to him. He has a right to rant and he has a right to be heard; he has a right even to throw up his hands in disgust and retire, whether it be into a Zen or a beatnick euphoria or simply into a flabby, unthinking, irresponsible lassitude. But Jimmy's tirades are not representative of any attitude. Osborne has given Jimmy a certain facility in composing biting remarks, but there is no real sense, no mature criticism in those remarks. Examined closely, Jimmy Porter's self-conscious orations are the veritablest sophomoric piffle.

Look Back in Anger was strenuously fiddled up into an epoch-making play by the London critics. It is nothing of the sort; but, on the other hand, it is by no means a worthless play either. Osborne has created an excellent, minutely accurate dissection of a perverse marriage in the style of Strindberg. Look Back in Anger irresistibly recalls the Swedish author's Dance of Death. Jimmy Porter's problem is not the vicious injustice and hypocrisy of the social order: it is his suppressed awareness of the insoluble psychological paradox caused by his desperate, overriding need to possess a woman's complete, unquestioning love and his simultaneous constitutional inability to get along with anyone. His outbursts are the overflow of his bitterness whenever his wife fails to measure up to the standards of devotion that he expects of her at the same time that he knows them to be impossible. Jimmy's biting sarcasms are in a sense really directed inwardly against himself in the manner of the guilt-ridden Dostoyevskian hero who tortures himself by torturing others. His real purpose, as he deliberately tries to destroy his wife's love for him because it is not the love he had envisioned, is self-laceration. Jimmy is the sort of man who needs, but is too proud to demand, absolute devotion. He needs it all the more from Alison because she comes from the sort of upper-class family which he, as a good socialist, despises as useless and effete and which at the same time he envies and resents because he knows that it looks down on him. In order to possess her he has had to marry her and submit to the conventionality that he hates. His dilemma is perfectly

226 THE NEW ENGLISH DRAMATISTS

presented in Alison's description of his reaction to her virginity: "afterwards, he actually taunted me with my virginity. He was quite angry about it, as if I had deceived him in some strange way. He seemed to think that an untouched woman would defile him." [5] By being a virgin she is pulling him into the vortex of social convention. She is what she is *expected* to be in *her* circle. But Jimmy cannot show pleasure because that would be the conventional reaction, though if his wife were not virginal he would have to resent it as evidence of her fickleness. What he really wants, as Alison explains to her friend, Helena (who becomes Jimmy's mistress when Alison leaves him), is "something quite different from us. What it is exactly I don't know—a kind of cross between a mother and a Greek courtesan, a henchwoman, a mixture of Cleopatra and Boswell." [6] Jimmy's tragedy is simply that he will never find this ideal, and he knows it. He will spend the rest of his life bathed in self-pity, yammering impotently at the misfortunes he himself has created.

Osborne's second play, *The Entertainer* (1957), was a clumsily constructed hodgepodge about a talentless vaudeville actor with the morals and feelings of a toad. It is chiefly interesting as a first fumbling attempt at the Brechtian episodic method which Osborne used later in *Luther*.

Epitaph for George Dillon (1958) was actually Osborne's first play, written in collaboration with Anthony Creighton, but it was not produced until the success of *Look Back in Anger* had established Osborne's name as "safe." It deals with a lazy and basically untalented young man who is trying to become a playwright with a minimum of effort. Unable to get anyone interested in his laborious attempts at serious drama, he sells out to a producer of honky-tonk road shows, and then submerges himself completely in the bourgeois milieu that he despises by marrying the brainless daughter of the family that has been supporting him. Dillon is a heartless chiseler, but his

5. John Osborne, *Look Back in Anger* (New York: Bantam Books, 1959), p. 28.
6. *Ibid.*, p. 113.

fall is the fall of the artist who finds the inertia of society too much for him and just gives up.

Another interpretation that could be applied to the play is that it is about the fragility of artistic integrity. Dillon starts out by attempting to be a serious playwright. He tries to gain time and comfort by sponging off an ordinary, middle-class family. He amuses himself by playing the part of the great and enigmatic artist for their benefit and sniggering to himself whenever their backs are turned. But sooner or later his bluff has to be called, and he has to sell out to the honky-tonk promoter to save the image he has manufactured. Someone once said— it was Hemingway, I think—that an artist's integrity is like a woman's virginity: once lost it can never be regained. Dillon illustrates the truth of this perfectly. Once he has compromised himself he *has* to sell out and do hack work. Thus when the family swallows him up at the end, it seems natural and inevitable to us. The power of inner resistance can only be maintained by constant use, Osborne and Creighton are saying; George Dillon bends once and is lost.

By the time *Look Back in Anger* and *The Entertainer* were produced, Osborne had been hailed as the angry young man so much that he had actually become one. If there is a prototype of the angry-young-man play, *The World of Paul Slickey* is it. Written as a musical, it failed when first produced. And no wonder. There is so much direct criticism of society (castigation would perhaps be a better word) in it that just about everyone must have been made uncomfortable. When criticizing social institutions on the stage it is advisable to use the gentle touch if one wishes to have a successful show. People will accept the offhand slaps of a witty mind because if they can laugh at the object of the satire they can feel superior to it: nobody consciously identifies himself with ridiculousness. But even if they will allow themselves to be slapped under the illusion that someone else is being slapped, they will not allow themselves to be openly and directly attacked. Osborne is no George Dillon. He does not compromise. He does not slip unobtrusively under his opponent's guard: he

beats it down with a two-fisted attack. He is an angry young
man, not a contemptuous one. *The World of Paul Slickey* is
pure spit and vomit thrown directly into the teeth of the audience. Commercially it has been Osborne's least successful play;
artistically it is his best. Inability to compromise may be disastrous from a diplomatic viewpoint, but art is not diplomacy:
it is truth.

In his dedication Osborne leaves no doubt as to his intentions:

> No one has ever dedicated a string quartet to a donkey
> although books have been dedicated to critics. I dedicate
> this play to the liars and self-deceivers; to those who daily
> deal out treachery; to those who handle their professions
> as instruments of debasement; to those who, for a salary
> cheque and less, successfully betray my country; and those
> who will do it for no inducement at all. In this bleak time,
> when such men have never had it so good, this entertain-
> ment is dedicated to their boredom, their incomprehension,
> their distaste. It would be a sad error to raise a smile from
> them. A donkey with ears that could listen would no longer
> be a donkey; but the day may come when he is left behind
> because the other animals have learned to hear.[7]

During the play Osborne lashes out indiscriminately at, among
other things, the cold war, the arms race, parliamentary double
talk, scandalmongers, debased public taste, vindictive legal
punishment (a character sings a song advocating a return to
beheading because hanging is too crude), income-tax evasion
by the rich, popular songs, and the prostitution act (get them
off the streets: see no evil, hear no evil, speak no evil—just do
it!). All these criticisms are embodied in the songs scattered
throughout the work. The framework of the plot is directed
against love as practiced in the modern world, which Osborne
sees as merely passionless lust.

It is a pity that the intensity and frankness of the anger in
The World of Paul Slickey will always prevent its being popu-

7. John Osborne, *The World of Paul Slickey* (London: Faber &
Faber, Ltd., 1959), p. [5].

lar, for it is a good play. In it Osborne finally becomes the angry young man.

In *A Subject of Scandal and Concern* (1960) and *Luther* (1961), Osborne continues to be the angry young man, but he seems to have absorbed the lesson of *The World of Paul Slickey*. In these two plays Osborne attacks the establishment indirectly instead of leaving his glove in its face. Both plays concern historical characters, and Osborne leaves the implication very clear for us that "it could happen again."

Despite the fact that the play is about a trial that took place in 1842, the very title, *A Subject of Scandal and Concern*, indicates Osborne's sense of the immediacy and urgency of the problem. This short television play is about the trial of George Jacob Holyoake, who was the last person tried for the "crime" of blasphemy in England. Holyoake's offense consisted in stating publicly that he did not believe in God and that the amount of money spent on religion was criminally large in view of the fact that a great many people were living in a poverty which could be substantially relieved by the diversion of church funds to charitable purposes. Curiously enough, although George Holyoake was the last person actually to be imprisoned in England for the "crime" of blasphemy, it would still be dangerous from a social and professional standpoint, if not from a legal one, for a man in a responsible public position (Holyoake was a teacher) openly to proclaim his atheism. That, of course, is the point over which Osborne is exercised. He gets it across by having a modern lawyer serve as narrator to the play. He treats the action patronizingly, as befits a modern lawyer talking about an archaic legal problem, but at the end of the play it becomes evident that the lawyer, who has been sitting in a prison interview room, is about to represent a client in a case similar to Holyoake's.

Luther presents a more difficult problem. Written in an imitation of Brecht's epic style, it presents a series of historically accurate episodes from Luther's career. Osborne takes Luther from the time he is admitted into the Augustinian Order in 1506 to his declining years, when he is living with his wife and child in the now abandoned convent in which he celebrated his first mass. At the beginning of each scene a knight carrying a banner appears and "Briefly barks the time and place of the scene following at the audience." [8]

Osborne's main purpose in *Luther* is to continue in a less offensive way the angry young man literature expected of him. *The World of Paul Slickey* was unpalatable because an audience likes to identify with at least one of the characters in a play—but the world of Paul Slickey was inhabited by uniformly despicable characters. The only angry young man in that play was outside it—John Osborne in person, dribbling black bile and trying to spatter the audience with it. In *Luther*, however, the angry young man is the hero, and the audience can easily identify with this hero—a universally respected religious reformer dead over three hundred years.

There is no harm at all in identifying with such a man and in feeling indignation with him at society. It is easy to feel rebellious and indignant when society is represented by such as John Tetzel. We all notice that Tetzel is nothing but a Madison Avenue or Tottenham Court Road huckster, but the effort to transpose him is too much. He remains a sixteenth century figure—painless and harmless. In short, *Luther* is the sort of thing that might and should have been written during the second World War if England had been occupied by the Nazis. Anouilh's *Antigone* would not have been acclaimed as a very effective play if it had been produced in 1961 either. It must be said in Osborne's defense, however, that when he did write a completely honest play—*The World of Paul Slickey*—the public reacted as if their seats were fitted with slowly emerging spikes.

As long as Osborne sticks to his point, emasculated as it necessarily is by the transposition of time and place and by the inevitable intrusion of purely religious considerations, he does well. The scene in which Tetzel gives his sales oration is first-class writing and first-class drama. But this scene and one other are the only ones in which Osborne is able to make a point. The other scene is the one showing Luther's dispute

8. John Osborne, *Luther* (New York: Criterion Books, Inc., 1961), p. 11.

with Johan von Eck at the Diet of Worms, in which Eck makes
the now all too familiar plea that we must stick together and
that anyone who thinks differently or questions the status quo
is an enemy since he gives the real enemy the impression that
there is dissension and, consequently, dissatisfaction. Besides
this there is nothing but pretentious, overblown rhetoric—
Osborne simply lacks a poetic style—and sloppy symbolism.
Osborne's repeated references to Luther's constipation may
lead the spectator to believe that he attributes the rise of the
Reformation to the constant exacerbation of Luther's mind
and spirit by the stubborn flabbiness of his lower intestine—
a theory which I would be the last to reject. Who knows what
world-shaking events are really ultimately traceable to some
great man's irritation with the chambermaid's lack of complacency or with the inordinate activity of the fleas in his wig?
Osborne's theory is surely a valid one—but what is one to do
with an author who can write lines like these: "I'm like a ripe
stool in the world's straining anus, and at any moment we're
about to let each other go"? [9]

Since *Luther*, Osborne has written two short plays, *The
Blood of the Bambergs* and *Under Plain Cover*, produced together at the Royal Court Theatre in July, 1962, under the
collective title of *Plays for England*. They reveal only too
clearly what one is to do with him—leave him unproduced.
That these two plays were accepted by a professional manage-
ment is in itself incredible, and is a disturbing indication of
how far the directors of the Royal Court have become bemused
by the mirage of the "movement" which they initiated and
nursed along. *The Blood of the Bambergs* is so unbelievably
bad, so monumentally inept, that it would have earned its
author instant and deserved expulsion from any competently
taught amateur playwriting class. *Under Plain Cover* illustrates
the fact that Shaw's remark about the net result of the English
stage censorship being to let through embarrassingly tasteless
exhibitions while it bars serious discussions of sexual relationships is as true now as it was in the eighteen-nineties.

9. *Ibid.*, p. 55.

The genesis of these two plays is not difficult to reconstruct. What happened, probably, is that Osborne, feeling that it was time to write a new play, started casting about for fresh things to be angry at. He decided to be angry at (i) the phoniness and extravagances of royalty, and (ii) the prejudicial attitude which the bourgeoisie adopts toward people who amuse themselves with some of the gamier practices described by Krafft-Ebing.

The Blood of the Bambergs seems to have been vaguely inspired by the Anthony Armstrong-Jones–Princess Margaret wedding. At any rate, it involves the wedding of a photographer with royalty. The real bridegroom has been killed in a car crash while speeding to the ceremony. The preparations have been so elaborate and costly that the organizers do not dare call it off. They explain that the government will inevitably fall if the ceremony is not held and cast desperately about for a solution to their difficulty. They are about to give up in despair when (surprise! surprise!) they find, fast asleep in the deserted cathedral, an Australian photographer who is really an illegitimate son of the Prince of Bamberg and the dead prince's double. The rest of the play is merely a witless farrago of disorganized scenes, none of them germane to anything in real life.

The critics did not have anything good to say about *The Blood of the Bambergs*, but they were kinder to *Under Plain Cover*. Kenneth Tynan was the most enthusiastic, as usual. He found that "Mr. Osborne's courage is doubly flabbergasting: not only does he state the facts about a sadomasochistic *ménage*, he also refrains from condemning it." He goes on to say that "perhaps the most audacious statement ever made on the English stage" is that "an anal-sadistic relationship need not preclude love." [10]

The second of the *Plays for England* is about a young married couple whose pleasure it is to dress up in various costumes and act out sadomasochistic sexual fantasies. Between charades they indulge themselves in lengthy and incredibly boring fetishistic discussions of female underwear. After a bit, a newspaper reporter ambles on and informs us that, unbeknownst to them,

10. *The Observer*, July 22, 1962, p. 20.

Tim and Jenny are really brother and sister. Parted as little children, they met and fell in love as grownups (by a coincidence no more or less contrived than the convenient discovery of a bastard Bamberg snoozing in the cathedral), married, had two children, and lived happily with their fetishes and their charades. Tim and Jenny are parted, and Jenny marries someone else. She then runs away and returns to Tim. For seven years they live together in their old house, never once going out and presumably parading happily around in their underwear. Then the reporter appears again, and gives us what is presumably Osborne's message: "To Timothy and Jenny I leave this message. You can't escape the world. Even if you want to, it won't let you. Come out then, I say. Show yourselves. Be brave. Be courageous. Fear not. Fear not." [11] Osborne seems to be suggesting here that sexual perverts should flaunt their abnormalities publicly—or at least that they should be permitted to do as they please. But the problem, surely, is that they find it necessary to do it. The immaturity of Osborne's thought processes can be seen by comparing *Under Plain Cover* to Pinter's *The Lover*, which deals with very much the same theme. Pinter's treatment is sophisticated, accurate, witty, and meaningful; Osborne's is jejune and tasteless. Instead of being a protest, *Under Plain Cover* is only the cheaply sensational story it purports to be protesting against.

It is doubtful that anything significant can be expected from John Osborne after *Plays for England*. He has become a victim of his own critical success. Left alone, he might have developed into a modestly talented writer of competently constructed, slightly acidulous hack plays. The strong streak of trite sentimentality which marred *Look Back in Anger* would undoubtedly have taken over had Osborne not been promoted into the figurehead of a new "movement," and he would have peacefully joined the ranks of the television and provincial repertory company playwrights. Osborne is now committed to being angry; but he got all his anger off his chest in *The World of Paul Slickey*. In *Luther* he tackled a subject far beyond his

11. John Osborne, *Plays for England* (London: Faber & Faber, Ltd., 1963), pp. 135–36.

intellectual powers. The result was ludicrous rather than enlightening. In *Plays for England* he is preaching—and making no more sense than if he were fulminating from a real pulpit.

ARNOLD WESKER
"Awake and Sing" in *Whitechapel*

SOME TWENTY odd years ago Clifford Odets wrote *Awake and Sing*, a play about Jewish family life in the Bronx. The play had a success in its day, though it was never very good, and then faded out. A production of *Awake and Sing* in the United States nowadays would be as anachronistic as a May Day parade down Fifth Avenue. Not so in England. Inspired by the hopeful, before-the-fact announcements of the critics that England is experiencing a dramatic renaissance under the second Elizabeth to rival the one under the first, Arnold Wesker has written a trilogy that does for the Jews of London's East End what *Awake and Sing* did for the Jews of the Bronx.

Wesker's trilogy is an extremely curious piece of work. Partly, I suspect, because Wesker is the first English playwright to announce anything as impressive as a trilogy of connected plays, and partly because Wesker himself has done a great deal of self-conscious talking about the "seriousness" of his art, it has had a distinct *succès d'estime* in England. The English look upon the Wesker trilogy as their answer to *Mourning Becomes Electra*: Englishmen can write epics about crumbling families too. Wesker, then, was extremely shrewd when he announced that he intended to write a trilogy. He was shrewd because (i) the series of plays is not a trilogy (the second play, *Roots*, is, strictly speaking, not connected to the other two plays at all); (ii) it assured the production of the last two plays once the first was produced; and (iii) the designation of "trilogy" gave the work an appearance of profundity, just as Galsworthy had given *his* scenes eavesdropped from family life an appearance of profundity 52 years earlier by calling them a "saga." Just how shrewd he was we can see from J. R. Taylor's remark that "he has already been hailed as 'the most promising and exciting young dramatist to come into the English theatre since the end of the war,' and the eventual performance of all three Wesker Trilogy plays in sequence at the Royal Court in 1960 found the critics almost without exception ready to bring out their most unequivocally enthusiastic adjectives, and hail the work as an unparalleled achievement." [1]

The trilogy is often called the "Chicken Soup trilogy" after the name of the first play, *Chicken Soup with Barley*. The other two plays are *Roots* and *I'm Talking About Jerusalem*, and the whole trilogy concerns the fortunes of a family of London East End Jews from 1936 to 1959. Actually only the first and third plays deal with the family. *Roots* is about an entirely different family, a family of Norfolk farmhands which is indirectly affected by a member of the Jewish family.

The stories of the plays are briefly told and are, in fact, comparatively unimportant. The real substance of the plays is in the quips and in the little pathetic vignettes scattered here and there throughout them. It takes no great perception to see that Wesker's literary forebears were the play doctors of the popular Yiddish theatre.

Chicken Soup with Barley (1958) is the story of the Kahn family. The family consists—naturally—of a strong mother; a weak father; a beautiful, sweet, and innocent young daughter of the biblical Ruth variety; and a brilliant, confused son whose portrayal is so blatantly autobiographical as to be positively embarrassing. In drawing Ronnie Kahn, the hero of the trilogy, Wesker seems to have compiled a catalog of all the clichés of adolescent behavior.

The whole trilogy is essentially the story of Ronnie's growing pains. In *Chicken Soup with Barley* Wesker shows us Ronnie's exposure as a child to the spirit of militant Communism prevalent among most East End Jews of the nineteen-thirties. Wesker portrays this Communism as purely nonideological, a reaction against the economic injustices of depression slum life rather than a rationally held belief. As Ronnie grows

1. Taylor, *op. cit.*, p. 143.

up, his character is formed by his fear, on the one hand, of becoming a failure like his weak-willed father, and, on the other, by his rebellion against his strong-willed, domineering mother. At the end of the play Ronnie, now twenty-five years old, comes back from Paris, where he has been working as a cook (just as Wesker himself did) and tells his mother that he has lost his faith in life and doesn't care about anything anymore. His confession is accompanied by much breaking of the voice, turning of head to wall, and impotent clutching of air. The literary style of the play as a whole might be described as Yiddish lachrymose.

Roots (1959) is about a young girl's visit to her family back on the farm. Beatie Bates has been away for three years, and now she has come back to the lonely flatlands of Norfolk where the men of her family have been farm laborers for generations, full of news about the man she hopes to marry. She has been working as a waitress in a café and has met and fallen in love with a fellow worker, a self-educated "intellectual." Throughout the play she tries to prepare her family for Ronnie's visit. He never appears, but he is the play's invisible protagonist. Practically everything Beatie says is a quotation from Ronnie— "Ronnie say . . ." and "Ronnie do it this way . . ."—until we almost feel that Ronnie is some sort of dybbuk speaking through Beatie. None of the other members of the family can understand this sort of talk. To them life is working on the land, cooking, eating, sleeping, drinking, and meekly accepting whatever happens. Reading is the daily tabloid. Recreation is popular music and movies. Talking is gossip. Into this atmosphere Beatie comes with her discussions of politics and moral problems, her classical music, her abstract painting, her books —and her quotations from Ronnie. For two weeks she pesters and reproaches her mother for her Philistinism and tries to change her with arguments from the fountainhead. But her mother remains unaffected. At the end of the two weeks Ronnie himself is supposed to arrive, and the family gather nervously around, creaking uncomfortably in their best clothes, to do him honor. Instead of Ronnie, however, a letter from him arrives. In it he tells Beatie that their relationship has been

a failure: for three years she has fought him, refused to listen
to him, made fun of his beliefs. She has refused to listen to his
kind of music, refused to read his kind of books, refused to
discuss his kind of politics, and derided his intellectual conversation and that of his friends. He has tried, he tells her, to
devote all his energies to making at least one human being better; and his experience with her has convinced him that it cannot be done. Beatie is shattered, and her mother, who is the
type that likes to exalt her ignorance into a virtue, crows
triumphantly that "the apple doesn't fall far from the tree."

Beatie's reaction to the letter is the turning point of the
play. Up to this it has appeared to be chiefly a cheap satire on
"pseudointellectualism," with Beatie's ridiculous aping of
Ronnie's attitudes and her Norfolk Ma Kettle mother's corn-
ball common-sense deflations. In short, television-level drama.
After her initial shock has worn off, Beatie turns on her complacent, self-satisfied family, who are openly pleased at her collapse, and starts tongue-lashing them. At first, tearfully and
angrily stammering, she bravely swallows her pride and prefaces
her accusations with the customary "Ronnie say . . ." Gradually during the long scene she gains confidence, forgets herself,
forgets Ronnie finally, becomes carried away. She says the same
things Ronnie has always said, but for the first time she says
them in her own words because for the first time she herself really believes them. For three years she has lived with
Ronnie and fought him and derided him exactly as her mother
has fought and derided her, but now at last she believes. Her
family and she were wrong; Ronnie, the intellectual whose
quoted clichés have been ridiculed throughout the play, was
right. The curtain falls on Beatie jubilantly shouting, "It can
be done, Ronnie . . ."

With this last scene Wesker alters the whole meaning of
his play, or, rather, gives it a meaning. What had seemed to
be a reassuring pat on the back for the fools and Philistines becomes a bold vindication of the intellectual's Weltanschauung,
made all the stronger by the sudden turnabout. The painstak-
ing realism of the first part of the play, the precise transcrip-
tion of the obvious, repetitive, cliché-ridden conversation, al-

most as if Wesker had been prowling around with a tape recorder under his coat, turns out to be a condemnation rather than a glorification. The only really serious objection that one can make against the play is that Wesker has put the commonly heard clichés of pseudointellectuals into Ronnie's mouth instead of something really sensible.

The less said about the final play in the Chicken Soup trilogy the better. I'm Talking About Jerusalem (1960) is an unmitigated disaster. Once again Wesker is trying to treat a theme of social significance in terms of his Jewish working-class family and once again he is unable to do anything except write Yiddish theater clichés. In Chicken Soup with Barley Wesker had tried to show the East End Jew's involvement in the Communist movement of the nineteen-thirties as a largely instinctive antifascist reaction. In I'm Talking About Jerusalem Dave Simmonds, Ronnie Kahn's brother-in-law, who had gone to fight for the Spanish Loyalists in Chicken Soup with Barley, tries to practice a sort of William Morris-type socialism in the Norfolk fields. Disillusioned by his experiences in Spain and in World War II, Dave decides that mass movements will never build Jerusalem (i.e., the ideal state of life on earth): only individual action will build individual Jerusalems. He and his wife decide to retire into the isolation of the Norfolk fens and live off the land, doing everything for themselves, relying on no one. Ronnie is still the hero since Wesker tells everything from his point of view—in other words, what we see is not so much Dave's experience in living but rather how Dave's experience affects Ronnie.

Dave's attempt to put socialism into action on an individual basis fails, as one English critic admiringly puts it, not only because of "the debased values of a hostile society debauched by materialism and its by-product cynicism," but also because of "inherent weakness" in Dave's own character.[2] This is perfectly true: the only thing wrong with it as a critical statement is that it is written admiringly. Wesker is obviously trying to write a play about individual socialism in action. Such a play

2. Robert Muller in Arnold Wesker, I'm Talking About Jerusalem (Middlesex, England: Penguin Books, 1960), p. 7.

can be significant only if it deals with the reasons why individual socialism is impossible today. Wesker's play fails to achieve significance because it deals mainly with one man's psychology. This is not to say that character drawing is unimportant. Of course the characters must be well-rounded, motivated people and not puppets on strings labeled "social forces." But the characters themselves must not cause the failure of this experiment. It *is* important to put individual socialism into practice today because of the "debased values of a hostile society, debauched by materialism and its by-product cynicism." To show, as Wesker does, that individual socialism is impossible because the person who practices it is congenitally stupid is defeating his own purpose. Wesker's main concern, however, is to show the effect of Dave's failure on the awkward, mawkish adolescent, Ronnie. Ronnie, according to Wesker, grows up a little more. At the end of the play he bursts into tears for the umpteenth time in the two plays of the trilogy in which he appears and then, affirming, I suppose, that Dave's failure is really in some mysterious sense a triumph, he yells, "We must be bloody mad to cry." On this sophomoric note the play and the trilogy closes.

The extent to which Wesker's reputation in England has been built up on the strength of the Chicken Soup trilogy is absolutely extraordinary. Wesker is regarded as the theater's leading creative thinker and even his most naïve outbursts are received with the sort of respect one imagines the more gullible among the ancient Greeks reserved for the latest bulletins from Delphi. Since the success of the trilogy, Wesker's earliest play, *The Kitchen*, has been produced, published, and made into a film. It has been received with the reverence usually accorded to the juvenilia of the masters.[3] *The Kitchen* is based on Wesker's experience as an apprentice pastrycook in Paris and Norwich. Naturally there is a Jewish pastrycook with an all-embracing love of humanity in the play—a sort of Whitmanesque figure constantly gazing into eggyolks to see the halo

3. Lawrence Kitchin, for example, calls it "a compressionist masterpiece." (Lawrence Kitchin, "Backwards and Forwards," *Twentieth Century*, CLXIX [February, 1961], p. 170).

I

round his head. Wesker himself has explained what he was trying to do in the play in these words: "The world might have been a stage for Shakespeare, but to me it is a kitchen: where people come and go and cannot stay long enough to understand each other, and friendships, loves, and enmities are forgotten as quickly as they are made."[4] Two things are notable about this remark: the willy-nilly dragging in of Shakespeare as a point of reference in order to show that the "New English Drama" represents a renaissance analogous to that of Elizabethan times; and the blissfully unconscious bathos of the comparison. From *Welttheater* to *Küche*. From a panorama of humanity to burnt crêpes suzettes, sausages and eggs, and fried flounder.

The Kitchen (1959) is what the French might describe as a *tranche de veau* drama. We see the kitchen of a large restaurant with the cooks standing round a huge circle of ovens performing their various specialties. The hero is the boiled-fish cook, a lunatic German who is having an affair with a married waitress. There is also an Irish fish-frier who keeps lamenting his fate in a rich brogue, an Italian pastrycook, the aforementioned Jewish pastrycook, another German cook, and a number of Cypriot chefs. The play consists largely of a series of vignettes between various chefs and waitresses. As might be expected, these vignettes deal with the usual stock situations of melodrama. There is the situation of the hero-cook and his waitress girl friend, who is pregnant by him but is reluctant to get rid of her well-to-do husband. There is the waitress who sprays plates of boiling Brown Windsor soup all over the place as she faints from the results of an attempted abortion; and of course there is the plain, elderly waitress who calls the German cook a dirty Boche when he annoys her.

What Wesker is trying to get across in this play is the lack of mutual understanding and affection between people—even between people who are constantly thrown closely together, such as the workers in the kitchen. Each person stands at his particular station around the huge stove, absorbed in his own

4. Thomas Maschler, ed., *New English Dramatists 2*, p. 7.

visions and totally unable to understand his neighbor. This is essentially the same theme that we find in Arthur Miller's *A Memory of Two Mondays*, in which the young hero realizes at the end that the people with whom he has worked in the automotive parts warehouse have not really been aware of his existence: they have just been going through the motions to keep the illusion of communication they need so much. It is instructive to compare Miller's method of getting his point across, for it gives us a capsule contrast between a mature playwright and a juvenile one. Miller's method is objective and demonstrative—he shows you what is happening and lets you observe it and learn from it; Wesker's method is subjective and explanatory: he beats the audience over the head with his moral and carefully holds the magnifying glass over his bleeding heart for us.

In 1961 Wesker published an article in which he reviewed his past work and made some predictions about his future. He concluded the article by saying, "I am becoming more conscious of style, and I bet the rest of my plays are no bloody good." [5] Wesker has proved himself to be a very on-and-off sort of prophet in the event: his next play, *Chips with Everything*, showed absolutely no increasing consciousness of style.

Chips with Everything opened at the Royal Court Theatre, London, on April 27, 1962. The scene is a Royal Air Force basic training camp, in which a group of new recruits has just arrived. The group, like the cooks in *The Kitchen*, is a variously assorted one, including the inevitable Jew, the Cockney, the Northern industrial slum boy, the Scotsman, and, most important of all for Wesker's purposes, the upper-class boy in rebellion against society. For *Chips with Everything* is not about the cruelty and stupidity of the military basic training routine, but about the ever-looming British class conflict.

Arnold Wesker has never been able to rid himself of the deep-seated inferiority complex he seems to have developed as a result of being born into the working classes. He appears to be unaware of the fact that, long before he was born, Shaw's

5. Arnold Wesker, "Art Is Not Enough," *Twentieth Century*, CLXIX (February, 1961), p. 192.

Pygmalion demonstrated that the so-called English class distinctions are pure, meaningless illusion, nor has he troubled to open his eyes to the fact that in modern England even these illusions have ceased to exist any more. In present-day England class distinctions have disappeared for all practical intents and purposes. It is no longer necessary even to change one's accent in order to get ahead. But to Wesker, class distinctions have not yet become the occasion for derisive laughter they now are for all normal Englishmen. He is still angry at the injustice of it all. Furthermore, he does not show his anger by spitting venom at what he dislikes, as Osborne's Paul Slickey does: his method is to whine, to hold his bleeding heart up to us and tell us how much it hurts. What Wesker does in this latest instalment of his saga of English *Klassenschmerz* is to show how "Pip" Thompson, the son of a banker and former general, who rebels against his background by enlisting in the ranks and refusing to become an officer, is broken by the "system." Thompson at first stirs up his fellow recruits against the officers and makes his stand when he refuses to participate in bayonet practice. The climactic scene of the play comes when Thompson is brought back to the bayonet range and charges the dummy, screaming maniacally. The breaking down is accomplished by a junior officer, who informs Thompson that the upper classes are invincible, that they see right through him, and that no act of rebellion he could ever think up could make the slightest dent in their self-assurance. Thompson thereupon gives up, charges the dummy, and becomes an officer. There are two good scenes in the play (the revolt in the recreation hut and the theft from the coal dump), but they depend for their effect exclusively on pantomime. Whenever a character has to talk, the writing becomes embarrassingly gauche. The most level-headed of the British reviewers was, predictably, the anonymous one in the *Times Literary Supplement*:

> . . . the play is a neat polemical exercise derived from the basic (highly arguable) assumption that service life is a microcosm of civil life, the class struggle and so on, and using all the resources of the theatre to bludgeon the point

home . . . one becomes uncomfortably conscious that for a good political cartoon a clear grasp of the real facts is required before they can be adapted to the particular requirements at hand. There are parts of *Chips with Everything* which are so blatantly far from the truth—any sort of truth —that the spectator rebels, and once the theatrical spell is off him there may not be very much left.[6]

It is instructive to compare this with the remarks of the journalistic reviewers, who, for the most part, went into an ecstasy of cringing abasement before the light of Wesker's "genius." [7]

In his desperate attempt to produce a working-class literature that would imitate the real life of ordinary people, Wesker has paradoxically been able to produce only a caricature of real life based on all the century-old literary stock situations. He has achieved precisely the opposite of what he wished to achieve. His drama is no more representative of the real life of the working classes than Mr. Crummles's was. Crummles and his type of company puffed out pipe dreams for the working classes so that they could temporarily forget the misery of their reality. Wesker puffs out pipe dreams for our contemporary, unctuously self-conscious "socially aware" intellectuals, who like to see visions of a working class that is both hairy-chested and introspective.

6. *Times Literary Supplement*, August 10, 1962, p. 606.
7. Harold Hobson in *Sunday Times*, May 6, 1962, p. 41: "*Chips With Everything* is the first anti-Establishment entertainment of which the Establishment need be afraid. It is this because it is a magnificent play, exceedingly funny, yet of complete tragic seriousness, informed with a passion which, despite its intensity, is always under control; and because it attacks the Establishment, not in some crumbling outpost which any intelligent Tory would be glad to abandon, but in the centre of its strength and the heart of its goodness. As no other play of its kind has done, it rises to the height and grandeur of its argument and purpose." Or Bernard Levin in *Daily Express*, May 6, 1962, p. 27: "It is shot through with Mr. Wesker's anger and compassion, throbbing with love and life, rocking with laughter. For sheer exhilaration, for the feeling it generates that it is good to be alive on the same planet as the author, it is his best play yet."

BERNARD KOPS
The Jew as "Everyman"

ACCORDING TO THE Bible, Judaism is a patriarchal religion; and indeed Jewish families always dutifully pay lip service to the father as the nominal head of the household. His position in the household, however, is somewhat like that of the President of France under the Third Republic: his function is mainly to find a new wife when the old one dies. The real power in the Jewish family resides with the mother, and young men like Bernard Kops and Arnold Wesker, who have been brought up in traditional Jewish families, usually grow up with what is best described as an unwhelped Oedipus complex: runny-nosed mama's boys looking up worshipfully at the all-encompassing Mother Earth figure. A few trips to those Yiddish theaters still remaining will convince anyone of this. The mothers are always large-bosomed, domineering figures and the fathers hollow-chested, runty little men skipping along behind their wives like coracles towed in the wakes of galleons. Watching Yiddish drama one wonders how the children were ever begot.

If Arnold Wesker demonstrates the disastrous consequences to the potential playwright of being formed in a traditional Jewish household, Bernard Kops demonstrates his possible salvation. This salvation lies in humor: if you can laugh at your heritage, you can transcend it.

This is precisely what has happened to Bernard Kops, another one of the promising young sparks of the "New English Dramatists" movement. Kops's work, like Wesker's, has been entirely determined by his Jewish heritage. So far he has published three plays: *The Hamlet of Stepney Green, The Dream of Peter Mann,* and *Enter Solly Gold.* Of these the second is an unfortunate attempt at writing a Jewish folk play in expressionistic style, while the other two are simple Jewish folk plays set in contemporary London but modeled on the type of Jewish folk literature written by Sholom Aleichem or Isaac Babel.

The Hamlet of Stepney Green and *Enter Solly Gold* are
opposite sides of the same coin. In the former, Kops takes
himself seriously and fails; in the latter, he does not take himself seriously and succeeds. It is as simple as that, and the lesson
for the Jewish playwright is inescapable. The Jew is apt to be
extremely emotional and to have a sharp, self-critical sense of
humor. Extreme emotion is dangerous on the stage at the best
of times. It is successful only when it is entirely impersonal
and objective, as in Shakespeare and in the Greek drama. The
Jewish form of emotion, as portrayed by Kops, is, however,
strictly of the breast-beating, mea culpa type, sung solo with
wailing-wall chorus obbligato; and this makes for embarrassed
rather than sympathetic audiences. Another drawback to Kops's
serious plays is that serious plays require some sort of philosophical orientation. When a man writes a serious play he has
to take a definite position with respect to his view of reality.
Now, Kops, though a first-class humorist, is anything but a
thinker. He feels that the world is really a wonderful place and
that everything would be all right if people would only jiggle
around flapping their arms and smiling through. To Kops
reality is one long, manic vaudeville act.

The Hamlet of Stepney Green (1958) transposes Shakespeare's hero to Stepney Green, one of the seedier districts of
Jewish East London. Hamlet becomes David Levy, a young
and rather feeble-minded good-for-nothing who wants to be a
crooner instead of following in his father's footsteps as a
pushcart peddler:

> DAVID: I want to be a crooner—I want to be a king
> —to be looked at—to be looked up to. I want people to
> nudge each other as they pass and say 'Look! there goes
> David Levy—the most famous—fabulous crooner in the
> world.' I want to hear my voice blaring from the record
> shops as I whizz by in my Jaguar—I want to switch on the
> radio—any time—and any day and hear my voice on records.
>
> . . . .
>
> I'd stun them—I'd be the greatest thing—don't ya see—

> I want to make people happy—I'VE GOT TO MAKE
> them listen—they'd love me.[1]

Hamlet's father becomes Sam Levy, Whitechapel's leading pickled-herring peddler. Sam has a habit of moving his bed into the back garden and announcing his death. One day he really does die out there, and David, thinking his father's last words accuse his mother of poisoning him, becomes even more cracked than before. The rest of the play concerns David's relations with his father's ghost who comes back to try and straighten him out—a fairly hopeless task. At the end of the play everything is resolved as David decides to become a singing herring peddler, and the ghost fades away announcing the moral of the play:

> Make the most of your youth—because youth is a wreath
> of roses—make the most of your life—because life is a holi-
> day from the dark—make the most of the world—because it
> is YOUR WORLD—because the world is a wedding—so—
> Let the wedding continue—.[2]

In *The Dream of Peter Mann* (1960) the hero has become a clothes peddler who dreams the world is coming to an end. He meets a tramp who persuades him to steal his mother's money and come away with him. While he is trying to get the money out of the safe, the safe falls on his head and he has the dream that is the main part of the play. In the dream Peter Mann—the name indicates that Peter is an Everyman symbol —comes back after twelve years of digging for uranium to find that everyone in his local pushcart market is also digging. He rallies them and persuades them all to go to work for him. In the next scene of the dream he has organized shroud factories all over the world. The shrouds are to be a protection against the Bomb, which duly explodes after Kops has let off a great many obvious, clumsily put reasons why it shouldn't. When Peter finds himself alone in the world, he wakes up, marries (of course), and bounds off into the middle distance spouting the following:

1. E. Martin Browne, ed., *New English Dramatists* (Middlesex, England: Penguin Books, 1959), pp. 108–109.
2. *Ibid.*, p. 170.

Don't you see—you can always make money, but you can't always make merry. You're saving up for nothing, going nowhere, hoarding nothing, losing—everything—What will YOU bid for LIFE? Here it is. A kiss in the dark. The one and only—all shapes and sizes—lovely, lousy, terrible, terrific. Magnificent! Ridiculous! But it's the only one we've got. A great opportunity never to be repeated—a unique bargain—going—going—so make the most of it before it's gone! [3]

When we come to *Enter Solly Gold* (published 1961) it is quite a different story. The plot is basically the same, but the approach is different. Once again we have the talkative, picaresque Jewish rogue, but this time that is all he is. Solly Gold has no notion of being a world-betterer. He spouts no juvenile pronunciamentos on how to live or on what to do about the bomb: he simply has fun. Solly's one idea in life is that getting a job is the ultimate horror. He starts out by confiscating some chickens by posing as a chicken inspector. Then he dresses up as a rabbi and peddles his chickens from door to door by announcing that it is the Rabbinical Chicken Sunday of the American Reform Orthodox Proxy Rabbi's Association. Finally he succeeds in convincing a harried millionaire that he (the millionaire) is the Messiah—or will be when Solly Gold has taken all his money. At the end, of course, poetic justice is served with Solly losing everything. The curtain falls as he picks cigarette butts out of the gutter and contemplates further grandiose confidence plans.

The contrast between Kops's first two plays and *Enter Solly Gold* is amazing. It seems hardly possible that the first two exercises in sophomoric philosophy were written by the same man who wrote the gay and witty *Enter Solly Gold*. And yet Kops seems to have committed the unforgivable crime in the eyes of the English critics by writing *Enter Solly Gold*. He is no longer part of the upsurge of the British drama. He is guilty of not being serious, which puts him on the level of Terence Rattigan (though Rattigan has of late been hailed, with breath-bereaving

3. Bernard Kops, *The Dream of Peter Mann* (Middlesex, England: Penguin Books, 1960), pp. 85–86.

insouciance, as a convert to the New English Dramatists because of *Ross*, his "study" of T. E. Lawrence). The latest round up of "new dramatists" (in *Twentieth Century*, February, 1961) does not even mention Kops. It seems he will not merit the favor of the English critics until he returns to the schoolboy solemnities of his two earlier plays. As Mervyn Johns says admiringly in his preface to *The Dream of Peter Mann*, the New English Dramatists had the effect of someone playing a guitar in a cathedral.[4] That appears to be the idea of daring and originality held by the English critics who are fostering the new movement.

DORIS LESSING
The Angry Young Cocoon

WITH DORIS LESSING, a British colonial writer who is known primarily as a novelist, the angry-young-man school of the New English Dramatists takes a new turn. More objective and realistic than Osborne, Miss Lessing shows contemporary society as it is rather than as she interprets it. In the angry-young-man drama the angry young man is always the author, who shows his irritation either by purposely exaggerating some aspects of society for satiric effect or by putting ranting, soap-box denunciations into the mouth of his hero. This is all very well, but it is purely subjective and gives us one man's view of society only. The fact is—and it must be painfully obvious to anyone who takes the trouble to keep his eyes open—that although there may be some angry young authors in contemporary society, there are no angry young men. The angry young man is a mythical creation born in the minds of some writers—novelists for the most part—who use it to criticize the complacency and inequity of society. What society is actually composed of is young men who are the very opposite of angry. Or, rather, if they are angry at all, they are angry at those who would force them to be involved in the problem

4. *Ibid.*, p. 9.

of society and therefore angry at it. The real representative of the younger generation is the angry anti-angry young man—the angry young cocoon.

Such a young man is the hero of Doris Lessing's *Each His Own Wilderness* (1958). Tony Bolton is twenty-two and the typical post-World War II young man. He has just come home from his two year stretch in the army, which he has served willingly and unthinkingly, and indeed, rather enjoyed: "Rather nice, the army—being told what to do, everything in its place, everything tidy . . ." [1] His one thought now is to settle down, to have a home and security. Politics does not interest him, and he has successfully anesthetized himself to the potentially mortal dangers of the international situation. In fact, modern young man—and Miss Lessing has observed him with amazing accuracy—has paradoxically reverted to the ideal of midnine-teenth-century woman—all he wants is *Kinder, Kirche, und Küche*. Tony's clash is with his mother, who belongs to the generation which grew up in the social turbulence of the nine-teen-thirties, when there really *were* angry young men. Myra Bolton is a totally unregenerate survivor of those times. Her whole life still revolves around social issues, and she spends all her time organizing committees to warn people against the Bomb and making plans to chain herself to the railings of the House of Commons in order to make her protest more effec-tive. She is, in fact, a sort of female Lord Russell. The only effect all this has on her son is to make him squirm with embar-rassment at the lack of social dignity implied in such actions. Tony, a representative of the younger generation, is a perfect prig. His only anger is directed against those who would draw him out of his cocoon of safe conventionality. His mother's carefree Bohemianism and humanitarian idealism mean noth-ing to him. All he wants to do is settle down placidly in his house and be left alone to live his life in a tight circle of secu-rity. The climax of the play comes when he learns that his mother has sold the house so that he can have money to travel around and enjoy himself. Mother and son realize that, coming

1. E. Martin Browne, ed., *op. cit.*, p. 15.

from different generations, they come from different worlds: they will never understand each other. He is furious that his carefully woven cocoon has been broken, and she, paradoxically, is the one who wants to go out into the world to seek more adventure:

> I'm nearly 50—and it's true there's nothing much to show for it. Except that I've never been afraid to take chances and make mistakes. I've never wanted security and safety and the walls of respectability—you damned little petty-bourgeois. My God, the irony of it—that *we* should have given birth to a generation of little office-boys and clerks and . . . little people who count their pensions before they're out of school . . . little petty–bourgeois.[2]

To which the younger generation's only reply is,

> . . . listen—never in the whole history of the world have people made a battle-cry out of being ordinary. Never. Supposing we all said to the politicians—we refuse to be heroic. We refuse to be brave. We are bored with all the noble gestures—what then . . . Leave us alone, we'll say. Leave us alone to live. Just leave us alone . . .[3]

SHELAGH DELANEY
The Drama of Alienated Youth

IN MAY, 1958, the Theatre Royal in Stratford, East London, which, under Joan Littlewood's direction, had become the leading experimental theater in England, produced a new play by a nineteen-year-old girl. The play was Shelagh Delaney's *A Taste of Honey* and it was an immediate success, so much so, indeed, that it was later moved to a West End theater and produced on Broadway soon thereafter. According to the story circulated at the time, Shelagh Delaney had been working as an usher in a theater and had become so fed up with the gritless pap being dribbled at the audiences that she decided to sit

2. *Ibid.*, p. 94.
3. *Ibid.*, p. 95.

down and do better herself. Sit down and do better is precisely
what she did when she turned out *A Taste of Honey*. To put
criticism of *A Taste of Honey* on its most elementary level,
there is at least nothing in the play that resembles what Helen,
one of its characters, complains of in the modern drama: "The
cinema," says Helen, "has become more and more like the theater, it's all mauling and muttering, can't hear what they're
saying half the time and when you do it's not worth listening
to." [1] Miss Delaney is talking about the general incompetence
of most present-day actors and the equally widespread unim-
portance of contemporary plays here, and she has taken particular care to avoid any suspicion of this sort of thing in her
first play.

A *Taste of Honey*, like so many other good modern plays,
sees the human condition as one of loneliness. In choosing this
theme—or rather, in having it chosen for her, since an artist is
compelled by his view of society—Shelagh Delaney tacks herself
on to the avant-garde movement of Beckett, Ionesco, Genet,
and Adamov, all of whom use the feeling of alienation from
the world and from its other inhabitants as their leading theme.

Miss Delaney's method of demonstrating the impossibility
of communication without at the same time "mauling and
muttering so that you can't hear what they're saying half the
time" is the direct-address technique. The two leading characters of *A Taste of Honey*, Helen and her daughter Jo, address
their opinions about each other directly to the audience so that
as far as the latter are concerned the barriers between people
are broken down. Essentially the device is the old nineteenth-
century technique of taking "asides" to the audience, brought
up to date by rapid-fire delivery and constant, almost imperceptible, switching back and forth from the actor to the audience. The result is very effective direct dramatic irony, with
the two characters remaining strangers to each other while the
audience is privy to their real thoughts. [2]

Shelagh Delaney resembles the current avant-garde writers

1. Shelagh Delaney, *A Taste of Honey* (London: Methuen & Co.,
Ltd., 1962), p. 27.
2. J. R. Taylor (*op. cit.*, p. 114) says that this device was one of
Joan Littlewood's contributions.

as far as theme is concerned, but she differs in technique. Her plays are not "theatre of the absurd," in which a segment of life is taken out of its context and exaggerated or distorted until the action itself becomes a wryly satiric commentary on reality. The Delaney plays are pure realism, slices taken directly from the life of the industrial North of England milieu in which the author was born and raised.

In A *Taste of Honey* Miss Delaney tells the story of a mother and daughter who never really come into contact with each other. The mother, who is described as a "semi-whore," earns just enough from her occasional encounters with men to keep them going. During the course of the play, one of her admirers, a man ten years younger than she, inexplicably marries her and she cheerfully abandons her daughter. The latter consoles herself with a brief affair with a passing Negro sailor and is nursed through her pregnancy by a young homosexual. Just before the birth of the child the mother comes back, chases the homosexual out, and takes over her daughter's problems herself. One gets the idea that nothing is solved and that the two will reach the same impasse as before.

The Lion in Love, so far Shelagh Delaney's only other play, was first produced in September, 1960, at the Belgrade Theatre, Coventry, and later moved to London. This play has even less of a definite plot than A *Taste of Honey*. It is simply a series of episodes in the life of an extremely unconventional family living in a semibombed out house in the North of England. Miss Delaney's implicit theme of revolt consists in the unexpected and unorthodox events within the framework of conventional family drama. The Fresko family is constantly on the verge of breaking up. Members come and go with gypsylike irregularity. The mother is constantly being locked up for drunk and disorderly conduct. The father is constantly thinking of running away with a fellow peddler from the street market where he "works." The daughter elopes with a casual pick up (although Miss Delaney is youthfully romantic enough to imply that this one will work out); and the whole raffish establishment is watched over by the grandfather, a lawless, Rabelaisian type who is full of the old vigor yet.

It is too soon yet to see how Miss Delaney will develop. Her greatest gift is her ability to write live, snappy stage dialogue; her greatest drawback is her inability to get a coherent plot together. Her future will depend on her ability to combine her considerable native talent and the cheerful iconoclasm that marks her first two plays to produce something with a definite meaning instead of only the hint of a meaning.

JOHN MORTIMER
The Apotheosis of Failure

The plays are . . . intended as comedy, comedy being, to my mind, the only thing worth writing in this despairing age, provided the comedy is truly on the side of the lonely, the neglected, the unsuccessful, and plays its part in the war against established rules and against the imposing of an arbitrary code of behaviour upon individual and unpredictable human beings.

There may, for all I know, be great and funny plays to be written about successful lawyers, brilliant criminals, wise schoolmasters, or families where the children can grow up without silence and without regret. There are many plays that show that the law is always majestic or that family life is simple and easy to endure. Speaking for myself I am not on the side of such plays and a writer of comedy must choose his side with particular care. He cannot afford to aim at the defenceless, nor can he, like the more serious writer, treat any character with contempt.[1]

With this statement John Mortimer puts himself firmly on the side of the drama of protest. Like most of the current English writers, however, his protest is a severely limited one. It is not a cosmic, nihilistic protest, as in the French avant-garde drama, but a protest against the oppressiveness of society's rules. It is a protest, furthermore, that has its feet firmly and distinctly

1. John Mortimer, *Three Plays* (London: Methuen & Co., Ltd., 1958), pp. 10–11.

planted within the society it protests against. Mortimer is not only against—he is also *for*. He is for those who have been unable to cope with society: for the failures, the flotsam, the drifting scum of society; for the rejects and the defeated; for the hopeless and the numb; and for those who have chosen to conceal their hopelessness even from themselves in a desperate pretence. John Mortimer's plays are the glorification of the failure.

A failure is hardly a heroic figure. Mortimer's failures receive their stature by analogy: they are the antitheses of the organization men. The efficient compromisers are the villains of Mortimer's plays, even though they do not appear in them personally. They are condemned by contrast. Mortimer has no use for the survival-of-the-fittest doctrine, since, as he sees it, the terms of the survival are dictated by those who know they will triumph under those terms, the sum of which constitutes the society we live in.

Although he began his writing career as a novelist, Mortimer's talent definitely does not lie in the direction of the longer stage forms. *The Wrong Side of the Park* (1960) is interesting only as the representative of a type of play much favored by the young English writers. It is a rather clumsily told story of an incipiently schizophrenic housewife in suburban London who is saved on the brink of lunacy by her husband's sudden awakening from the torpor into which his job as a civil servant has sunk him. The interesting thing about this play is its exemplification of a syndrome that appears to afflict most of the current young English playwrights. The syndrome is the writer's need to exorcise his personal drab middle-class background by producing a work in which his origins are denigrated and ripped apart. In Mortimer's play, as well as in Osborne's *Epitaph for George Dillon*, Bolt's *Flowering Cherry*, and Shaffer's *Five Finger Exercise*, we see the writer serving his apprenticeship with a play about family life in suburban, semi-detached houses where restless adolescent children rebel against their parents, usually a weak-willed and ineffectual husband married to a stronger but unpleasantly neurotic wife. N. F. Simpson's *A Resounding Tinkle* shows the same thing in a rather slanted way, as do Shelagh Delaney's *The Lion in Love* and Arnold Wesker's *Chicken Soup with Barley* in a somewhat different social milieu.

The real value and originality of Mortimer's drama lies in his one-act plays. Like Jean Tardieu in France, Mortimer seems to have made the one-act form peculiarly his own. It is here that his failures come into their own—here that they become successes at last by alienating themselves completely from the society that has trodden them down through decreeing terms they have found impossible to honor.

The most successful of Mortimer's one-act plays, and the best-known in the United States because of their presentation on television here, are *The Dock Brief* and *What Shall We Tell Caroline?* Both of these plays take place in Mortimer's world of the misfits and failures. It may be possible, Mortimer tells us, to write plays about "successful lawyers . . . wise schoolmasters, or families where the children can grow up without silence and without regret." But such plays are not John Mortimer's cup of tea. *The Dock Brief* and *What Shall We Tell Caroline?* are about unsuccessful lawyers, blundering schoolmasters, and families where the children grow up in silence and regret. The lawyer in *The Dock Brief* is a pathetic figure who has gone gray waiting for a "dock brief" (charity case) to show up. Now, at sixty-three years of age, he has finally been chosen to try his first case. It is a murder case, and he has no doubt at all that it will make him famous. Already he sees visions of himself on the bench, his chambers besieged by befurred and bejeweled society people, his name in the headlines as the most famous barrister in London. He spends most of the time allotted to him for interviewing his client in acting out his pipe dreams of success with the result that when the time comes to go to trial he is totally unprepared. The case is hopeless, anyway. In the second scene we learn that the lawyer has failed again. Instead of the brilliant two or three day address to the jury which was going to move strong men to tears and cause women to faint, he said nothing. No words would come; and so he just sat down again and gave up. His client is convicted, of course, but is immediately afterwards pardoned on the grounds that the incompetence of his lawyer rendered the trial an unfair one. Momentarily depressed, the lawyer cheers up again at the thought that his client, with whom he has become quite friendly, may need some little legal advice in the future. As the curtain falls, both men happily dance out of the cell whistling a gay tune. After a brief excursion into the cruel world of reality for which he is simply unfitted, Morgenhall, the lawyer, scampers back into the dream world where he fiddles away his existence with his crossword puzzles and his dreams of glory. His address to the jury fails for the same reason as his attempt to propose to the woman he loved failed:

> MORGENHALL: . . . It was the moment when I should have spoken, the obvious moment. Then, something overcame me, it wasn't shyness or fear then, but a tremendous exhaustion. I was tired out by the long wait, and when the opportunity came—all I could think of was sleep.
>
> FOWLE: It's a relief. . . .
>
> MORGENHALL: To go home alone. To undress, clean your teeth, knock out your pipe, not to bother with failure or success.
>
> FOWLE: So yesterday . . .
>
> MORGENHALL: I had lived through that moment so many times. It happened every day in my mind, day-dreaming on buses, or in the doctor's surgery. When it came, I was tired of it. The exhaustion came over me. I wanted it to be all over. I wanted to be alone in my room, in the darkness, with a soft pillow round my ears. . . . So I failed.[2]

He simply does not have the stamina to make his way in the everyday world; and Mortimer's sympathy is entirely with him and with his kind.

In *What Shall We Tell Caroline?* the debonair pretender becomes a faded London roué who has been an assistant master at a small boys' boarding school on the bleak Norfolk coast

2. *Ibid.*, p. 50.

for eighteen years. For eighteen years he has kept his spirits up by reminiscing about his days as a gay young blade on the Earl's Court Road. Accompanying himself on a banjo as he tells stories of lurid escapades that probably never happened, he brings a little light into the drab life of the school. It cheers things up, as he says, when "the results of the squash rackets competition and the state of the weather and the suspicion about who pinched the nail brush off the chain in the downstairs loo have been powerless to quicken the pulse." [3] The one thing wrong with the household is that Caroline, the headmaster's daughter, has not spoken to anyone for a long time. At the end of the play she finds her voice again and announces that she is going to London. But the play is really about the aging roué who has been hiding out from the reality he constantly talks about and dreams about for eighteen years.

Mortimer's other plays, *I Spy, Call Me a Liar, Lunch Hour, David and Broccoli, Collect Your Hand Baggage,* and *Two Stars for Comfort* are all similar efforts. All of them deal with people who are unable to cope with the world and who seek refuge in their illusions. Mortimer's sympathy is entirely with these characters, for he feels that their rejection of the conditions of society—their mute rebellion as it might be called—is justified. To function in society and be a success is commendable only if we accept the conditions set up by society as correct. This there is no reason to do. The laws of society are purely arbitrary, and there is nothing wrong, Mortimer feels, in receding into an individual world of one's own. Mortimer's view of people is one of personal sympathy, much like Brendan Behan's: "I respect kindness to human beings first of all, and kindness to animals. I don't respect the law; I have a total irreverence for anything connected with society except that which makes the roads safer, the beer stronger, the food cheaper, and old men and old women warmer in the winter, and happier in the summer." [4]

3. *Ibid.,* p. 105.
4. Quoted in program of *The Hostage* production at Wyndham's Theatre, London, 1959.

BRENDAN BEHAN
The Irish Primitive

LACK OF respect for the law and total irreverence for
anything connected with society are even more pronounced in
Behan than in Mortimer. Mortimer, indeed, might be described as a genteel and refined Behan. Where Mortimer shows
us gentle characters who have been too weak to cope with
life or who have politely declined to have anything to do
with it as it is lived in modern society, Behan shows us rough-
and-ready types who have kicked society in the teeth.

Brendan Behan is a primitive author in the best sense—
instinctive, untutored, uninfluenced. The two plays by which
he is known—*The Quare Fellow* and *The Hostage*—both
show this primitivism even in their published forms, which
have been considerably reworked by Joan Littlewood. Brendan
Behan, it should be noted, is emphatically not a member of
the New English Dramatists movement. His first play, *The
Quare Fellow* (1945), was written well before Osborne's breakthrough with *Look Back in Anger*, and his second, *The Hostage*
(1957), is related neither in theme nor in style to the angry-
young-man syndrome. For Brendan Behan is most definitely not
an angry young man, though he has far more reason to be one
than any of the writers dubbed with that title by the critics.
Behan has spent nine of his forty years in some kind of penal
institution. Every minute of those nine years imprisonment
was an injustice since Behan was no criminal but a nationalist
who had been caught acting in a manner considered rebellious
by people whom he considered usurpers of his country's sovereignty. Instead of making him "angry," all this has served to
do has been to make him an ever-bubbling wellspring of elemental good cheer. The main thing that strikes one about
Behan's work is the compassion and understanding that he has
for both sides of any conflict—for jailed and jailers in *The
Quare Fellow*, for English and Irish in *The Hostage*. The only
type of person that Behan cannot stomach is the person who
tries to impose his authority and swell his dignity in the name

of some abstract ideal, which, Behan implies, is not really sincerely held but manufactured to justify the person's behavior. Behan's villains are thus the mealy-mouthed, hypocritical prison visitor Holy Healey in *The Quare Fellow* and the puritanical, self-important I.R.A. leader, whose behavior ironically apes that of the British upper-class officers, in *The Hostage*.

Brendan Behan began playwriting more or less accidentally. After his release from prison in the late nineteen-forties, he worked as a painter for a bit and then began writing a column for the *Irish Press*. In his spare time he wrote a radio script originally entitled *The Twisting of Another Rope*. This was rejected by Radio Eireann and by the Abbey Theatre, and finally came to the attention of Alan Simpson, the producer, director, founder, and owner of the Pike Theatre, a tiny house he had built himself in a Dublin back-street garage. Simpson helped Behan rewrite the play, gave it its new title of *The Quare Fellow*, and put on its first performance anywhere, at the Pike Theatre in 1954.[1] The published text of *The Quare Fellow* is a later version, rearranged with the help of Joan Littlewood.[2] According to Simpson, this is an inferior version since it tends to mix up the characters of Donnelly and Regan, two of the warders.[3]

The Quare Fellow is a highly specialized slice-of-life play —nothing more or less than that. It is a play that becomes powerful and interesting through its situation, which is that of life in a cell block on the eve of an execution. The events leading up to an execution are perhaps the easiest of all possible theatrical situations to ruin through tastelessness, mawkishness, and misplaced social fervor. Behan avoids all the traps, most notably the one involving the condemned man's appearance. The "quare fellow" (prison slang for a condemned man) never does appear, and all we see is the reaction his fate has

1. Alan Simpson, *Beckett and Behan and a Theatre in Dublin* (London: Routledge & Kegan Paul Ltd., 1962), pp. 39–41.
2. Brendan Behan, *The Quare Fellow* (London: Methuen & Co., Ltd., 1961).
3. Alan Simpson, *op. cit.*, pp. 44–45.

on his fellow prisoners. Behan makes his play a success by rigidly avoiding any hint of sentimentality and by displaying an equal feeling of sympathy and understanding for the prisoners and the guards, both trapped victims of an invisible system that is beyond their power to comprehend.

Behan's other important play is *The Hostage*.[4] This was originally written and performed in Gaelic, having been commissioned by Gael Linn, an organization devoted to the revival of the Irish language. As *An Gáill* it was first performed in Dublin in 1957. After being translated, it was reworked with the help of Joan Littlewood and directed by her at the Theatre Royal, Stratford, in 1958. Alan Simpson remarks very justly that it was this play, Miss Littlewood's most successful author-director collaboration, that helped bring about the widespread acceptance of her type of dramatic production.[5] Simpson gives this the rather vague name of "dramatized social realism," but actually it is a form of exuberant, perpetual-motion communication between audience and actor. *The Hostage*, with its constant stops and starts, its songs and dances, its jokes and vaudeville routines, is the perfect vehicle for this kind of production. The fact that *The Hostage* has a plot and a purpose is almost obscured under the blanket of sheer nonsense covering the whole action. This "nonsense," however, is itself an integral part of the action since it serves to imply that it is nonsensical to take seriously the problem that the plot deals with. The situation that Behan deals with in *The Hostage* is at one and the same time deadly serious and ridiculous. An eighteen-year-old I.R.A. member—a boy far too young to have had any personal experience or knowledge of the Irish Rebellion—is to be hanged by the British in Belfast for terrorist activities. The British thus compound the idiocy of the boy's misguided and anachronistic terrorism by another idiocy; which is then further compounded by the fanatical, self-conceited I.R.A., who capture a young British soldier and announce they

4. He has also written *The Big House*, a radio play recently adapted for the stage by Alan Simpson, as well as two radio sketches, *The New House* and *The Garden Party*.

5. Alan Simpson, *op. cit.*, p. 28.

will shoot him in retaliation for their member's execution. The action takes place in a Dublin whorehouse on the night before the execution. The British hostage has been brought here for safekeeping since a whorehouse is the last place the police would associate with the I.R.A. The head of the house is a real veteran of the Irish Rebellion. He is roused into a positive ecstasy of withering contempt by the posturings of the strutting young I.R.A. officer and absolutely refuses to take the matter seriously. One of the weird inmates of the house finally betrays the place to the police, and the hostage is inadvertently killed in the ensuing raid. But Behan immediately has him spring up and lead the cast in a mocking song that sums up the whole "devil take it" attitude of the play: "The bells of hell/Go ting-a-ling-a-ling,/For you but not for me,/Oh death where is thy sting-a-ling-a-ling?/Or grave thy victory?" [6]

In *The Quare Fellow* and *The Hostage* Brendan Behan has written two of the best plays of the contemporary English theater. They are completely original and owe nothing to anyone. We can only hope now that Behan, unlike most primitive artists, is able to produce more good work without falling into repetitiousness.

NIGEL DENNIS
The Return of Intellectual Satire

FOR A man born as long ago as 1912 Nigel Dennis's literary output has been unusually small—two novels and three plays.[1] As a rule, the cliché that lack of quantity indicates high quality does not hold true in literature: a writer who says little usually has little to say. That, however, is not the case with Nigel Dennis. His work seems to be small in bulk for much the same reason that the end product of a refining

6. Brendan Behan, *The Hostage* (London: Methuen & Co., Ltd., 1962), p. 108.
1. Dennis's third play, *August for the People*, is a farce about the British aristocracy's vested interest in democracy. It cannot compare with his first two plays.

process is small in bulk: what remains after all the distillations is the pure, ultimate essence of the substance.

Perhaps the reason for Dennis's excellence is that he is an unabashedly intellectual dramatist. At the same time his plays are vastly entertaining and first-rate theater. They do not, however, resemble the average Broadway or West End play. They are not, like commercial dramas, built around a situation into which some references to serious problems have been injected. Dennis's plays, like Shaw's, are built around a serious moral or intellectual problem, and the situation of the play grows out of the problem (that is to say, it is created solely for the purpose of theatrically illustrating the problem).

The problems that Dennis chooses to discuss in *Cards of Identity* and *The Making of Moo* are nothing less than the two basic problems with which the mind of man is confronted; namely, religion and psychology: his relationship to the universe and his relationship to himself. The two plays are preceded by a long and brilliantly written essay that further strengthens Dennis's right to be looked upon as a worthy, direct-line descendant of Shaw.

The two plays are philosophically related, as Dennis emphasizes in his preface, although they deal with totally different situations. *The Making of Moo* is subtitled "A History of Religion in Three Acts." It is Dennis's expression of his atheistic beliefs. Despite his nonbelief, he is not particularly opposed to religion per se. Dennis is an extreme individualist, and as such he feels understandably irritated by the attempt of believers to whittle him down into their image. One might get the idea that Dennis suffers from a paranoid complex about religion. Not so! He simply wants to be let alone to do as he pleases. He does not want to bother anyone, and he expects the same treatment in return. He does not want to be bothered by proselytizing busybodies or by prescriptive pronunciamentos on morals and mores from a dogmatic Olympus. He contends that the sickness lies rather with those who cannot be content to find peace for themselves and insist on enjoining the "joys" of their "peace" on everyone else, forcibly if necessary. Furthermore, Dennis feels that all evangelical zeal is based on a huge, mushrooming chain reaction of swindle since all religions originate in one man's idea and his need to fortify it with fellow believers (known as disciples). In short, Dennis's views of the beginnings of religion can be summed up in the well-worn saying, "Religion began when the first knave met the first fool." *The Making of Moo* is about the origin of a religion—the religion of Moo. The implication is that all religions begin and develop like the religion of Moo.

Moo is the name of a new god created by an English civil engineer to replace Ega, an old god whom he has inadvertently "killed." It seems that Ega was a river god who was suffocated when the engineer (Frederick Compton by name) built a dam across the African stream he inhabited or haunted or permeated. Compton's British sense of the white man's burden and all that sort of thing is deeply disturbed when he hears of this, especially as the crime rate seems to be going up sharply now that Ega is no longer around to punish wrongdoers. He determines to whip up another god for the natives before he leaves. Moo, named after the lowing of the cows which infest Compton's front lawn, is the result. Moo starts out as a purely rational, personified code of ethics which Compton is going to work out for the benefit and improvement of the natives—a sort of mathematically systematized Taoism. But then Compton's wife and secretary join in. She wants to write the Bible of Moo, and the secretary, an amateur musician, wants to write the liturgy of Moo. Pretty soon Compton himself gets carried away with all this emotionalism, and the first act ends as he harangues his butler on the subject of Moo in the manner of St. Paul to the Corinthians.

In the second act we see the Moo religion two years later. The Comptons and their secretary have remained in Africa as "prophets"; their butler has been appointed pope. Moo is now in the primitive state of religion: barbaric ceremonies, human sacrifices, prophecies direct from the horse's mouth, rampant emotionalism, and so on. No trace of Moo's proposed rationalism remains. The religion is now based exclusively on emotion, revelation, and atavism. This is what happens to all religions, Dennis tells us in his preface. The theologians create something Invisible and Intangible, and consequently Inexplicable. Something Inexplicable can either be rejected out of hand as ridiculous or it can be accepted on blind faith. The latter is usually the case, since people have a psychological need to cling to something. Since it is Inexplicable and, therefore, believed in blindly, the theologians—the impresarios of the show—can manipulate it at will without danger of being scoffed at. Thus the religion, in order to survive, pronounces such dogmas as "Love Moo—and you will never think again" or "And Moo has said: 'In my arms there is no room for reason, and where there is no room for reason there is no room for doubt, and where there is no room for doubt there is room for Moo only.' " [2] Persons who point out flaws in the religion at this point are usually accused of heresy and eliminated at an auto-da-fé, a ceremony designed to make new men out of the onlookers while it makes no men out of the participants. This edifying ritual, which took the form of burning alive among the European Christians and heart gouging among the Aztecs, is here represented by the beheading of Fairbrother and his clerk. This stage gradually leads into the religion's solidified form.

In the third act, which takes place many, many years later, Compton is a senile patriarch, and the Church of Moo is so well-established that businessmen are donating funds to it and scientists are "discovering" in carbon deposits evidence of its existence millions of years ago. Barbarities are no longer practised; everything is staid and respectable; and religion is transacted over teacups instead of buckets of blood. In short, the Moovian religion at this stage is similar to the Church of England today, or, as Dennis puts it in his preface, "Protestantism retains its barbarities only in verbal form: worshippers still sing 'There is a fountain filled with blood' and even ask to be washed in it; but by now the blood has ceased to register as such and would create sheer disgust were it not regarded simply as a colourful word in a fanciful jug." [3] At the end of the

2. Nigel Dennis, *Two Plays and a Preface* (New York: Vanguard Press, 1958), p. 194.
3. *Ibid.*, p. 12.

play Compton's son, a Moovian priest, goes off into the wilderness to seek the "original purity" of the religion, and the allegory thus comes full circle.

The Making of Moo is essentially an attack on universal-
ized absolutism—there would be nothing wrong with Moovian-
ism (or with any other religion), according to Dennis, if its
devotees did not insist that its truth is absolute. For if it is
absolute it follows that nothing else is right and, therefore,
everyone should believe in it. And that is where the individualist stands up and begs to be excused: " 'Everything absolute
belongs to pathology,' says Nietzsche—which does not mean
that no one may give tongue to an absolute if he pleases, only
that its pathology should not be enjoined on others. The intellectual may, if he please, make God in his own image: we rebel
only when we are made in it as well." [4]

The intellectual with the established idée fixe is unhappily
concerned with our social life as well as with our transcendental
life. The religious fanatic's counterpart is the social brain-
washer, the planner who wants to mold individual psyches to
conform to his preconceived blueprints. The Moovian prophets, who want to control our lives by forcing their religious
"beliefs" on us, are supplemented in modern society by the
Identity Club members, who wish to impose their personal
dogma of social behavior on us.

Cards of Identity illustrates Dennis's thesis that modern
psychology, with its emphasis on making people "adjust" to
the society around them, is stifling individualism. For Dennis
personal conspicuousness is not a sign of mental aberration,
and his play is a protest against the pressing-iron technique of
modern psychiatry. The process of psychoanalysis is analogous
to the process of religious conversion: the Fisher for souls
and the Fisher for minds are essentially one and the same.
Man, according to the modern political brainwashers and psychoanalysts, must submerge his identity if he is to be "saved":
"only when he swallows his pride can he be hooked to safety
by the Great Fisherman. Once this has happened, his life

4. *Ibid.*, p. 21.

and identity become utterly changed. Packed in a tin with other decapitated fish, his broken loneliness disappears; he is now a segment of the One Truth." [5]

The way the psychoanalysts accomplish this is by playing on the patient's inner life, on his memories, Dennis tells us. A man is made what he is by the experiences he has undergone. These experiences are all in the past and consequently exist only in the man's memory of them. It follows that if a man's memory of things is changed, the things themselves are actually changed; and the man's personality becomes reformed in accordance with the new set of experiences he now remembers. Thus, if a man can be made to "remember" things that never really happened (through suggestion, hypnosis, persuasion, terror, etc.) and if his personality is contingent upon his memory of his past experiences, then a man can be molded into any desired psychic shape. He becomes a piece of wet clay on a potter's wheel.

Cards of Identity is about a club, the Identity Club, whose members occupy themselves with changing other people's personalities. Three members, posing as husband, wife, and son, have taken over a country estate. They proceed to "make over" various people of the neighborhood. The doctor becomes a gardener, his nurse becomes a mental patient, another local character becomes the butler, complete with memories of alcoholism and crime in his younger days. At the annual meeting of the Identity Club the three conspirators plan to do away with the president, who is senile, and replace him with their leader. After an abortive attempt to poison the president, which results in the death of the founder's daughter, they incite another member to shoot him. After this the club clears out, and, its influence removed, the victims slowly come back to their senses.

That is all there is to the plot. The interest lies in Dennis's thesis that the Identity Club is comparable to all modern organizations dedicated to the standardization of personality, e.g., psychiatrists and psychoanalysts, totalitarian political

5. *Ibid.*, p. 40.

parties, absolutist religious sects, and similar groups. Dennis is strictly for the individual's right of self-determination. If we *must* have a religion then he is for the worship of the fourth-century divine, Pelagius, the opponent of St. Augustine, who is Dennis's bête noire. The main tenet of Pelagianism is that man has complete freedom of the will—no matter what his past may have been he has the ability at any given moment in his life to make a decision for good or evil. He must, therefore, accept full moral responsibility for each and every one of his acts. If he does this, he is safe. The Identity Club and the Moovians can only gain control of those who think they are not responsible for what they do—of those who feel they are determined by factors outside themselves.

In Nigel Dennis the English-speaking intellectual drama has found a new representative. *Cards of Identity* and *The Making of Moo* are superbly written plays with an innate and instinctive sense of the theater. They, together with the brilliantly witty preface (so witty in spots that the brilliance outsparkles the clarity) constitute the best that the British drama has produced since the death of Shaw.

JOHN ARDEN
Too Much Too Soon

THERE IS one respect in which the theatrical situation is better in America than in England. It is a commonplace thing to hear an American playwright say that he has a trunkful of unproduced plays. I would venture a guess that none of the new English dramatists is able to say the same. Once one of them has had a first play produced in one of the "clique" theaters, such as the Royal Court, the Belgrade Theatre, Coventry, or the Theatre Royal, Stratford, the production of his future work is virtually assured. One would suppose that this would be an excellent thing for the young playwright, but it is not. Instead of producing better plays, this state of affairs fosters a decline of craftsmanship because young playwrights are encouraged to submit, for public viewing, works that are really only experimental essays. The fact that these experimental essays are treated as finished works of art by the critics does not help matters. The place for such plays is the experimental or academic theater, not the professional one. Nothing illustrates this better than the plays of John Arden.

Could it be that the British and American critics are about equally detrimental to the rise of good drama in their respective countries—but for precisely opposite reasons? Do not American critics reveal their lack of education or intelligence (in many cases, both) by consistently writing bad reviews for good plays, while the English critics nurse their chauvinism by giving good reviews to bad plays? As a result of this kind of encouragement, English playwrights are deprived of a chance to serve an apprenticeship. They are hurried into professional production without adequate preparation. John Arden has had seven plays produced in as many years. Of these seven the three most successful have been published, yet they all read like muzzily thought-out first or second drafts. Typical of the sort of "white hope" dramatic criticism that is written about Arden and his fellow playwrights is the following excerpt from Bamber Gascoigne's review of Arden's latest play, *The Workhouse Donkey*:

> John Arden's very high but entirely just reputation is based on one play, "Serjeant Musgrave's Dance." It was grossly under-estimated at the time of its first production, but enthusiasts immediately began saying that his next play would prove him beyond dispute to be a major dramatist. It was "The Happy Haven," a very feeble affair, and it didn't. A mere lapse, we all said; his next play will be a masterpiece. . . . I shall continue to bleat that John Arden's next play is likely to be very good, . . . I repeat that his next play will be magnificent.[1]

Arden's very high but certainly not just reputation is un-

1. *The Observer*, July 14, 1963, p. 26.

doubtedly based on *Serjeant Musgrave's Dance* (1959). How
this reputation came about is fairly obvious. *Serjeant Musgrave's Dance* <u>looks</u> like a good drama at first glance. It is
written in a pretentious style, and it has the appearance of
being a drama of ideas. The style is made distinctive by having
the characters interrupt the action with song and dance every
so often. This is a device that has been used before, but
Arden misuses it. He makes the mistake of trying to super-
impose this style on a play which demands the suspension of
our disbelief in its situation. The song and dance thus has no
other effect than to break the audience's concentration on the
plot. The song-and-dance style can be effective only when the
action is frankly suspended for the duration of the song and
dance, as in Brecht; or when the play makes no attempt to
induce our belief in the action at any time, as in Behan's *The
Hostage*. As far as the ideas in *Serjeant Musgrave's Dance* are
concerned, the kindest word that can be applied to Arden is
that overworked term of psychological jargon "confused." He
tells the story of four deserters from Queen Victoria's army.
Led by Serjeant Musgrave, they come to a snow-bound mining
town in the North of England, carrying with them a skeleton
and a small arsenal of guns and ammunition. The skeleton
(not the least important "character" in the play since Arden
rather tastelessly gives it a love scene to "play") used to be
covered with the flesh of Billy Hicks, a home-town boy who
ended up with a knife in his back in one of the remoter spots
of the ever-sunlit Empire. Five natives were gunned down to
expiate the crime. All of the soldiers thereupon experienced a
revulsion at the barbarity of their calling and have come to
convince the townspeople of the evils of killing. Musgrave,
however, turns out to be an insane religious fanatic who claims
that he lives by absolute logic—"logic" in this case consisting
of five eyes for an eye, for he proposes to kill twenty-five leading townspeople in expiation for the five natives. This proposal
is received with the scorn it deserves, and the situation is saved
as loyal dragoons come trotting up in the nick of time over the
snow-topped slag heaps, à la the Relief of Lucknow.

What Arden is *trying* to do in *Serjeant Musgrave's Dance*

is to show how fanaticism can turn even excellent intentions such as Musgrave's into abominations. Musgrave believes himself to be the direct instrument of God's vengeance. Instead of being a study of the tragic paradox of militant pacifism, the play becomes simply a clumsily written case study of a lunatic. John Russell Taylor has tried to show that Arden never takes sides with any of his characters: all are observed dispassionately and all are felt to have some good in them.[2] This is true, but it is precisely what makes Arden's play exasperating and, in the last analysis, uninteresting. Either an author must show a point of view or he must show that no point of view is worth having. Arden does neither, and as a result his plays are theatrically boring and intellectually inept.

A year before he made his reputation with *Serjeant Musgrave's Dance*, Arden had had *Live Like Pigs* produced at the Royal Court. In this play he gives a hint of his real talent. Like Bernard Kops, Arden founders every time he tries to deal seriously with significant themes; unlike Kops, he has not yet discovered that his real talent is for writing pure farce. Insofar as *Live Like Pigs* is pure farce it is an excellent play of its kind; but Arden ruins it by trying to turn it into a sociological commentary. In his introduction to the play, Arden says that he intended the play to be "a study in differing ways of life brought sharply into conflict and both losing their own particular virtues under the stress of intolerance and misunderstanding."[3] In order to do this, Arden sets his play in a low-cost municipal housing project. One of the houses has been given to a raffish and unwashed family that had been living in an abandoned tram on the outskirts of town and supporting itself by petty thieving and prostitution. Naturally, as soon as they move in, the house is turned into an incredibly filthy shambles. The "conflict" comes when the Sawneys are thrown against their new neighbors, a typical lower-class bourgeois ménage. This is a situation rich in comic possibilities and even of a certain amount of serious-minded satire, since it shows up, by

2. Taylor, *op. cit.*, pp. 72–86.
3. Thomas Maschler, ed., *New English Dramatists 3* (Middlesex, England: Penguin Books, 1961), p. 95.

implication, the hidebound muddle-headedness of municipal
bureaucracy. Unfortunately, Arden is not content with so simple and unambitious an object. He tries instead to instill some
sort of "tragic" quality into his play by telling us in his preface that the Sawneys are really fine old English stock whose
behavior is due to the impasse between their traditional "free"
way of life and the modern regularized one to which the
neighbors are accustomed:

> The Sawneys are an anachronism. They are the direct de-
> scendants of the "sturdy beggars" of the sixteenth century,
> and the apparent chaos of their lives becomes an ordered
> pattern when seen in terms of a wild empty countryside and
> a nomadic existence. Put out of their fields by enclosing
> landlords, they found such an existence possible for four
> hundred years. Today, quite simply, there are too many
> buildings in Britain, and there is just no room for nomads.
> The family in this play fails to understand this, and be-
> comes educated in what is known as the "hard way," but
> which might also be called the "inefficient way." [4]

The trouble with this kind of thinking is that it has nothing to
do with reality. If there are people in England today who act
as the Sawneys do, it is not because the building boom has left
no room for nomads, but because they are criminal types of
low mentality and primitive living standards who do not deserve sympathy but rather require coercion. To look upon
people who wallow in verminous filth, disturb their neighbors
with earsplitting noise, destroy their houses with wanton van-
dalism, and live off thievery and prostitution, as wide-eyed,
innocent children of nature who deserve commiseration because the building boom has dispossessed them from their
idyllic life among the flower-bedecked hedgerows is the merest
muzzy-headed romanticism.

Arden's other published play is *The Happy Haven*, produced at the Royal Court Theatre in September, 1960. This
received a far less enthusiastic critical reception than his previ-

4. *Ibid.*

K

ous plays, although it deserved a better one. The Happy Haven is an old folks' home run by an obsessed young scientist who thinks he is on the track of the Fountain of Youth. Out of the bubbling, rainbow-hued fluids in his chromium-plated retorts and alembics he hopes to concoct something that will make old people young again. Dr. Copperthwaite is endowed with all the irresponsible, self-centered callousness so common among scientific researchers, whose goal is all too often fame and fortune at any cost. The old people, who have all been failures in their lives, find out about Dr. Copperthwaite's plan and, full of resentment at being used as guinea pigs, steal the solution and jab it into the doctor. The play thus ends as the scientist, hoist with his own petard, is transformed into a squalling baby and wheeled out. Arden has hit upon an excellent dramatic idea here, but the eccentricities of his style mar it as a stage piece. Most of the comment on *The Happy Haven* has centered on Arden's use of masks, which most of the characters wear. These masks are actually unimportant and are in no way integrated into the play, which could be just as effective, if not more so, without them. What really ruins the play as theater is the continued use of song and dance. Again Arden has failed to integrate the verse into the context of the action, so that every time one of the characters chants a verse or two there is a sense of jarring incongruity. To make matters worse, the verse is the clumsiest kind of doggerel.

In his latest play, *The Workhouse Donkey* (1963), magnificently produced at the Chichester Festival, Arden has at last solved his problems. In it he has found his niche as a dramatic author. *The Workhouse Donkey* is a superbly comic farce about municipal corruption in a North of England industrial town. Both the Conservatives and the Laborites are depicted as unmitigated scoundrels (although the Laborites are amiable ones), and the only honest man is the neutral Police Commissioner, the "man who stands alone." Roguery triumphs in the end, of course. In *The Workhouse Donkey*, also, Arden has hit upon the correct way to integrate his songs and dances into the action: he makes no pretense at suspension of disbelief and has the whole play written half at the audience in the manner of vaudeville skits. Despite all this, the critics generally agreed with Bamber Gascoigne's estimate, quoted above. They look to Arden to produce something more "serious," more "profound," and they deplore such lapses into farce as *The Workhouse Donkey*. What they cannot understand is that farce can very often be more serious than any other art form. Arden perfectly symbolizes the dilemma of the new English dramatists. Because the critics have decreed that theirs is a "philosophical" movement, they are not to be permitted to develop in their own way. Whenever they produce something like *The Workhouse Donkey*, which does not pontificate in the requisite pseudointellectual manner, they are brought sharply to heel. No drama of lasting value can develop under these circumstances.

Hope Deferred

The New American Drama

EVER SINCE the now almost historic first production of
Look Back in Anger in 1956 the English drama critics have
been beating their drums for a renaissance of the English
drama.   They have succeeded in creating a hypnotic atmosphere in which their readers could be made to believe that
the plays being produced by Osborne, Wesker, Kops, et al.
were really significant. The persistent rhythm of their verbal
tom-toms convinced almost everyone that there was something
called the angry-young-man movement, which had crystallized
out of the infinite aridity of the drawing-room desert over
which Terence Rattigan hovered like a too frequently descend-
ing sandstorm. This movement was later expanded into the
more inclusive—and, indeed, as it has turned out, catch-all—
New English Dramatists movement. American playgoers have a
right to be puzzled as to why this English drama movement
has not been paralleled in their own country. The fact is that
there have been plenty of new American dramas, most of them
every bit as interesting as their English counterparts. The lack
of a "movement" in the United States is due to the much
greater difficulty of getting a play produced in the commercial
theater and to the stubborn refusal of the New York drama
critics to get together and form a cheering section for the
American drama.[1]

1. John Mason Brown, one of the leading American theater critics, in
writing an article on the state of the current theater, recognized that

274

The American writers whose plays have been successful and interesting enough to provide the kind of counterbalance to the Tennessee Williams type of drama that the New English Dramatists have provided to the Terence Rattigan type of drama are Edward Albee, Jack Richardson, Jack Gelber, and Arthur Kopit. With one exception, to be considered later, these writers have shown more promise than achievement so far, but the promise is definitely there.

EDWARD ALBEE

IN THE unlikely event that anything like a "movement" of young American dramatists will ever get off the ground, the world premiere of Edward Albee's *The Zoo Story* will undoubtedly be commemorated as its starting point. Characteristically enough, this world premiere did not take place in the United States, where the critics seldom hail anything new in the arts until they have had the green light from across the Atlantic. In this case the green light came all the way from West Germany, where *The Zoo Story* was first produced in Berlin on September 28, 1959. The story of how *The Zoo Story* was first produced in Germany and subsequently became a success in New York after having previously been rejected right and left over here is extremely instructive for those trying to understand the fantastic world of the New York theater with its Alice-in-Wonderland economics, according to which the producers and theater-owners rake in all the money (and pay the featherbedding stagehands, house managers, and

"Within the last ten years . . . a generation has appeared, writing in a different manner, with a different purpose, from a different view of man in a melodramatically altered world. This new generation has by no means taken over the whole of the theatre. It is as yet mainly a force on the fringes. How long its vogue will last and how abiding its influence will be, no one can say. But its coming was needed and its impact has been healthy." But his list of the best plays produced on the American stage in recent years does not include any of Richardson's works and finally boils down to *J.B.*, *Becket*, and *A Man for All Seasons* (John Mason Brown, "What's Right with the Theatre," *Saturday Review*, May 11, 1963, pp. 19–21).

public relations men with it) while the actors and authors, unless the play is exceptionally "successful," starve. Naturally enough, if the sole purpose of theatrical productions is the personal enrichment of the producer and the theater-owner, new plays such as *The Zoo Story* have not the faintest chance of being put on unless they come with some built-in guarantee of success such as a European reputation. That is exactly what happened to Albee's play. After being passed around New York for a bit, it was sent to Europe by a friend of the author, and there it was finally produced. When it came back, it came with critical acclaim behind it and labels reading "avant-garde," "philosophy of the absurd," and "disciple of Beckett" plastered all over it. It was thus safe to produce and duly opened at the Provincetown Playhouse in New York on January 14, 1960, being obediently accorded enthusiastic reviews by critics who almost certainly didn't understand a word of it but who had done their homework on the European press notices and the academic pronouncements.

The Zoo Story is both an extremely simple and an extremely mystifying play. It is mystifying *because* it is so simple. Like Ionesco, who is clearly his literary progenitor, Albee is not *saying* anything with his play, which is nothing but an excessively fantastic slice-of-life pastiche: he is exemplifying or demonstrating a theme. That theme is the enormous and usually insuperable difficulty that human beings find in communicating with each other. More precisely, it is about the maddening effect that the enforced loneliness of the human condition has on the person who is cursed (for in our society it undoubtedly *is* a curse) with an infinite capacity for love.

There are only two characters in the play, which is essentially a monologue. A rather seedy, down-and-out young man approaches a somewhat older, pillar-of-society type sitting on a bench in a remote section of Central Park on a sunny Sunday afternoon. The man on the bench is middle-aged, well-to-do, respectable. He has a good position, a happy family, a comfortable home life. The desperation that Albee feels the human condition must engender in a sensitive man does not touch him. Not because he is a naturally insensitive being—he isn't. He is a cultured, well-read man, perfectly aware of all the things that are bothering his companion; but he is aware of them only in the abstract. Because he is walled-in by the protective barricades of society, they do not disturb him. Our social order, as Albee sees it, is a set of devices that protect the individual from the realities of the human condition. As a respectable member of society (family man; business executive; registered voter; college graduate; civic, social, and fraternal club member) Peter is granted immunity from the discomforts and anxieties of real human emotion. Man in society need no longer recognize that he is really naked and afraid, that he is really a helpless mote drifting in a hostile void governed by the elemental forces of the "Savage God." Albee sees society, in other words, as a sort of Chinese Wall protecting those within from the barbarian hordes outside. Occasionally, though, one of the inhabitants of this artificial enclosure inadvertently strays too near the line and is overcome by an intruder. This is what Albee shows us happening to Peter on his peaceful bench in Central Park. Jerry is an outsider—rootless and aimless, he is the absolute antithesis of Peter. Nothing protects him and, consequently, he feels the full agony of knowing the world as it *really* is (as do, for example, Beckett's two tramps or Adamov's cripples or any number of other characters from the current French avant-garde theater). He meets Peter and tries to make him understand. He fails, of course, and finally, in utter despair, tries to achieve a sort of communication through enmity by baiting Peter into a fight.[1] In the end, Jerry immolates himself by running onto his own knife, which Peter is holding out to ward him off, and thus finally forces a sort of human relationship between them by creating a perverse blood brotherhood.

The Zoo Story is not only remarkable as a young writer's first play: it is remarkable by any standards for the spareness of its construction and the daring of its conception. It takes a man

1. Bertolt Brecht used the same device as early as 1922 when he wrote *Im Dickicht der Städte*.

who has in him at least the germs of a master writer to bring
off as fantastic a situation as the one in which the schizoid
Jerry suddenly switches personalities, picks a fight with his
companion, and then impales himself on his own knife. Albee
manages to make this entirely believable and—what is even
more important—entirely understandable once the initial shock
has worn off.

Between *The Zoo Story* and his next significant play, *The
American Dream*, Albee wrote two more short plays, *The
Sandbox* and *The Death of Bessie Smith*. Both plays were
written in 1959, and, like *The Zoo Story*, *The Death of Bessie
Smith* was first produced in Berlin. Neither of these plays is
worth much comment. *The Sandbox* is a skillful piece of writing in the current avant-garde vein, but it is essentially merely
a preliminary sketch for *The American Dream*, several of whose
characters it duplicates. *The Death of Bessie Smith* is Albee's
impressionistic recreation of the circumstances surrounding
the death of the famous Negro blues singer who died in an
automobile accident in Memphis, Tennessee, in 1937. The
main character (Bessie Smith herself does not appear) is the
admissions nurse at one of the hospitals that refused to treat
Miss Smith because she was a Negro. Through her Albee tries
to probe the mentality of a typical Southern white woman. He
tries to show that the viciousness of such a person's resentment
against the Negro is the result of a series of constant frustra-
tions. His attempt, unfortunately, fails. The nurse is an entirely incredible character as portrayed, and the whole play
collapses with her. Albee plans the entire action around the
nurse, and the death of the Negro blues singer is treated only
as something that accidentally impinges upon her life. James
Baldwin very acutely points out that the trouble with the play
is that it is bloodless: there is nothing in it to "illuminate
the contrast between the wonderfully reckless life and terrible
death of Bessie Smith and the whited sepulchre in which the
nurse is writhing." [2] This ties in with Henry Goodman's per-
ceptive remark that Albee's enmity to the false values of society

2. James Baldwin, "Theatre: The Negro In and Out," in John A.
Williams, ed., *The Angry Black* (New York: Lancer Books [1962]), p. 21.

seems to be more a case of personal revulsion than of social conscience.[3]

In *The American Dream*, his most important play to date, Albee has picked an ideal subject and title with which to start a movement. As he notes in his preface, several critics have taken sharp exception to the play on the grounds that it is negative in approach, that it tends to denigrate its subject, and that it is "nihilist, immoral, and defeatist" in content.[4] All these things are undoubtedly true. But what did the critics expect? A play that *celebrates* the American dream would be utterly pointless, would, indeed, strictly speaking, be precisely what the critics called Albee's play. It would be nihilist, immoral, and defeatist because it would be perpetuating a lie. The "American Dream," the principle of freedom and individuality for which the country was founded has, as any clear-thinking and courageous person cannot hesitate to admit, become thoroughly corrupted by precisely the things Albee is attacking in his play: by misplaced hero worship; by values based exclusively on the crassest commercialism; by flabby, unthinking complacency; and by brutal destruction of human emotions. To *celebrate* the "American Dream," even supposing there were anything left to celebrate, would be utterly useless. What would be the point of flattering an audience and sending them away with hands folded in self-congratulatory complacency on their comfortably rounded stomachs? This is a function performed efficiently enough by our annual open-air, massed-voice, historico-patriotic pageants, most of which are staged, significantly enough, in the South. The function of the drama is not to celebrate what is good but to protest against what is bad. Progress can come about only through criticism.

Albee's technique in *The American Dream* is caricature. He takes the traditional elements of the American dream—the happy family, the efficient go-getter, the idealistic hero—and shows them in the grotesquely distorted form that he feels they

3. Henry Goodman, "The New Dramatists, 4: Edward Albee," *Drama Survey*, II (Spring, 1962), pp. 72–79.
4. Edward Albee, *The American Dream* (New York: Coward-McCann, Inc., 1961), p. 7.

have assumed. The happy family becomes an emasculated money supplier dominated by an emotionally sterile, nagging wife; the efficient go-getter becomes a sexless female machine; the idealistic hero becomes a handsome, empty-headed, hollow shell of a man with the outlook and philosophy of a professional pimp. Interestingly enough, as the critics might have known had they been the competent drama scholars they should be instead of the ill-educated journalists casually kicked onto the drama desk by their editors that they are, Albee is by no means the first man to treat the American dream theme in this way. Back in 1933 George O'Neil, who might well have become one of America's greatest dramatists had he not died early, wrote a play called *American Dream* which deals with the degeneration of the American ideal using even more "nihilism, immorality, and defeatism" than Albee's play. O'Neil used the panoramic method, showing the moral disintegration of one American family through several generations, while Albee shows us a caricatured version of the end product; but the general idea is the same. It would be instructive to be able to see parallel productions of the O'Neil and Albee plays.

Albee sets his little parable in his conception of a typical slice of *Suburbia Americana*. Mommy and Daddy sit opposite each other in their foam-rubber and fumed-oak living room, the former babbling vacuous inanities, the latter keeping himself just conscious enough to register what she is saying. The scene is irresistibly reminiscent of Ionesco's *The Bald Soprano*, in which Mrs. Smith sits and mumbles the English equivalents of Mommy's inanities. Here, as in *The Bald Soprano* and *The Zoo Story*, we see the impossibility of communication even in the closest of relationships. The parallel between the two plays is carried further when Mrs. Barker comes in. She has been sent for, but she does not know why; nor do Mommy and Daddy know why they have sent for her, although they have both been eagerly awaiting her. Like Mr. and Mrs. Martin in *The Bald Soprano*, who have to go through a long chain of inductive reasoning to find out that they were married to each other (but only possibly, since the maid points out a fatal flaw in their reasoning immediately afterwards), Mrs. Barker

has to probe around interminably. She is, however, so en-
tangled in all the commitments she has made in her capacity
of "professional woman," that she is totally unable to find out
what she is supposed to be there for. It takes Grandma,
Mommy's somewhat jaundiced eighty-six-year-old parent, to set
her straight finally. Grandma is easily Albee's most memorable
character; his play, indeed, stands or falls on her, for nothing
is easier than for the actress playing her to make her cute and
precious. The danger is that the actress will play the tough-
talking, wisecracking Grandma for laughs. This would be
tempting and easy to do but ruinous for the play since
Grandma is its only admirable character. Grandma is an
anachronism: she represents the solid pioneer stock out of
which the American Dream might have come had it not been
corrupted instead. Grandma reveals to Mrs. Barker that she
is there in her capacity of fieldworker for an adoption agency.
Twenty years before, it seems, Mrs. Barker had provided
Mommy and Daddy with a baby that had turned out to be a
disappointment. To discourage its disobedience, Mommy
found it necessary to gouge its eyes out, cut its hands off and
its tongue out, and emasculate it. Finally it died and now
Mommy and Daddy want either their money back or a new
and more satisfactory baby. At this point a caricature of the
traditional "All-American boy" enters—big, muscular, handsome in a glossy, Hollywood-studio way, utterly brainless, and
ready to do anything—*anything* (the emphasis is his)—for
money. He was not always like this, though; and he can still
grope around in the dim recesses of his mind for memories of
a time when he had an identical twin brother (who represents
his potentialities for good) from whom he was separated a
long time ago. Since the separation he has been steadily going
downhill until now he is totally unable to feel anything: "I
cannot touch another person and feel love. . . . I have no emotions. I have been drained, torn asunder . . . disemboweled. I
have now only my person . . . my body, my face. . . . And it
will always be thus." [5] The young man's story touches the old

5. *Ibid.*, pp. 78–79.

woman deeply, for it rouses the stirrings of a distant racial memory she had thought long dead. Grandma is not merely an exceptionally spry eighty-six-year-old; she is Albee's conception of the Great American Earth Mother who recognizes deep within herself the memory of the original dream that the founding of the New World gave to the human race. She, the pioneer stock, remembers the real dream: "I don't know you from somewhere, but I knew . . . once . . . someone very much like you . . . or, very much as perhaps you were . . . Someone . . . to be more precise . . . who might have turned out to be very much like you might have turned out to be." [6] But it is too late for that now, so Grandma conceives the idea of persuading Mrs. Barker to give the young man to Mommy and Daddy as their new son. Grandma leaves at the end of the play, and Mommy and Daddy enthusiastically accept the flawed, maculate image of the dream that they deserve. Few plays have shown up the sterility of the society in which they were written so uncompromisingly and savagely as this play of Albee's. As James Baldwin points out, it is hardly a "dream" anymore: "Its vision of the antiseptic passivity of American life, and the resulting death of the masculine sensibility makes it more closely resemble a nightmare." [7]

Albee's latest play, Who's Afraid of Virginia Woolf?, is his first full-length effort. It is unhappily considerably more than full-length since it lasts well over three hours. Although the play could be tightened (it has at least one hour of purely excess dialogue), the process would merely result in making meaninglessness more playable. After the promise of The American Dream, Who's Afraid of Virginia Woolf? is a disappointment. It was perhaps too much to hope that Albee would produce something as significant as The American Dream for his first Broadway effort; too much to hope that the production of Who's Afraid of Virginia Woolf? would mark the entrenchment and acceptance of the off-beat, paradoxical, enigmatic plays of Albee, Richardson, Kopit, and Weinstein that constituted the off-Broadway seed of the putative new

6. *Ibid.*, p. 79.
7. Baldwin, *loc. cit.*

American drama. In *Who's Afraid of Virginia Woolf?* Albee has succeeded merely in producing a long piece of intellectualized *kitsch*.

There are only four characters in Albee's play, which takes place in a small New England college. The scene is the living room of a history professor who has been married for over twenty years to the daughter of the college's president. Theirs appears to be a marriage based by now almost exclusively on a sort of vaguely good-humored bickering which flares out every so often into open savagery. Their bickering is automatic and off-hand, with the touch of professionalism brought by years of practice. His main gambit is her drinking and the fact that she is six years older than he is; hers is his spinelessness and his failure to rise in academic circles despite his connections as the president's son-in-law. Just now they are returning at 2:00 A.M. from a party at the president's house and are preparing to receive a late visit from a young biology professor and his wife. The rest of the play is taken up with George and Martha's constant hacking away at each other while the biologist and his wife watch and are slowly and unwillingly dragged into the vortex of their hosts' affairs.

During the play Martha repeatedly humiliates George in front of the guests, even going so far as to try to seduce the young biology professor. George gets even at the end by announcing that a telegram has arrived saying their son, who is supposed to return home for his twenty-first birthday celebration the next day, has been killed in an automobile accident. This reduces Martha to a state of sniveling hysteria; and we learn that the son we have been hearing about all through the play is purely imaginary—an illusion George and Martha have maintained between themselves. Martha, in telling the guests about him, has violated the compact she has had with George never to mention the imaginary son to anyone else, so he revenges himself by publicly, i.e., irrevocably, destroying the comforting little teddy-bear secret they have been hugging together for so long. At the end the guests leave, and George and Martha are left to rearrange their perspectives and pick up the pieces.

There is nothing more in this than a dissection of an extremely ambiguously conceived sick marriage. In writing *Who's Afraid of Virginia Woolf?* Albee looks like a man expending a tremendous amount of energy on furiously pedaling backwards.

JACK RICHARDSON

OF THE TWO young American dramatists who have shown the greatest promise of future achievement, Edward Albee has perhaps the more imagination and originality, while Jack Richardson has definitely the more powerful intellect. If Albee has learned his lesson from Ionesco, Richardson has as clearly been influenced by Shaw. The three remarkable plays Richardson has written so far are distinguished by the excellence of their construction, the clarity of their style, and the powerful intellect they display. Although Richardson resembles most other modern dramatic authors in that the subject matter of his plays is based on paradox, he is definitely not a member of the avant-garde as far as style is concerned. His closest affinity with living dramatists is with Dürrenmatt and Frisch. He has the same sardonic view of the world, the same precision of technique, the same effect of intellectual stimulation. The first impression that a careful reading of Richardson's plays gives one is that here at last is a playwright with brains, an intellectual who, like Shaw and Dürrenmatt and Frisch, has the ability to get a didactic message across and be entertaining at the same time. He resembles Dürrenmatt more than Frisch or Shaw perhaps in that he has a detached rather than an involved attitude towards humanity. He is interested and observant rather than evangelistic.

The use of the ancient Greek dramatic legends has been fairly common in the modern theater, but rarely, if ever, has one of the Greek legends been transposed so brilliantly as in Jack Richardson's *The Prodigal.* Using the *Oresteia* legend as a framework, Richardson has written a parable about man's enforced subservience to the demands of society. In Richardson the philosophy of determinism is placed on a purely temporal

level: there is nothing to prevent man doing as he pleases except the laws and conventions of society, but these bind him
as effectively as the vague cosmic forces of the metaphysicians.

The Prodigal opened at the Downtown Theatre, a small off-
Broadway house, on February 11, 1960. It received a moderately good press and had a moderately good run. Later on it
achieved a sort of consolatory *succès d'estime*, being produced
in a few of the higher-class summer-stock theaters and in some
college theaters. But the fact that nobody thought *The Prodigal*
fit for a full-scale Broadway production, that it remains an unknown quantity to the vast majority of theater-goers, and that
the name of Jack Richardson is still as obscure after the production of his first play as before speaks ill for any hopes that
we can have for a new movement of young American dramatists to parallel the enthusiastically accepted new movement in
the English drama. For *The Prodigal* is not merely a solid, well-
written play, as sophisticated in content as it is precisely constructed in form: it is undoubtedly the most brilliantly written
new American play to come out since the end of World War
II.

In Richardson's retelling of the Orestes legend, Orestes becomes a modern "angry young man" who wishes to dissociate
himself completely from the duties society requires of him.
He has neither patriotism nor family feeling and looks upon
Agamemnon and Aegisthus with equal contempt. His mother's
betrayal of his father and her liaison with Aegisthus merely
inspire him with cynical amusement. His one care in life is
not to become "involved": in a world he considers mad he intends to remain detached and sane. The play shows how
Orestes is forced to ab^ndon this sensible and entirely admirable position. The two forces that work upon him and in-
exorably squeeze him into acquiescence are the opposing views
of Agamemnon and Aegisthus. The latter, in an extremely skillful portrait, is shown at the beginning as a combination of
eighteenth-century rationalist and Italian Renaissance Machia-
vellian politician. During Agamemnon's absence he has introduced a new state religion which clearly resembles Protestant
fundamentalism in its emphasis on simple faith and the equal-

ity of each man's offering in the sight of the gods. Aegisthus' simple verses (he writes all the hymns and prayers for the new religion) reassure the people that their lives are valuable and worthwhile, and that tilling the soil and herding sheep are occupations as worthy and virtuous in the eyes of the gods as performing heroic deeds in battle. Later on, once he has got rid of Agamemnon and has become secure in his power, Aegisthus of course becomes unbalanced and, in accordance with Lord Acton's dictum about the corrupting influence of power, starts hanging everyone who opposes him.

Agamemnon, on the other hand, is totally unable to see that his life-long emulation and pursuit of the heroic ideal has been useless and mischievous. Unable to persuade his son to join him in opposing Aegisthus, he deliberately goads the latter into killing him so that Orestes's hand will be forced. And forced it is. Although Orestes is sent on a long journey by Aegisthus, he can get no peace. He has no interest in either Agamemnon or Aegisthus and certainly has no wish ever to rule. His one wish is to settle down peacefully somewhere and be forgotten. But his destiny—not the destiny the gods have mapped out for him, as in the ancient Greek plays, but the destiny required of him by the conventions of society—pursues him relentlessly. Even his cynical friend, Pylades, deserts him: he does not want to have his social reputation besmirched by being associated in the public mind with a man who will not avenge his father. Even the peasant girl whom Orestes had hoped to marry and settle down with in obscurity so that he could "cultivate his garden" is forced to desert him by family pressure:

> Yes, I loved her—both for herself and what she offered me. I was to have children, I was to tell them stories with happy endings, and to make love with gentleness. I wanted to stay within our small garden and watch conception, birth, decay, and death, and to give myself to the same process.[1]

Finally Orestes realizes that he is too weak to struggle any

1. Jack Richardson, *The Prodigal* (New York: E. P. Dutton & Co., Inc., 1960), p. 107.

further—as anyone but the most superhumanly single-minded
and self-righteous person would be—and succumbs. He will go
back, kill Aegisthus and Clytemnestra, assume his rightful place
on the Argive throne and become involved in the affairs of the
world:

> The world demands that we inherit the pretensions of our
> fathers, that we go on killing in the name of ancient illu-
> sions about ourselves, that we assume the right to punish,
> order, and invent philosophies to make our worst moments
> seem inspired. Who am I to contradict all this any longer?
> I will return to Argos. I belong to no other place.[2]

Jack Richardson continues his commentary on man's entrapment by social forces in his second play, *Gallows Humor. Gallows Humor* is actually two separate but interrelated one-act
plays, one dealing with the condemned and one with the executioner. Richardson's thesis here is that a large number of people
have become so deindividualized by the routine of their social
existences, so unthinkingly obedient to the prescribed routine,
so "automated," in fact, that it has become difficult to distinguish the quick from the dead. Many people are just walking
dead—meekly going through the motions until the day they
finally stop breathing and keel over, officially dead. The two
plays are preceded by a prologue speech delivered by the
"Death" character from the old morality plays. He explains
that he has not been permitted to appear in the play and has
been relegated to the prologue because he has lost his touch.
The living and the nonliving are no longer as precisely differ-
entiated as they used to be, and Death consequently has become rather confused:

> . . . in the last years, I seem both to have expanded and
> blurred my activities without knowing it. The grave's dimen-
> sions suddenly have grown to include those who have not
> yet achieved the once necessary technicality of ceasing to
> breathe. It appears I now infiltrate those still bounding to
> music, still kissing their wives, still wiggling their forefingers

2. *Ibid.*, p. 109.

in the air to emphasize those final truths by which they think their lives are lived. But are they, after all, living? [3]

The two playlets which make up *Gallows Humor* illustrate this theme. In Part One a condemned man with just a little over an hour to live is visited in his cell by a prostitute, compliments of the State. It is the State's charitable idea that the condemned should mount the gallows with sprightly step and gleaming eye so as to confute the opponents of capital punishment. Walter, the condemned man, has other ideas, however. He is, in every sense of the word but the technical one, dead already and understandably he does not want to be revivified at this point. He is quite happy, indeed. In prison his life has once again taken on the ordered tranquillity that it had before he broke out and became a murderer. Except for one brief period he has lived his life in a substitute womb of business, social, and family life in which everything was prescribed, even the number of times to make love (four times a month, only with his wife and always in bed). Now he is looking forward to his actual physical death as if he were a stray bit of protoplasm instinctively straining to be remerged with the mother mass. The prostitute's presence disturbs him since it reminds him of the one terrible period of his life, which began with his losing a cut-and-dried court case because his client developed hiccups, continued with a round of Bohemian parties and extramarital affairs, and culminated when he administered forty-one strokes of a golf club to his wife's head. The prostitute wins out, of course, and Walter goes to the gallows paradoxically more alive than the hangman, who forms the subject of Part Two of Richardson's play. The hangman really is dead in effect, because he is never able to break out of the grooves prescribed for his particular existence. During the play he makes a couple of feeble attempts to break out of the routine, first by trying to persuade the warden to let him wear a medieval execution-er's black hood at hangings so that he can have more "indi-viduality," and then by threatening to leave his wife after he

3. Jack Richardson, *Gallows Humor* (New York: E. P. Dutton & Co., Inc., 1961), pp. 14–15.

catches her kissing the warden. This last attempt is really pathetic. The executioner tells his wife he plans to go to the tropics, where nothing is hard-and-fast and everything shimmers in the heat. After he has recuperated there, he plans to go to work again as a free-lance executioner, strangling the living dead —all those whose days are precise copies of each other and whose lives are regulated by rules they unquestioningly obey. But he has waited too long: he cannot even open the kitchen door to go out, although it opens quite easily when the time comes for him to go out to work. Nor can he strangle his wife: although he strains as hard as he can, his muscles refuse to do the work. He goes out to hang Walter, but he is less alive than his victim.

Gallows Humor failed when it was first produced off-Broadway in 1961. Perhaps it is too intellectual and objective to appeal to the mass and at the same time not so obviously cynical as *The American Dream* to appeal to the few. Whatever its commercial success, however, it confirms the impression made by *The Prodigal* that Jack Richardson is America's best young playwright.

One of the most intriguing aspects of the 1962–1963 theatrical season was to have been the first Broadway productions of plays by America's two most promising young playwrights, Edward Albee and Jack Richardson. Albee got his entry in first and scored a major hit with his chronicle of sexual perversity in an upper-class American home. Richardson's play, *Lorenzo*, folded quietly after four performances. Once again the New York drama critics displayed their total incompetence and irresponsibility as they wildly applauded Albee's cunningly calculated combination of Behrman's finesse with Williams' perversity while shouting down Richardson's sophisticated and beautifully written *Lorenzo*. Unlike Albee, Richardson makes no compromises in his first Broadway work. He has refrained from pandering to the mass audience of Broadway, as Albee has done with his pretentious, supposedly authentic picture of the private life of the degenerate American intellectual. Eschewing Albee's "drama through the keyhole" technique, Richardson has written a work on a universal theme.

Written with Richardson's usual mastery of language, *Lorenzo* is about a group of strolling players caught in one of the frequent factional skirmishes between the city-states of Renaissance Italy. Lorenzo's company is by no means a good one —it is irresistibly reminiscent of Mr. Vincent Crummles's— but, goaded by the single-minded devotion of its leader, it is a dedicated one. It plays anything anywhere, and it always honors its contracts. Lorenzo adheres fanatically to the old theater adage that the only excuse for not going on is personal death —and even then an effort should be made. To him reality is what happens on the stage, and, as far as he is concerned, nothing else matters. The play shows what happens when reality as it really is obtrudes into his comfortable, make-believe world. His son goes off to fight, his daughter runs off to become the mistress of the ruthless mercenary general who represents the harshness of life as it is, and his best actor is killed defending her. Goaded at last out of his protective shell of illusion, Lorenzo challenges the general, and, in attempting to match his flashy stage sword play with the soldier's efficient professionalism, is easily killed. Lorenzo's son comes back from the battle, sated with reality by what he has seen of it, and gathers the decimated company together. He urges them on in his father's old manner: they will fulfill their engagement in Padua after all. The force of illusion has triumphed over reality; and perhaps, reality being what it is, it is better so in Richardson's view.

ARTHUR KOPIT

ASIDE FROM Albee and Richardson the future looks rather bleak for the "new American drama." The only other playwrights produced so far who show any signs that they might some day produce significant drama are Arnold Weinstein and Arthur Kopit. Both these writers are represented so far by only one play. Weinstein's play is *Red Eye of Love*, a clumsily overwritten parable that tries to show America in terms of a skyscraper meat market with one floor for each state. Nevertheless, it is obvious that once Weinstein is able to curb his exuberant bad taste, his genuine talent for satire and wry humor will enable him to write significant plays. Kopit has made a greater public impression than Weinstein because of his long-run hit, *Oh Dad, Poor Dad, Mamma's Hung You in the Closet and I'm Feelin' So Sad.* It can be safely said, without in any way detracting from the play's real qualities, that a good part of Kopit's success, particularly as far as getting the play produced in the first place was concerned, is due to his bold and shrewd composition of the title. Some of Kopit's other titles, as yet unproduced on the professional stage, such as *On the Runway of Life You Never Know What's Coming Off Next* and *Sing to Me through Open Windows* might lead people to believe that his chief talent lies in title writing, but that would be a serious mistake. Like most modern playwrights —like most modern thinkers of any kind—Kopit has a distinct tendency to view the rotting underside of life from below. There is nothing particularly new about this—Kopit's contribution lies in the wry imagination he brings to his description of life as he sees it:

> Life is a lie, my sweet. Not words but Life itself. Life in all its ugliness. It builds green trees that tease your eyes and draw you under them. Then when you're there in the shade and you breathe in and say, "Oh God, how beautiful," that's when the bird on the branch lets go his droppings and hits you on the head. Life, my sweet, beware. It isn't what it seems. I've seen what it can do.[1]

In a way it would be quite unfair to form any judgment of Kopit's abilities as a playwright and thinker on his one produced play. *Oh Dad, Poor Dad . . .* is essentially a huge practical joke. Kopit has written a brilliant satiric take-off on the conventions of the avant-garde drama, and most of the play's popularity undoubtedly stems from the fact that it is wildly funny without being at the same time even vaguely disturbing. Passages like the one quoted above, while they certainly ex-

1. Arthur Kopit, *Oh Dad, Poor Dad, Mamma's Hung You in the Closet and I'm Feelin' So Sad* (New York: Hill & Wang, Inc., 1960), p. 44.

press a probably seriously held view of life, are easily accessible
to the most uncomplicated senses of humor while losing none
of their savor for more sophisticated ones. Kopit's method of
playwriting consists chiefly of creating fantastic characters, placing them in fantastic situations, and giving them either *non
sequiturs* or facilely suave pessimistic comments to utter. Thus
we have Madame Rosepettle, who is both fabulously rich and
fabulously eccentric, traveling around Latin America measur-
ing yachts and protecting her son from life. She has just arrived
in Havana, where she finds Commodore Roseabove's yacht, the
biggest of them all. She captivates the Commodore and then
tells him the story of her life, which is mainly that she married
the ugliest man she could find and then had him stuffed when
he died. He is now hanging in her bedroom closet, and she
slyly invites the Commodore to take a peek. The latter, understandably, crawls out of her overpowering presence, all thoughts
of romance gone. Besides leading on admirers and then dis-
couraging them in this unique manner, Mme. Rosepettle also
amuses herself by walking along the beach at night, kicking
sand into lovers' faces. Her main interest, however, is to keep
her son away from life. He is never permitted out of the hotel
room lest he be contaminated, and his one attempt to break
out ends in disaster as he strangles a young girl who is trying
to seduce him on his mother's bed. He then buries her under
a small mountain of stamps, rare coins, and books, leaving his
father's body, which had fallen out of the closet during the
tussle with the girl, lying on the floor. The play ends as Mme.
Rosepettle returns from one of her nocturnal beach rambles
and discovers the mess:

> *Robinson!* I went to lie down and I stepped on your father!
> I lay down and I lay on some girl. Robinson, there is a
> woman on my bed and I do believe she's stopped breath-
> ing. What is more, you've buried her under your fabulous
> collection of stamps, coins, and books. I ask you, Robinson.
> As a mother to a son I ask you. *What is the meaning of
> this?* [2]

2. *Ibid.*, p. 89.

On this somewhat vaudevillian-joke curtain line the play unexpectedly ends. We can hope much from Kopit on the basis of the little we have received.

JACK GELBER

THE RELUCTANCE of the American drama critics to get together, wind their red, white, and blue mufflers around their necks and raise their beer steins in a toast to a new American dramatists movement has now been remedied by Kenneth Tynan who was the ringleader in the creation of the angry-young-man myth when *Look Back in Anger* came out. In his preface to the published edition of Jack Gelber's *The Connection,* Tynan hails it as "the most exciting new American play that off-Broadway has produced since the war." [1] He goes on to say that the play "explores a frightening territory with clear, unprejudiced eyes and a gift for words that makes its vision ours." [2] The "frightening territory" that Gelber explores is that of drug addiction in its more unpleasant forms—that is to say, as practised by mental degenerates, congenital morons, and the inevitable jazz musicians. This is a territory which, I fear, no gift for words can make intelligible to an outsider—and if there is a contemporary dramatist who is more incoherent and has less sense of the precise nuances of words and of the niceties of verbal rhythms than Mr. Gelber, we can only give thanks that he remains unproduced. Furthermore, Gelber does not look at the problem of drug addiction with "clear, unprejudiced eyes"—he looks at it with a strong bias in favor of the addict.

The Connection has no plot. A group of drug addicts sit around waiting for their "connection" or drug supplier. While they wait they chat aimlessly, boringly, and stupidly. Gelber's purpose in all this is to try and convince us that these people

1. Jack Gelber, *The Connection* (New York: Grove Press, Inc., 1960), p. 11.
    2. *Ibid.*

are not actors playing addicts, but real addicts. This is, of course, a project that is doomed from the start since even the most gullible member of any given audience will know that he is watching actors and not addicts. Recalling a distant and incorrect reading of Pirandello, Gelber begins by having two actors playing the producer and the author come on stage (from the audience, naturally) to announce that we are about to see a play improvised by real addicts. In a way this constitutes a technical tour de force: right away Gelber has actors playing addicts who are improvising a play about addicts—who are in other words, playing actors who are playing addicts. A play within a play within a play within a play right off the bat. This is impressive, certainly, but hardly the way to write a play; and definitely not a basis for hope of a new American drama movement which would drag our theater away from the Williams-Inge axis of psuedopsychological drama. Gelber's attempt to achieve verisimilitude with the pretense of an immediately organized improvisation fails because of his fundamental ignorance of the true function of the theater. The theater is an illusion, and there is no way to get around that. The use of an improvisational technique, which is necessarily self-conscious on the part of the actors (it is possible to improvise but not to *pretend* to improvise, which is what the actors in Gelber's *The Connection* and *The Apple* are doing), a self-consciousness that is accentuated by Gelber's insistence that the actors in *The Apple* use their real names, is merely embarrassing and ultimately offensive. In *The Connection* the actors have fictitious names but the director's real name and the name of the theater is mentioned. Gelber does not realize that all theater is a cooperative effort in which the audience has a very definite part. The audience's contribution to the theatrical experience is suspension of its disbelief. Mr. Gelber, who totally fails to recognize this, spends most of his time trying to coax the audience into suspending its disbelief, never realizing that the audience automatically does this as soon as it enters the theater. Consequently, Gelber attempts an exercise in absolute realism, which in the theater is merely a contradiction in terms, by having actors play addicts who are putting on an amateur and naturally clumsy imitation of themselves; the point being that when they seem to forget to act the audience will accept them as real junkies. If this is not Gelber's aim, then there is no sense to the play's introduction, which is only silly pretense to people who know what goes on in a theater. And with all this fake rigmarole, what has Gelber to say about drug addiction? [3] Nothing. Presumably his transcript of junkie talk and his picture of junkie life are accurate, since he claims he has lived among these people. But what of it? Gelber presents us with an apparent slice of life, but he has nothing to say about it. His purpose is probably to make us *understand* these people and to sympathize with them. The actual effect is precisely the opposite.

Gelber's other play to date, *The Apple*, is, if possible, totally without meaning. The play, if it can be called that, takes place in a coffee shop, but Gelber works very hard at trying to convince the audience that the theater *is* the coffee shop by having a drunken patron of the shop circulate among the playgoers in the lobby before the performance and by spending most of the time in having his actors discuss what they are going to improvise that evening. Since they can never make up their minds very clearly and since their improvisations once they do make up their minds are utterly incomprehensible, *The Apple* becomes an exercise in mass boredom and nothing more.

With the exception of Jack Gelber, who has shown neither promise nor achievement but has received more notoriety through the shock value of his plays, the new American playwrights considered here definitely show the nucleus of a movement that, if given the chance to develop by the peculiar production economics of the New York theater, may turn out to be more lasting and more influential than the highly touted New English Dramatists movement. All in all, the prospect for a renaissance of dramatic writing in the United States is bright. The plays are being written—the only question is, will the off-Broadway theater be able to survive long enough to produce them?

3. Bernard Dukore ("The New Dramatists, 5: Jack Gelber," *Drama Survey*, II [Fall, 1962], pp. 146–57) says that Gelber is trying to show that all of us need a "connection," a "fix," to go on living in society. This seems to me to be reading things into the play. It may be what Gelber meant; it is certainly not what he succeeds in putting across.

SELECTED BIBLIOGRAPHY

General Works

Abel, Lionel. *Metatheatre*. New York: Hill & Wang, Inc., 1963.
Esslin, Martin. *The Theatre of the Absurd*. Garden City, N. Y.: Doubleday & Company, Inc., 1961.
Fowlie, Wallace. *Dionysus in Paris*. New York: Meridian Books, Inc., 1960.
Grossvogel, David I. *The Self-Conscious Stage in Modern French Drama*. New York: Columbia University Press, 1958.
————. *Four Playwrights and a Postscript*. Ithaca, N. Y.: Cornell University Press, 1962.
Guicharnaud, Jacques. *Modern French Theatre from Giraudoux to Beckett*. New Haven, Conn.: Yale University Press, 1961.
Pronko, Leonard C. *Avant-Garde: The Experimental Theatre in France*. Berkeley, Cal.: University of California Press, 1962.

French-Speaking Drama

ARTHUR ADAMOV

Lynes, Carlos, Jr. "Adamov and 'le sens littéral' in the Theatre," *Yale French Studies*, No. 14 (1954–1955), pp. 48–56.
Regnaut, Maurice. "Arthur Adamov et le sens du fétichisme," *Cahiers de la Compagnie M. Renaud - J. L. Barrault*, Nos. 22–23 (1958), pp. 182–90.
Weber, Jean-Paul. "Adamov (Arthur Sourenovitch), de Kislovodsk, Auteur dramatique français (1910–19—)," *Figaro littéraire* (April 3, 1960), p. 3.

ANTONIN ARTAUD

Arnold, Paul. "Antonin Artaud et le théâtre de la nouvelle vague," *Revue générale belge* (January, 1960), pp. 75–83.
Fowlie, Wallace. "New French Theatre: Artaud, Beckett, Genet, Ionesco," *Sewanee Review*, LXVII (1959), pp. 648–51.
Hahn, Otto. "Portrait d'Antonin Artaud," *Temps Modernes*, No. 192 (1962), pp. 1592–1619; No. 193 (1962), pp. 1854–82.

SAMUEL BECKETT

Barbour, Thomas. "Beckett and Ionesco," *Hudson Review*, XI (1958), pp. 271–77.
Chadwick, C. "*Waiting for Godot*: A Logical Approach," *Symposium*, XIV (1960), pp. 199–212.
Champigny, R. "Interprétation de *En attendant Godot*," *PMLA*, LXXV (1960), pp. 329–31.
Cohn, Ruby. "The Comedy of Samuel Beckett: Something Old, Something New," *Yale French Studies*, No. 23 (1959), pp. 11–17.
———. "*Endgame*: The Gospel According to Sad Sam Beckett," *Accent*, XX (1960), pp. 223–34.
———. "Plays and Players in the Plays of Samuel Beckett," *Yale French Studies*, No. 29 (1962), pp. 43–48.
———. *Samuel Beckett: The Comic Gamut*. New Brunswick, N. J.: Rutgers University Press, 1962.
———. "*Watt* in the light of *The Castle*," *Comparative Literature*, XIII (1961), pp. 154–66.
Dobrée, Bonamy. "The London Theatre, 1957," *Sewanee Review*, LXVI (1958), pp. 146–60.
Driver, Tom F. "Beckett by the Madeleine," *Columbia University Forum*, IV, iii (1961), pp. 21–55.
Flood, Ethelbert. "A Reading of Beckett's *Godot*," *Culture*, XII (1961), pp. 257–62.
Friedman, M. J. "The Achievement of Samuel Beckett," *Books Abroad*, XXXIII (1959), pp. 278–81.
Gregory, Horace. "Beckett's Dying Gladiators," *Commonweal* (October 26, 1956), pp. 88–92.
Hamilton, Kenneth. "Negative Salvation in Samuel Beckett," *Queen's Quarterly*, LXIX (1962), pp. 102–11.
Harvey, Lawrence E. "Art and the Existential in *En attendant Godot*," *PMLA*, LXXV (1960), pp. 137–46.
Hesse, Eva. "Die Welt des Samuel Beckett," *Akzente*, VIII (1961), pp. 244–66.
Hoffmann, Frederick J. *Samuel Beckett: The Language of Self*. Carbondale, Ill.: Southern Illinois University Press, 1962.
Hooker, K. W. "Irony and Absurdity in the Avant-garde Theatre," *Kenyon Review*, XXII (1960), pp. 436–54.
Hubert, Renée Riese. "The Couple and the Performance in Samuel Beckett's Plays," *L'Esprit Créateur*, II (1962), pp. 175–80.
Hughes, Catherine. "Beckett and the Game of Life," *Catholic World*, CXCV (1962), pp. 163–68.
Iser, Wolfgang. "Samuel Becketts dramatische Sprache," *Ger-*

manisch-romanische Monatsschrift, XI (1962), pp. 451–67.

Karl, Frederick R. "Waiting for Beckett: quest and re-quest," *Sewanee Review*, LXIX (1961), pp. 661–76.

Kenner, Hugh. "Beckett: The Rational Domain," *Forum (Houston)*, III, iv (1961), pp. 39–47.

Kern, Edith. "Beckett's Knight of Infinite Resignation," *Yale French Studies*, No. 29 (1962), pp. 49–56.

——. "Drama Stripped for Inaction: Beckett's Godot," *Yale French Studies*, No. 14 (1954–1955), pp. 41–47.

Lamont, Rosette C. "The Metaphysical Farce: Beckett and Ionesco," *French Review*, XXXII (1959), pp. 319–28.

McCoy, Charles S. "*Waiting for Godot*: A Biblical Appraisal," *Religion in Life*, XXVIII (1959), pp. 595–603.

Mercier, Vivian. "Samuel Beckett and the Sheela-na-gig," *Kenyon Review*, XXIII (1961), pp. 299–324.

Metman, Eva. "Reflections on Samuel Beckett's Plays," *Journal of Analytical Psychology*, V (1960), pp. 41–62.

Nadeau, Maurice. "Samuel Beckett, l'humour et le néant," *Mercure de France*, CCCXII (1951), pp. 693–97.

Pritchett, V. S. "Irish Oblomov," *New Statesman* (April 2, 1960), p. 489.

Radke, Judith J. "The Theatre of Samuel Beckett: 'Une durée à animer,' " *Yale French Studies*, No. 29 (1962), pp. 57–64.

Rexroth, Kenneth. "The Point is Irrelevance," *Nation* (April 14, 1956), pp. 325–28.

Scott, Nathan A., Jr. "The Recent Journey to the Zone of Zero: The Example of Beckett and his Despair of Literature," *The Centennial Review of Arts and Science*, VI (1962), pp. 144–81.

Strauss, W. A. "Dante's Belacqua and Beckett's Tramps," *Comparative Literature*, XI (1959), pp. 250–61.

Touchard, Pierre-Aimé. "Le théâtre de Samuel Beckett," *Revue de Paris* (February, 1961), pp. 73–87.

Walker, R. "Love, Chess and Death: Samuel Beckett's Double Bill," *Twentieth Century*, CLXIV (1958), pp. 533–44.

Weales, Gerald. "The Language of *Endgame*," *Tulane Drama Review*, VI, iv (1962), pp. 107–17.

JEAN GENET

Clark, E. "The World of Jean Genet," *Partisan Review*, XVI (1949), pp. 442–48.

Dort, Bernard. "Le jeu de Genet," *Temps Modernes*, XV (1960), pp. 1875–84.

Ehrmann, Jacques. "Genet's Dramatic Metamorphosis: From Appearance to Freedom," *Yale French Studies*, No. 29 (1962), pp. 33–42.

Fowlie, Wallace. "The Case of Jean Genet," *Commonweal*, LXXIII (1960), pp. 111–13.

———. "New Plays of Ionesco and Genet," *Tulane Drama Review*, V, i (1960), pp. 43–48.

Genet, Jean. "To a Would-be Producer." Translated by Bernard Frechtman, *Tulane Drama Review*, VII, iii (1963), pp. 80–81.

McMahon, Joseph H. "Keeping Faith and Holding Firm," *Yale French Studies*, No. 29 (1962), pp. 26–32.

Markus, Thomas B. "Jean Genet: The Theatre of the Perverse," *Educational Theatre Journal*, XIV (1962), pp. 209–14.

Melcher, Edith. "The Pirandellism of Jean Genet," *French Review*, XXXVI (1962), pp. 32–36.

Nelson, Benjamin. "*The Balcony* and Parisian Existentialism," *Tulane Drama Review*, VII, iii (1963), pp. 60–79.

Pierret, Marc. "Genet's New Play: *The Screens*." Translated by Rima D. Reck, *Tulane Drama Review*, VII, iii (1963), pp. 93–97.

Pronko, Leonard C. "Jean Genet's *Les Paravents*," *L'Esprit Créateur*, II (1962), pp. 181–88.

Pucciani, Oreste F. "Tragedy, Genet and *The Maids*," *Tulane Drama Review*, VII, iii (1963), pp. 42–59.

Reck, Rima Drell. "Appearance and Reality in Genet's *Le Balcon*," *Yale French Studies*, No. 29 (1962), pp. 20–25.

Sartre, Jean-Paul. *Saint Genet: Comédien et Martyr*. Paris: Gallimard, 1952.

Taubes, Susan. "The White Mask Falls," *Tulane Drama Review*, VII, iii (1963), pp. 85–92.

MICHEL DE GHELDERODE

Abel, Lionel. "Our Man in the Sixteenth Century: Michel de Ghelderode," *Tulane Drama Review*, VIII, i (1963), pp. 62–71.

Draper, Samuel. "An Interview with Michel de Ghelderode," *Tulane Drama Review*, VIII, i (1963), pp. 39–50.

———. "Discovery of Ghelderode." *Commonweal*, LXXIII (1960), pp. 113–15.

———. "Michel de Ghelderode: A Personal Statement," *Tulane Drama Review*, VIII, i (1963), pp. 33–38.

Ghelderode, Michel de. "Lettres à Catherine Toth, André Reybaz, René Dupuy, Jean Le Poulain, Marcel Lupovici, Gilles Chancrin," *Revue d'histoire du théâtre*, XIV (1962), pp. 118–56.

Grossvogel, David I. "The plight of the comic author and some new departures in contemporary comedy," *Romanic Review*, XLV, (1954), pp. 268–70.

Hauger, George. "Dispatches from the Prince of Ostrelande," *Tulane Drama Review*, VIII, i (1963), pp. 24–32.

———. "The Plays of Ghelderode," *Tulane Drama Review*, IV, i (1959), pp. 19–30.

Herz, Micheline. "Tragedy, Poetry and the Burlesque in Ghelderode's Theatre," *Yale French Studies*, No. 29 (1962), pp. 92–101.

Italiaander, R. "Michel de Ghelderode," *Deutsche Rundschau*, LXXVII (1951), pp. 279–81.

Stevo, Jean. "Visages de Michel de Ghelderode," *Revue générale belge* (May, 1962), pp. 45–57.

Valogne, Catherine. "Michel de Ghelderode et ses interprètes," *Revue d'histoire du théâtre*, XIV (1962), pp. 113–17.

Weiss, Aurélieu. "The Theatrical World of Michel de Ghelderode" Translated by Ruby Cohn, *Tulane Drama Review*, VIII, i (1963), pp. 51–61.

EUGÈNE IONESCO

Coe, Richard N. *Eugène Ionesco*. New York: Grove Press, Inc., 1961.

Daniel, John T. "Ionesco and the Ritual of Nihilism," *Drama Survey*, I, i (1961), pp. 54–65.

Doubrovsky, J. S. "Ionesco and the Comic of Absurdity," *Yale French Studies*, No. 23 (1959), pp. 3–10.

———. "Le rire d'Eugène Ionesco," *Nouvelle revue française* (February, 1960), pp. 313–23.

Dukore, Bernard. "The Theatre of Ionesco: A Union of Form and Substance," *Educational Theatre Journal*, XIII (1961), pp. 174–81.

Eastman, Richard M. "Experiment and Vision in Ionesco's Plays," *Modern Drama*, IV (1961), pp. 3–19.

Esslin, Martin. "Ionesco and the Creative Dilemma," *Tulane Drama Review*, VII, iii (1963), pp. 169–79.

Glicksberg, Charles I. "Ionesco and the Aesthetics of the Absurd," *Arizona Quarterly*, XVIII (1962), pp. 293–303.

Greshoff, C. J. "A Note on Ionesco," *French Studies*, XV (1961), pp. 30–40.

Guicharnaud, Jacques. "A World Out of Control: Eugène Ionesco," *American Society of Legion of Honor Magazine*, XXXI (1960), pp. 105–15.

Hughes, Catherine. "Ionesco's Plea for Man," *Renascence*, XIV (1962), pp. 121–25.

Ionesco, Eugène. "The Avant-Garde Theatre," *Tulane Drama Review*, V, ii (1961), pp. 44–53.
———. "Notes on My Theatre." Translated by Leonard Pronko, *Tulane Drama Review*, VII, iii (1963), pp. 127–62.
———. "The Tragedy of Language: How an English Primer Became My First Play." Translated by Jack Undank, *Tulane Drama Review*, IV, iii (1960), pp. 10–13.
Knowles, Dorothy. "Ionesco and the Mechanisms of Language," *Modern Drama*, V (1962), pp. 7–10.
Lamont, Rosette C. "The Hero in Spite of Himself," *Yale French Studies*, No. 29 (1962), pp. 73–81.
———. "The Proliferation of Matter in Ionesco's Plays," *L'Esprit Créateur*, II (1962), pp. 189–97.
Murray, Jack. "Ionesco and the Mechanics of Memory," *Yale French Studies*, No. 29 (1962), pp. 82–87.
Schechner, Richard. "The Enactment of the 'Not' in *Les Chaises* of Eugène Ionesco," *Yale French Studies*, No. 29 (1962), pp. 65–72.
———. "The Inner and the Outer Reality," *Tulane Drama Review*, VII, iii (1963), pp. 187–220.
———. "An Interview with Ionesco," *Tulane Drama Review*, VII, iii (1963), pp. 163–68.
Strem, George. "The Anti-Theatre of Eugène Ionesco," *Twentieth Century* (Melbourne), XVI (1962), pp. 70–83.
Touchard, Pierre-Aimé. "L'itinéraire d'Eugène Ionesco," *Revue de Paris*, LXVII (1960), pp. 91–102.
———. "Un nouveau fabuliste," *Cahiers de la Compagnie Madeleine Renaud - J. L. Barrault*, No. 29 (1960), pp. 3–13.
Vannier, Jean. "A Theatre of Language." Translated by Leonard Pronko, *Tulane Drama Review*, VII, iii (1963), pp. 180–86.
Watson, Donald. "The Plays of Ionesco," *Tulane Drama Review*, III, i (1958), pp. 48–53.

ALFRED JARRY

Shattuck, Roger. *The Banquet Years*. New York: Harcourt, Brace & World, Inc., 1958.
York, Ruth B. "*Ubu* Revisited: The Reprise of 1922," *French Review*, XXXV (1962), pp. 408–11.

JEAN TARDIEU

Jaccottet, Philippe. "Notes à propos de Jean Tardieu," *Nouvelle revue française* (July, 1960), pp. 107–11.

German-Speaking Drama

FRIEDRICH DÜRRENMATT

Askew, Melvin. "Dürrenmatt's *The Visit of the Old Lady*," *Tulane Drama Review*, V, iv (1961), pp. 89–105.

Brock-Sulzer, Elisabeth. *Friedrich Dürrenmatt: Stationen seines Werkes*. Zürich: Verlag der Arche, 1960.

Davian, Donald G. "Justice in the Works of Friedrich Dürrenmatt," *Kentucky Foreign Language Quarterly*, IX (1962), pp. 181–93.

Drese, C. H. "Friedrich Dürrenmatt," *Eckart*, XXVIII (1959), pp. 385–89.

Guth, Hans P. "Dürrenmatt's *Visit*: The Play Behind the Play," *Symposium*, XVI (1962), pp. 94–102.

Johnson, Peter. "Grotesqueness and Injustice in Dürrenmatt," *German Life and Letters*, XV (1962), pp. 264–73.

Klarmann, Adolf D. "Friedrich Dürrenmatt and the Tragic Sense of Comedy," *Tulane Drama Review*, IV (1960), pp. 77–104.

Loram, Ian C. " 'Der Besuch der alten Dame' and 'The Visit,' " *Monatshefte*, LIII (1961), pp. 15–21.

Muschg, Walter. "Dürrenmatt und die Physiker," *Moderna Språk* (Stockholm), LVI (1962), pp. 280–83.

Peppard, Murray B. "The Grotesque in Dürrenmatt's Dramas," *Kentucky Foreign Language Quarterly*, IX (1962), pp. 36–44.

Scherer, Josef. "Der mutige Mensch: Versuch einer Deutung von Friedrich Dürrenmatts Menschenbild," *Stimmen der Zeit*, CLXIX (1962), pp. 307–12.

Schneider, Marcel. "Friedrich Dürrenmatt, le fils prodigue de l'occident," *Revue de Paris* (August, 1961), pp. 99–105.

Temkine, Raymonde. "Friedrich Dürrenmatt," *Lettres nouvelles*, No. 7 (1960), pp. 140–45.

Waidson, H. M. "Dürrenmatt: The Comedy of Despair," *Nation*, CXC (1960), pp. 34–35.

MAX FRISCH

Bänziger, Hans. *Frisch und Dürrenmatt*. Berne and Munich: Francke, 1960.

Müller, Joachim. "Max Frisch und Friedrich Dürrenmatt als Dramatiker der Gegenwart," *Universitas* (Stuttgart), XVII (1962), pp. 725–38.

Seidmann, Peter. "Modern Swiss Drama: Frisch and Dürrenmatt," *Books Abroad*, XXXIV (1960), pp. 112–14.

L

Ziolkowski, Theodore. "Max Frisch: Moralist without a Moral,"
    Yale French Studies, No. 29 (1962), pp. 132–41.

English-Speaking Drama

GENERAL

Marowitz, Charles. "New Wave in a Dead Sea," X, A *Quarterly
    Review*, I (1960), pp. 270–77.
Taylor, John Russell. *Anger and After*. London: Methuen & Co.,
    Ltd., 1962.
Trilling, Ossia. "The Young British Dramatists," *Modern Drama*,
    III (1960), pp. 168–77.

JOHN OSBORNE

Deming, B. "John Osborne's War against the Philistines," *Hud-
    son Review*, XI (1959), pp. 411–19.
Dennis, Nigel. "Out of the Box," *Encounter*, XVII (1961), pp.
    51–53. (On *Luther*.)
Denty, Vera D. "The Psychology of Martin Luther," *Catholic
    World*, CXCIV (1961), pp. 99–105. (On *Luther*.)
Marowitz, Charles. "The Ascension of John Osborne," *Tulane
    Drama Review*, VII, ii (1962), pp. 175–79.
Popkin, Henry. "Williams, Osborne, or Beckett?" *New York
    Times Book Review*, November 13, 1960, pp. 32–33, 119–21.
Weiss, S. A. "Osborne's Angry Young Play," *Educational Theatre
    Journal*, XII (1960), pp. 285–88.

HAROLD PINTER

Cohn, Ruby. "The World of Harold Pinter," *Tulane Drama Re-
    view*, VI, iii (1962), pp. 55–68.
Dick, Kay. "Mr. Pinter and the Fearful Matter," *Texas Quarterly*,
    IV (1961), pp. 257–65.
Dukore, Bernard. "The Theatre of Harold Pinter," *Tulane Drama
    Review*, VI, iii (1962), pp. 43–54.
Esslin, Martin. "Pinter and the Absurd," *Twentieth Century*,
    CLXIX (1961), pp. 176–85.
Hoefer, Jacqueline. "Pinter and Whiting: Two Attitudes Towards
    the Alienated Artist," *Modern Drama*, IV (1962), pp. 402–
    408.

ARNOLD WESKER

Findlater, Richard. "Plays and Politics," *Twentieth Century*,
    CLXVIII (1960), pp. 235–42.

Goodman, Henry. "The New Dramatists, 2: Arnold Wesker,"
    Drama Survey, I (1961), pp. 215–22.
Jones, A. R. "The Theatre of Arnold Wesker," *Critical Quarterly*,
    II (1960), pp. 366–70.

EDWARD ALBEE

Zimbardo, Rose A. "Symbolism and Naturalism in Edward Albee's
    The Zoo Story," *Twentieth Century Literature*, VIII (1960),
    pp. 10–17.

JACK GELBER

Abel, Lionel. "Living Theatre," *Commentary*, XXXIII (1962),
    pp. 331–34.
———. "Not Everyone is in the Fix," *Partisan Review*, XXVII
    (1960), pp. 131–36.

Index